Managing Product Recall

Managing Product Recall

A COMPREHENSIVE GUIDE TO ESTABLISHING A PRODUCT RECALL PLAN

Howard Abbott

Pitman

Pitman Publishing
128 Long Acre, London WC2E 9AN

A Division of Longman Group UK Limited

First published in 1991

© Howard Abbott 1991

British Library Cataloguing in Publication Data
Abbott, Howard
  Managing product recall.
  I. Title
  658.5

ISBN 0 273 03449 9

Typeset, printed and bound in Great Britain.

The ability to foresee that some things cannot be foreseen is a very necessary quality.

Jean-Jacques Rousseau 1712–1778

Contents

Figures

Tables

Foreword

Unsafe or defective products can have disastrous consequences for both the consumer and the supplier. Preventing these products from reaching the market must therefore be the main priority, but if they do slip through it is vitally important to be able to withdraw them from distributors and from consumers as quickly and effectively as possible.

Reducing the risk of injury is clearly paramount, but the legal and economic impact on a business of a badly handled product recall can also be serious. This is especially true in a world where safety considerations are increasing in importance.

Howard Abbott's book offers sound practical advice and examples of how to develop the techniques and understanding needed to deal with product recalls. Each case will be different and the decisions facing business managers will vary in both severity and circumstances. Howard Abbott provides a framework for these decisions and I hope that his book will encourage managers to review and, where necessary, improve their approach to product recall.

It may not only save lives, but their business as well.

Edward Leigh
Parliamentary Under Secretary of State
for Industry and Consumer Affairs

Acknowledgements

I am grateful to the following who kindly provided me with information for this book: Christian Bouckaert, Jeantet & Associés, Paris; Michael Brownlee, National Highway Traffic Safety Administration, Washington; Nigel Churton, Control Risks Group, London; Mike Culver, Mori Sogo Law Offices, Tokyo; G A Hamil, Vehicle Inspectorate Executive Agency, Bristol; Brian Hartley, The Medicines Inspectorate, London; Larry Hurst, Association of British Pharmaceutical Industry, London; Christian Joerges, Universität Bremen, Bremen; Yoshimi Kanemitsu, Tokio Marine & Fire Insurance Company, Tokyo; Jocelyn Kellam, Blake Dawson Waldron, Sydney; Martin Langford, Burson-Marsteller, London; Peter Madge; Paul Marriner, Transport Canada, Ottawa; David Miller-Randle, Kmart Australia Limited, Victoria; Mike Murray, Association of British Pharmaceutical Industry, London; Takeo Oyanagi, Ministry of Transport, Tokyo; Carlos Perez, US Consumer Product Safety Commission, Washington; Nils Ringstedt, National Swedish Board for Consumer Policies, Vallingaby; Mikael Rosenmejer, Plesner & Lunoe, Copenhagen; Ken Ross, Popham Haik Schnobrich & Kaufman, Minneapolis; Ewen Todd, Health & Welfare, Canada, Ottawa; Sean Wadmore, Society of Motor Manufacturers and Traders, London; Margrit Wallek-Heldtke, Jauch & Hubener, Mulheim.

Special thanks are due to Stuart Ashworth, the Editor of Product Liability International, Lloyd's of London Press, for much help and advice.

There are many other people to whom I am indebted but who wish to remain anonymous. These are the men and women of the companies I have worked with in establishing product recall plans or in managing a recall. Although generous with their help they prefer not to have public acknowledgement. Nevertheless, I must also record my thanks to them.

I am particularly grateful to Sheila Richards who typed the considerable research correspondence as well as the manuscript.

Howard Abbott
Richmond, Surrey

Preface

Driving a car backwards at speed with little warning is difficult. Especially if one has not done it before. A major product recall can be a little like that. Problems arise when managers assume it would be just another business task to be solved because they can drive forwards quite satisfactorily.

This book is based on ten years' experience helping companies recall products, both in prevention by planning ahead and in actual recalls occasioned by accidental defects or deliberate contamination of products. No two situations are identical but there are some general principles that can apply. I have set these out in the pages that follow but they will not all be required in every case. Each company has to decide for itself what will meet its unique circumstances. The best advice I can give is to hope for the best but plan for the worst.

Looking back, I see that managing a national recall is excellent management training for the men and women involved. However, I do not recommend that such an exercise should be included in all company training programmes, but there are advantages for those who find they have a part to play when quick decisions can have very significant consequences.

Howard Abbott

PART ONE

The background

1 *Product safety management*

Introduction

At one time the decision whether or not to withdraw or recall a product from the market was largely in the hands of manufacturers. On occasion, management might decide that it would be economically more advantageous to risk a small number of court actions than incur the substantial costs of a recall, with the accompanying publicity. Even if a recall was initiated, the action could perhaps be kept quiet and become a silent recall.

Today things are very different. There are three reasons for this:

1 National legislation and EC Directives provide the consumer with greatly enhanced protection, extensive powers for regulatory bodies and increased penalties for errant companies.
2 The growth of consumerism has made people far more aware of their rights, with the establishment of consumer advice centres and government publications explaining how to complain.
3 The increase in product complexity has made some products more prone to failure and at the same time increased consumer expectations of performance. One expert estimates that the automobile has undergone a four-fold increase in the number of its parts in four decades.

The best recall is no recall. But no company, however prestigious, can guarantee that it will never make a defective product. One has only to look at the great and the good that have made a bad one to realise that this is true. It is one of the penalties we have to accept for the society in which we live: mass-production, for all its advantages, employs fallible human beings who on occasions make mistakes.

People expect products to be safe, even though this has to be an unattainable absolute. Every product carries with it some risk for someone, somewhere. A product on recall is usually, but not always, unsafe. To avoid this situation, a professional attempt must be made not to have an unsafe product in the first place.

Today the management of product safety has become an activity in its own right, as companies realise that it involves far more than just having a good quality function. The tried and trusted methods of yesterday may not be sufficient for a regime of strict liability and increased consumer awareness.

This review of some of the key elements of product safety management looks at how companies can reduce the chance of having to recall a product. The book is not concerned with scientific or engineering safety, in the sense of preservatives in food or guards on machines, but rather with overall management. Every function has a contribution to make, some not realising the significance of their role.

Product safety policy

As corporate conduct is inseparable from the collective conduct of the individuals who make up the corporation, it is vital that those individuals act in concert on important issues. By having a written product safety policy, management by principle can be substituted for management by expediency and assumption. It should be expressed in broad terms and not attempt to cover every contingency in detail.

An illustration of the need for a policy occurred when the managing director of a subsidiary of a multinational was talking about the liability exposure presented by his products, which incorporated both water and electricity. He declared with some vehemence his determination by saying, 'I want my products to be absolutely safe and not be a danger to anyone, employee or member of the public.' It took some time to convince him that he was seeking an unattainable absolute, and that he needed time and discussion to formulate a reasoned approach to product safety, which could then be developed into a policy. International corporations often establish product safety policies as they are well aware of the changes taking place in their product liability exposure.

The policy should be signed by the chief executive and have the total commitment of the board. By itself it is useless. To achieve the aims of the policy, a strategy is needed and a director should be given responsibility to see that it is carried through. The means must be provided to achieve the aims set out in the policy.

As we are primarily concerned with recall, we will concentrate on the ways in which a strategy can help prevent a product becoming defective: design, manufacture and information. A failure in one of these can lead to a recall, with varying degrees of impact.

Design or formulation

Some of the tragic design failures that have led to products being removed from the market have concerned drugs (Thalidomide, Opren) and medical devices (Dalkon Shield, heart valves and pacemakers). These illustrate the fact that a design failure can have a very severe impact, with the costs running into millions. Widely distributed products with latent defects, which only appear after a period of time, attract much publicity when they are withdrawn from the market. But some design defects can hit the headlines with a single incident such as the *Amoco Cadiz* running ashore in France and the *Challenger* space shuttle exploding shortly after take-off. Others lie dormant for years until scientific developments enable them to be detected as the source of much illness and death, such as that which resulted in asbestosis.

The case histories in Part III have examples of design defects which resulted in a recall (see Nova Fritex deep-fat fryer, p.190; Formula Shell Petrol, p.207; and Snecma aeroengines, p.234).

There can be no simple answer to the reduction of design-related defects, and each company will have to develop its own checklist of the factors that have to be taken into consideration. The points that follow are those that can be important from the point of view of safety and, therefore, potential recall. They should be taken into account during the design review process.

End-user

The most sensitive users of products are children, geriatrics and pets because they have limited powers of understanding and discrimination. People use products in ways which the designer may not have intended, but of which he should have been aware. The designer should have a description of the end-user and the possibilities of foreseeable misuse; for example we use screwdrivers to open tins of paint, because paint manufacturers do not bother to provide the means of opening their packaging. There are numerous cases of children's toys being recalled because of apparent misuse, but teddy bear designers are expected to know that small children will attempt to pull the eyes out. And if they can, a recall will be necessary.

If the product is likely to be sold to an ethnic minority this should be known, as the physical characteristics may be important. For example, Afro-Caribbean hands are significantly larger than those of Europeans, Asians or Indians, while Japanese have smaller anthropometric dimensions.

Ethnic minorities require communication in a manner they can understand. This may involve pictograms and designing out hazards that cannot be accommodated by the use of a warning label. In Australia, companies recalling products sold to ethnic minorities may be required by the Federal Bureau of Consumer Affairs to use the ethnic language press in a recall.

Designing for product safety can be both positive and negative, and it may be necessary for the designer to ensure that the product will not do certain things. All household fridges must have doors that can be pushed open from the inside to prevent children being trapped while playing inside one that has been discarded; and some household products, such as bleach, must have child-resistant packaging so that a child cannot get at the product.

Environment of use
The proximity of children and animals may be important, as may the periods for which a product is left unattended. The optimum and extremes of temperature, humidity, sunlight, vibration, noise and pressure are all factors that should be known where necessary.

Reliability
This is 'the ability of an item to perform a required function under stated conditions for a stated period of time.' If a product is not reliable it may become unsafe and have to be recalled. The safety-critical parts should be identified so that particular attention is paid to them during the design process. With some products it may be possible to weight the importance of different parts according to their effect on safety. Parts that could need replacing in a recall, which involves a repair or a retrofit, should be accessible.

Model identification
The means by which a user can rapidly identify the unit he has bought needs some thought. Model numbers, serial numbers, batch codes and the like will be familiar to the manufacturer but can be confusing to the layman. For consumer products the code must be easily found and be legible. A plate with the necessary data on the back of a domestic appliance will not be sought; the code edge system for labels, for example, cannot be understood without a special plastic card.

Warnings, directions and instructions

These are considered to be part of the product when defectiveness is being determined. The user has a right to expect that sufficient information will be given so that the product can be used safely. A *warning* is a communication about the dangers associated with or inherent in a product, eg 'Danger high voltage'. A *direction* specifies a related command or prerequisite to the use of the product, eg 'Disconnect from the mains before use'. An *instruction* explains how to use the product most effectively, eg 'To empty turn the valve anti-clockwise'.

A failure to communicate with the user can result in an accident and a recall (see the Renault case history in Part III, p.233). In a trial on the effect of the proposed change in European law on the labelling of medicines, a pack was labelled in accordance with the new draft law and shown to a sample of patients. Eighty-five per cent could not understand from the instructions how often they were supposed to take the medicine, 20 per cent could not work out the maximum daily dose, and 30 per cent were unable to see in what circumstances they should not take the medicine at all.

Standards and Codes of Practice

These should be treated as minima. It should be remembered that the standards do not necessarily have anything to do with safety but may only be concerned with measurement or performance. This means that, although conformance with relevant standards and codes of practice is required, it does not follow that an entirely safe product will result. The Nova Fritex deep-fat fryer was recommended by prestigious organisations but it still had a design defect which led to a recall (see the case history in Part III, p.190).

Hazard analysis and risk assessment

The use of risk identification techniques can reveal areas of potential danger and provide a valuable warning of possible trouble ahead. A major vehicle manufacturer, for example, requires firms supplying safety-critical components to use such techniques to demonstrate that risks have been reduced to a minimum.

Packaging

Products that are vulnerable to deliberate contamination by criminals would benefit from tamper-evident packaging. The designer should take into account the possibilities available and select that which provides the greatest protection. See the product extortion and malicious product tamper case histories in Part III (p.213).

Manufacture

A manufacturing error is probably the most frequent cause of a product recall. The important management attribute is to know that a bad one has been made and be in a position to withdraw it from the market fast. The quality function will have a big part to play in reducing the chance of a manufacturing error and much published information is available on the management of quality.

The case histories in Part III have examples of manufacturing errors which have resulted in a recall (see John West canned salmon, p.144; Farley's baby food, p.151; Perrier mineral water, p.165; Remington electric shaver, p.182; and Wall's canned stewed steak, p.209).

Records

From a recall point of view the rapid availability of full records will be critical. The use of computers is often essential here and they play a crucial part in computer-aided manufacture (CAM) and computer-integrated manufacturing (CIM). Essentially, one needs to know which incoming raw materials or components have gone into which end-product and to whom it has been sent. This is the core of product traceability, which is critical in the management of a product recall, and is dealt with in Part II.

Specification changes

Inevitably the specification of a product will change with time as design or formulation improvements are made, costs are cut or suppliers replaced. It is important to track such changes so that exactly what has been made with what is recorded. Unauthorised changes in the specification of incoming goods can lead to recalls. Danger can arise if reliance is placed on certification without surveillance – and more than one recall has been the outcome of such a practice. Another danger arises when price and availability relegate specifications to second place because of commercial pressures.

BS 5750 (ISO 9000)

This deals with quality management systems and will do much to ensure discipline and correct working practices. However, the standard itself does not mention recall and any requirements in that field will depend on the technical schedule used by the accreditation body. Although BS 5750 is to be recommended, gaining approval does not necessarily indicate that adequate recall management systems are in place. Indeed, there are examples which demonstrate that, even when product recall has been included and approval gained, the recall plan has been woefully inadequate.

Information

The field covered by information is very wide. It includes not only the words and illustrations that accompany the product itself but also the marketing literature, the point-of-sale advertising, the TV commercials, the mailshots, the posters, price lists, videos, and so on. Indeed, 'information' includes anything that will influence the way in which a customer or consumer will use – or not use – the product.

A recall can be the consequence of a mistake in product information which misleads or presents a danger to the public (see the Wall's canned stewed steak, p.209; Renault Owners'

Handbook, p.233; and Larousse cookery dictionary, p.234, case histories in Part III.

The Consumer Protection Act 1987 specifies what will be taken into account when the defectiveness of a product is being considered. It cites all the circumstances including:

'the manner in which, and the purposes for which, the product has been marketed, its get-up, the use of any mark in relation to the product and any instructions for, or warnings with respect to, doing or refraining from doing anything with or in relation to the product; (S3(2)(a)).'

There are usually two main sources of product information in a company – technical and marketing. The position of warnings, directions and instructions will be a technical responsibility and these have been mentioned above. The marketing people will influence the impression which the product makes on the public: the get-up or style, its characterisation or the manner in which it is perceived. If a product is marketed in such a way that its image is one of safety in operation, then the public are entitled to assume that the reality will reflect the image. If it does not and injury results, an action is possible under strict liability in tort.

This is a difficult area for management because the responsibility for information will lie with a number of different departments. The technical and marketing functions will often have an informal system of cross-checking to make sure that published information is accurate. But informal systems have a weakness because they are informal, and it is advisable to institute a mandatory sign-off system to ensure that nothing can be published unless the approvals have been completed.

A manufacturer must be aware of his responsibility to provide warnings about products which he has already supplied and which have subsequently become potentially dangerous. In tort it can be argued that a producer would be failing in his duty of care if he did not do whatever was reasonably practicable to prevent injury. In Germany it is a legal requirement for a manufacturer to monitor a product's performance in use to detect any possible latent defects. If a danger is revealed, the manufacturer must take all necessary steps to remove it (see Chapter 2, p.20). In the UK a leading case is *Walton* v *British Leyland*: the manufacturer did not publish a warning about a defect and was severely censured by the judge for not doing so and initiating a recall (see case history, p.210).

Product safety data sheets

Product safety data sheets are an advanced form of more commonplace product information and are used for chemicals and electronic components, for example. They are more often found in connection with industrial products than with consumer products. Inaccurate information in a product safety data sheet could result in the need for recall and replacement with an updated issue. In these circumstances it may be important for the manufacturer to be able to prove that a customer did receive the document. If a customer was injured because he did not follow the information in a product safety data sheet, then the supplier of the information would have a defence if he could prove that he actually did supply it but the customer chose to ignore it.

The requirement to supply safety information to customers was formalised in the revision of Section 6 of the Health and Safety at Work Act 1974 by the Consumer Protection Act 1987.

2 *The law and product recall*

International

It has been estimated that each year between 15,000 and 30,000 deaths are due to product–related injuries in the European Community, and in addition perhaps four or five million people are injured. Studies in the Netherlands, UK, US and Japan show that 10 per cent of the patients using emergency services in hospitals have been injured by products.

There is a considerable difference between countries in the way in which they seek to protect their population from defective products. Some have advanced laws to protect consumers as with the United States' Consumer Product Safety Act 1972, France's Consumer Protection Act 1983, and the UK's Consumer Protection Act 1987; some establish regulatory bodies with wide powers such as the United States' Consumer Product Safety Commission, France's Consumer Safety Commission, and Australia's Federal Bureau of Consumer Affairs. The European Community is beginning to address the problem with the Directive on Liability for Defective Products and the Draft General Product Safety Directive, (see below).

The legal powers vary not only from country to country but also within one country from product to product, with such things as electrical appliances, food, vehicles and pharmaceuticals being the subject of special legislation. Products withdrawn from the market in one country may still be available in another, while products banned in a developed country may be exported to the Third World. Some initiatives are being taken to prevent these abuses, and public and private bodies have set up systems for the international exchange of information concerning hazardous products.

There is a growing legal obligation to ensure that only safe products are put into the marketplace in the first place, although this has to be an unattainable absolute in every single case.

Once a potentially dangerous product has left the factory gate there are four actions that an authority should be able to take, depending on the seriousness of the risk:

1 Ban further production or sale so that the product is withdrawn from the market.
2 Recall the product already in the hands of the end-user or consumer.
3 Issue a warning to the public.
4 Prohibit the export of the product.

From this it will be seen that recall is but part of a greater whole, fragmented and uneven though it may be. Some countries have mandatory powers of recall for certain products, such as the United States, Japan, Australia, France and Germany. Other countries which do not include such powers in their legislation may achieve the same result by what is often called indirect coercion, which can force a recalcitrant manufacturer into a 'voluntary' recall. Frequently, companies will recall a product without the need for pressure or threat of legal action because the commercial penalty for not doing so would be severe.

A wise company will monitor its products once they are on the market to ensure that dangerous latent defects do not develop; this is particularly important for drugs. The German civil code imposes this duty on manufacturers while the common law and civil law system of other countries have provisions which have a similar effect.

The following is a brief survey of some of the legal provisions in a selection of countries. It is not intended to be comprehensive but rather reflect the variety of legislation that can influence recall. A product recall plan (PRP) should contain a statement of the company's legal obligations in the countries in which it sells its goods.

Australia

The 1986 amendments to the Trade Practices Act introduced a new Division 1 'A 'Product Safety and Product Information' into Part V of the Act. The provisions became operative on 1 July 1986 and apply to goods supplied after that date. The Act is the major Commonwealth consumer protection law. It gives rights to consumers and prohibits unfair business conduct.

The Act gives the relevant Minister (in practice the Minister for Consumer Affairs or the Attorney-General) powers to:

- declare compulsory consumer product safety and information standards;
- ban the supply of unsafe consumer goods;
- order suppliers to recall consumer goods with safety-related defects if a voluntary recall is considered to be inadequate; and
- issue public warning notices concerning goods with safety-related defects.

These powers affect suppliers who may be manufacturers, importers, wholesalers, distributors or retailers. The Act also requires that a supplier must notify voluntary recalls to the Minister when goods will or may cause injury to any person. The enforcement of these powers is undertaken by the Federal Bureau of Consumer Affairs.

The types of compulsory consumer product standards under the Act are:

- safety standards which require goods to comply with particular design or construction rules (e.g. for motor-cyclists' helmets and pedal bicycles) or carry certain warning labels (e.g. on children's nightwear and flotation toys);
- information standards which require prescribed information to be given with goods (e.g. care labelling of garments and

household textiles to indicate the most suitable cleaning method).

It is a criminal offence to supply goods which do not comply with a compulsory standard under the Trade Practices Act.

The Minister may place an immediate ban on goods which pose an imminent risk of death, serious illness or serious injury. Where the risk is not imminent, the Minister is required to notify suppliers that a ban is proposed. A ban applies for 18 months, after which it may be renewed permanently by the Minister. If suppliers object to an immediate, a proposed or a permanent ban they may request a conference with the Trade Practices Commission. Bans apply to manufacturers, importers, wholesalers, distributors or retailers. It is a criminal offence to supply goods which have been banned under the Trade Practices Act.

The product recall system under the Trade Practices Act is essentially a voluntary system with reserve compulsory recall powers. Suppliers who voluntarily recall goods, which will or may cause injury to any person, are required to provide details in writing to the Minister within two days of taking the recall action. If there is a voluntary or compulsory recall of goods supplied to overseas customers, the supplier is required to notify them of details of the recall. In addition, the supplier is required to provide a copy of this notice to the Minister within ten days of issuing the notice.

The Minister may order a compulsory recall of consumer goods which:

- will or may cause injury to any person; or
- do not comply with a consumer product safety standard; or
- have been banned.

In each case the compulsory recall can only be ordered if the supplier has not taken action satisfactory to the Minister to prevent the goods causing injury to any person.

If goods create an 'imminent risk of death, serious illness or serious injury', the Minister may order an immediate compulsory recall (i.e. without suppliers being given the opportunity for a conference with the Trade Practices Commission). If the safety risk is not imminent, the Minister is required to notify suppliers that a compulsory recall is proposed, in which case a conference with the Trade Practices Commission may be requested by the supplier to consider any objections to the recall.

Information on goods currently subject to compulsory or voluntary recalls may be obtained from the Federal Bureau of Consumer Affairs.

Where the supplier is made the subject of a compulsory recall order, it is a criminal offence for the supplier to continue to supply goods subject to the compulsory recall, or to breach the conditions of a compulsory recall.

The Minister may publish notices:

- warning that goods are under investigation because of a possible safety problem; and/or
- warning of possible risks involved in the use of goods.

After an investigation is completed, and provided that no banning and/or recall action has been taken, the Minister is required to publish a further notice advising on the outcome of the investigation. The Minister may also announce any further action that is proposed to be taken, such as a ban or recall.

If goods are subject to a ban or compulsory recall proposed by the Minister, the supplier of these goods may seek a conference with the Trade Practices Commission. The conference will be held before the ban or recall takes effect. Where goods pose an imminent risk of death, serious illness or serious injury, a conference may be requested only after the ban has taken effect. Suppliers will be notified by the Federal Bureau of Consumer Affairs of their rights to request a conference. This will be done by direct correspondence or by press advertisement. Having requested a conference, a supplier should quickly lodge a submission with the Commission, setting out its case concerning the ban or recall. Time limits apply for requesting a conference (generally ten days) and holding the conference (a further fourteen days).

Following a conference, the Commission is required to recommend to the Minister that:

- the proposed ban or compulsory recall proceed, be modified or not proceed; or
- the existing ban either remain in force, be varied or be revoked.

If the Minister does not accept the Commission's recommendation, the reasons for the Minister's decision must be published in the *Commonwealth Government Gazette*. So far there have been three conferences for condoms, blow gum and smokeless tobacco.

The Federal Bureau of Consumer Affairs may take action in the federal court for breaches of standards, bans or recalls. The maximum penalties are A$100,000 for corporations and A$20,000 for individuals. Businesses or consumers who suffer either physical or financial harm as a result of a breach of a compulsory standard, ban or recall may take action in the federal court. The action may be taken against the business from which the goods were purchased, i.e. the retailer, the manufacturer or any supplier in the distribution chain. The court can order the offending business to pay compensation to those who have suffered harm (see Appendix 2 for Australian recalls 1 July 1986 to 30 June 1990, p.247).

France

The recall from the market of defective or dangerous products is treated under a number of French statutes. The principal one is Law No. 83–660 of 21 July 1983, the Consumer Safety Act (see overleaf). This allows the government in the case of 'an immediate and serious danger' to order the recall of a product for up to one year.

For pharmaceutical products, Article R 5–124 para 4 of the Public Health Code provides that, in the case where the authorisation to market a pharmaceutical product is withdrawn, the manufacturer must take all action to ensure that the product is withdrawn from the market.

For food products, Article 18 of Decree No. 84–1147 of 7 December 1984 provides for the withdrawal from the market of food products whose time limits for sale have expired. There have been cases where the courts have ordered manufacturers of pharmaceutical products to withdraw products from the market where a competing product has been shown to be less dangerous.

The Consumer Safety Act 1983 gives the Government the general power to prohibit or regulate the production, import, offer, sale, distribution, possession, labelling, packaging and use of any products. The powers are exercised by decrees (décret du Conseil d'Etat) on advice from the Consumer Safety Commission. The Minister for Consumer Affairs can order the withdrawal or recall of dangerous products by ministerial decree, without the advice of the Consumer Safety Commission, in cases of serious and immediate danger.

Specifically, the government can order the withdrawal of products from the market or their recall by the producer for modification, reimbursement or exchange. Withdrawal could be ordered under the Consumer Protection Act 1978, although the power was scarcely ever used, but the new Act adds mandatory recall. The Government can order the provision of information to consumers and the destruction of a product if that is the only action which will avert danger.

The measures taken have to be proportionate to the danger. Mandatory recall of products which are subject to particular statutory controls or EC regulations is prohibited, except for the emergency procedures; these products include drugs, cosmetics and chemicals.

The Consumer Safety Commission (Commission de la Sécurité des Consommateurs) is composed of members of the Conseil d'Etat and the administrative and judicial courts, trade organisations, consumer organisations and experts nominated by the Minister for Consumer Affairs; the chairman is appointed by the Government.

Under the Act the following products have been ordered to be recalled from the market: erasers which resemble food products; certain types of glue which may have hallucinatory effects; cigarette lighters in the form of cars; gymnastic bars unable to bear more than 75 kilograms; and underwater masks incorporating a tube containing a ping-pong ball.

The EC Directive on Liability for Defective Products (see p.43) applies to France.

Germany

There is no legislation in Germany that sets out the specific cases in which a manufacturer is obliged to recall his goods. This is because a manufacturer's civil law duties and sanctions, as well as possible criminal sanctions, make it unnecessary.

Only Article 69.I of the AMG (Arzneimittelgesetz or Pharmaceuticals Act) expressly refers to recall. It establishes not only the obligation to recall drugs, but also the power of the supervisory authorities of the German Lander (Parliament) to issue directives, including recall directives, to enforce the provisions of the AMG. Independently of this law the regulatory authorities are also empowered, under the general clause in Article 14 of the OBG (Gesetz über Aufbau und Befungnisse der Ordnungsbehorden or Regulatory Authorities' Organisation and Powers Act), to take the steps required to avert danger in the interests of safety and good order.

Any such step is an administrative act which, following the lodging of an unsuccessful protest under Article 68 or the VwGO (Verwaltungsgerichtsordnung or Rules of the Administrative Courts), is subject to examination by the administrative courts; the authorities have to prove that prerequisites exist for the action they have taken.

According to case law and the literature, a manufacturer's obligation to recall products can arise out of Article 823.I of the BGB (Bundesgesetzbuch or German Civil Code) under certain conditions.

Supreme court case decisions, particularly those of the BGH (Bundesgerichthof or Federal Court of Justice), have inferred from these provisions – including those connected with manufacturer's liability – that anyone creating a dangerous situation, or allowing such a situation to continue, is obliged to take those safety measures which are materially required and reasonable, for the protection of other persons. In principle, everything necessary to remove the danger is materially required.

A manufacturer who fails to take adequate measures is liable, through breach of the 'duty to safeguard trade'. This duty does not stop when the product is put on the market because the manufacturer then has a 'product compliance duty'. To fulfil this duty it is necessary to carry out active product compliance, by monitoring a product's performance in use to detect any possible latent defects. A manufacturer's 'duties of diligence' in design, manufacture and instructions become a 'compliance duty', which may eventually become a passive duty for products with a history of freedom from complaints.

As it is the manufacturer who makes the decision to recall or not, the consequences of failure are important. In addition to possible disciplinary provisions under public law arising out of Articles 69.I of the AMG and Article 14 of the OBG (ban on sales, heavy fines or technical product obligations), there is also the threat of recourse against the company under Article 823.I (and, where applicable, Article 826) of the BGB.

If the senior executives fail to furnish proof of their non-culpability, they will be jointly and severally liable with the company to pay compensation under Article 823.I and/or Article 826 (in conjunction with Article 840) of the BGB.

The reason for this is a Federal Court of Justice case in 1975 against former executives of Metzler AG. It was decided that the duty of diligence towards consumers under the law of tort also applied to senior executives, such as works managers and production managers. Within their area of accountability, such officials are responsible for faults committed unless they can convincingly refute a presumption of negligence. If, upon the occurrence of a loss, there is a suspicion of any omission on the part of the company's management in its duties to avert danger, the persons responsible have to demonstrate convincingly why they did not implement any recall action.

The introduction of strict liability and the state of the art defence does not alter the position. Even if a manufacturer contends that the fault was not detectable on the basis of the state of science and technology at the time of marketing, he can still be held liable for an unlimited sum for breach of product compliance (failure to recall) on the principle of concurring claims with traditional product legal liability.

Should failure to carry out a recall lead to impaired health or death as a result of a defective product, senior officials can also be held criminally liable on the basis of the Metzler judgement. In particular, Article 230 (bodily injury caused by negligence) and Article 222 (negligent homicide) of the StGB (Strafgesetzbuch or Penal Code) apply here; the latter lays down, in addition to very heavy fines, terms of imprisonment of up to five years. If a manufacturer knows that a danger exists and does not recall, because he is willing to chance the breach, he will be guilty of wilful intent which, under Articles 212 and 211 (manslaughter and murder) of the StGB, carries penalties of between not less than five years and life imprisonment. The obligation necessary for default to be deemed a criminal offence arises in such cases out of 'prior endangering deeds' or marketing a defective and dangerous product.

The following general conclusion can be drawn regarding recall in Germany: action must be taken by a manufacturer if that manufacturer finds that a series of products could have defects or deficiencies which are likely to endanger life and limb or property; the defects must appear in a number of cases. The hazard and the degree of risk it presents will determine the action required, as will the circumstances in which the product will be used.

The Product Liability Act (Produkthaftungsgesetz: Prod-HaftG) of December 1989 implements the EC Directive of July 1985 into German law. The Act applies only to products placed in circulation after 1 January 1990. A comparison of the

Directive with the Act reveals many differences in the wording. This is a result of the Directive's transcription into usual German statutory language. In content, however, the Act corresponds with the Directive. The Act does not apply to pharmaceuticals and so does not affect the provisions of the Pharmaceutical Act (Arzneimittelgesetz).

Liability attaches to a defendant under the Product Liability Act irrespective of fault when a defective product causes damage (paragraph 1(1) ProdHaftG). Defendants under the Act are producers of a finished product, raw materials and component parts, any person who represents himself as the producer, importers and suppliers of the product when the producer cannot be identified (paragraph 4). Liability can neither be excluded nor restricted by the use of contractual clauses. If multiple defendants exist, they are jointly and severally liable (paragraph 5).

'Product' refers to chattels or chattels attached to land (paragraph 2). Electricity is included, but agricultural products and game are not. 'Defect' is defined in accordance with the EC Directive (paragraph 3).

Compensation above DM1,125 is awarded for death and bodily injury, generally, and for property damage (but not for the product itself) (paragraph 11), when the product was intended, and predominantly used by the consumer, for private use. The ceiling on liability for personal injury caused by a product or defective line of products is DM160 million (paragraph 10(1)). Compensation for pain and suffering will continue to be regulated by paragraph 847 of the BGB (see p.21).

There are six defences to an action under the Act. The onus of proof is on the injured plaintiff to establish the existence of the defect, the damage and a causal connection between the two (paragraph 1(4)). The defendant bears the onus of proof regarding exclusion of liability (paragraph 1(4)).

A statute of repose, a concept previously unknown in German law, is introduced by the Product Liability Act. Claims are extinguished ten years after the product causing injury was placed into circulation. The statutory period of limitation is three years from the date the plaintiff knew, or must have known of, the relevant damage (paragraph 12(1)).

Japan

There is a growing body of administrative safety regulations in Japan designed to prevent health and safety hazards. However, the majority of product recalls are voluntary, although certain state regulatory agencies have authority to mandate recalls concerning specific products under certain Acts. Among the regulatory agencies are the Ministry for Health and Welfare, the Ministry of International Trade and Industry and the prefectural governors of the autonomous local governing bodies, for instance Tokyo, Osaka, Kyoto and Hokkaido, each of which has independent legislative authority.

The Japanese Acts concerning product recall include the following:

Pharmaceutical Affairs Law 1960

(Article 70) regulates human and animal drugs, toiletries, cosmetics and medical devices. The Minister for Health and Welfare or a prefectural governor can order a manufacturer, importer, distributor or retailer of a defective product to recall it.

Foodstuffs Sanitation Law 1948

(Article 22) regulates foods, additives, packaging, etc. The Minister for Health and Welfare or a prefectural governor can order a manufacturer, importer, distributor or retailer of a defective product to recall it or eliminate the hazards it presents to consumers.

Consumer Products Safety Law 1973

(Articles 35 and 82) regulates consumer products with a number of exceptions such as foodstuffs, road vehicles, medical supplies and electrical appliances. A recall can be ordered by the Minister for International Trade and Industry if it is found that a product endangers consumers, because it does not carry the seal (see below) showing that it has been inspected and meets safety standards. Where serious injuries have occured, or where there is an imminent danger of this occurring because of a defect in a product, the Minister can order a recall.

Harmful Substances Used in Household Products Control Law 1974 (Article 6) regulates household products with a number of exceptions including foodstuffs, toys, detergents, drugs and medical devices. The Minister for Health and Welfare or a prefectural governor may order the manufacturer, importer, distributor or retailer of defective products to dispose of them or take emergency measures to prevent consumers being injured.

An outstanding development in consumer protection has been the enactment of local ordinances by prefectures. These adopt a comprehensive approach to product safety as opposed to the national government's product-by-product approach. Among the provisions are prohibitions on the supply of defective products and powers to order a recall.

The Product Safety Association was established under the Consumer Goods Safety Act. It draws up safety standards and checks products for conformance. A seal is fixed to products that are approved and consumers who suffer damage from such a product can receive guaranteed compensation of a fixed amount.

Despite numerous injuries caused by products, there have been few court decisions relating to product liability; perhaps 50 where manufacturers of defective products have been sued by injured consumers. However, there have been several multiple injury incidents which received wide media coverage. They include: the Thalidomide (Isomin in Japan) litigation; the Morinaga milk case in which 131 babies died and 12,000 were harmed; the Kanemi rice oil case in which 40 people died and 10,000 were affected in 31 prefectures; and the Smon case in which 5,000 plaintiffs demanded damages in 26 district courts after suffering drug-related injuries.

In 1990 Sony recalled 390,000 TV sets in Japan to replace high-voltage components that could catch fire. Pioneer

Electronics, Matsushita Electric Industrial and Toshiba also recalled TV sets. The Ministry of International Trade and Industry warned electronics companies to improve quality control and adopt regular product recall procedures. It was reported that in an annual inspection the Ministry found that more than 30 per cent of manufacturers had violated government safety standards. See Vehicles case histories in Part III (p.218) for Japanese car recalls.

Netherlands

Although the Government has no formal power to initiate a recall, the regulatory bodies can take certain initiatives because the distribution of unsafe goods is a criminal offence.

The Commodity Act, which came into force in August 1988 and replaced a previous statute of 1935, is the basis for regulations dealing with the quality and safety of goods in general. Special acts and regulations deal with particular products, such as medical devices, cars and electrotechnical consumer products.

Article 18 prohibits the sale of unsafe goods. Article 21 of the Commodity Act gives the Minister for Welfare, Health and Cultural Affairs (Welzijn, Volksgezondheid en Cultuur (WVC)) power to require the distributor of a dangerous consumer product to notify the purchasers; if no action is taken the Minister can issue a public warning. The Minister is responsible for product safety policy, which is developed by the Product Safety Department (Hoofdafdeling Produktveiligheid).

The Consumer Safety Institute (Stichting Consument en Veiligheid (SCI)) is funded by the Ministry and initiated several recall actions before the new Commodity Act came into force. The Consumentenbond is an independent consumer organisation with half a million members and has taken part in actions to remove dangerous products from the market, including a lamp containing prohibited asbestos, an inflammable carpet and a dangerous expander. The Economic Investigation Department (Economische Controle Dienst (ECD)) is the authority for electrotechnical products, which can advise companies to recall products and can seize goods if it considers them to be dangerous. The Commodity Inspection Service (Keuringsdienst van Waren) is attached to the Ministry and deals with non-electrotechnical products with powers similar to those of the Economic Investigation Department.

Article 2 of the Environmental Hazardous Substances Act (Wet Milieugevaarlijke Stoffen) provides for an explicit legal obligation: 'Anyone who in the course of a profession manufactures, delivers, imports into Holland or puts into circulation a substance or device, and who knows or ought to know that as a result of his action with these substances and devices man or the environment can get into danger is obliged to take all reasonable measures to prevent or minimise this dangerous situation.'

The EC Directive on Liability for Defective Products (see p.43) applies to the Netherlands.

Spain

Article 5 of the General Law for the Defence of Consumers and Users of 19 July 1984, stipulates that '. . . in any event, as a guarantee of human health and safety, the obligation must be observed . . . to recall or suspend, through effective means, any product or service that does not conform to the conditions and requirements demanded of them, or that for any other cause, supposes a foreseeable risk to human health or safety.' Further regulations are still outstanding in order to develop this law.

The EC Directive on Liability for Defective Products (see p.43) applies to Spain.

Sweden

In 1982 the Government appointed a committee to look into the legislation on product safety and three years later widened the committee's terms of reference to include the possibility of prohibiting the export of hazardous goods. The committee was under the chairmanship of a Justice of the Supreme Court and included representatives from the unions, industry, ministries and the National Board for Consumer Policies. In 1987 the committee presented its proposals for a new statute which became the Product Safety Act of 1 July 1989. This law did not make any provisions concerning the export of hazardous goods, but supplementary regulations on export prohibitions are being considered. The Product Safety Act provides powers to prohibit, recall and inform about products. The aim is to prevent goods and services from causing injury or damage to property; it is concerned primarily with goods and services provided to consumers. An entrepreneur may be required to supply safety information, forbidden to supply goods and services, or required to supply cautionary information and to recall goods and services.

An injunction for safety information can require such information to be provided at the point of sale, as part of the instructions for use, by signs or posters, advertisements, pamphlets or by other means. It is intended that an entrepreneur will voluntarily co-operate in such matters; if this fails, the regulatory body can refer the matter to the Consumer Ombudsman requesting that the case be brought before the Market Court, where the Ombudsman can apply for an injunction or a prohibition. There is no appeal granted from the Market Court.

A sales prohibition will usually be of a general nature and absolute, but it can be partial and apply to a certain category of users or products only.

Cautionary information applies when hazardous goods or services have already reached consumers and present a risk of personal injury or property damage. The entrepreneur can be forced to inform those possessing the goods, or holding property that has been serviced, about the risk of injury and how it can be prevented.

A recall can be ordered only when there is a risk of personal injury and can be an alternative to cautionary information. Repair, replacement and refund are the three actions associated with a recall. *Repair* implies that a product's defect has been corrected. *Replacement* means an exchange for a faultless product of a corresponding kind. *Refund* is the payment of compensation in return for the hazardous product. The recall powers can be used in connection with services but only for a repair or a refund.

When recalling products the entrepreneur has to offer the users concerned his assistance and specify the conditions involved. The latter must be generally acceptable but not unreasonable to the entrepreneur. The offer must be without significant cost or inconvenience to the user of the product. Repair and replacement must take place within a reasonable time. If the goods on recall are regarded as particularly dangerous, or when the risk is great, the entrepreneur may be ordered to destroy the goods.

Co-operation between entrepreneurs to carry out a recall is enforceable under the Act. There is a ten-year limitation period for recall but no limitation clause for cautionary information.

Two cases under the Product Safety Act which have been brought to the Market Court concerned catapults and a smoke alarm; a Danish test house reported that the smoke alarm would not issue a warning until people in the room were already unconscious or dead, and the Consumer Ombudsman has issued a number of injunctions, including those for a child's car seat, a pretzel, a toy aeroplane, a candy lipstick, catapults and a blow pipe.

United States

Some of the US Government bodies that impact significantly on product recalls are the:

- Consumer Product Safety Commission (CPSC);
- Food and Drug Administration (FDA);
- National Highway Traffic Safety Administration (NHTSA);
- Department of Transportation (DOT);
- Bureau of Mines (BOM);
- Department of Agriculture (USDA);
- Federal Aviation Agency (FAA).

Most of these agencies require prompt notification in the event that either the risk of injury or the severity of possible injury, or both, is suspected to be substantial, or if applicable mandatory standards or regulations are violated. The agencies conduct enquiries based on complaints and on their own research; some can force a product recall depending on the severity of the situation.

A brief review of the activities of the Consumer Product Safety Commission and the Food and Drug Administration follows; the work of the National Highway Traffic Safety Administration is under Vehicle recalls in Part III (see p.218).

Consumer Product Safety Commission

The responsibilities of manufacturers, importers, distributors and retailers of consumer products are defined in Section 15(b) of the Consumer Product Safety Act 1972. Each is required to notify the Consumer Product Safety Commission (CPSC) if they believes that a product:

- fails to meet a consumer product safety standard or banning regulation; or
- has a defect which could create a substantial hazard to consumers.

The intent of this section is to encourage widespread reporting of potential product hazards. The CPSC is an independent regulatory agency charged with reducing unreasonable risk of injury associated with consumer products; it has jurisdiction over 15,000 types of consumer products found in the home, schools and in leisure activities. It regulates all consumer products that are not specifically under the jurisdiction of other federal regulatory agencies such as automobiles, boats, guns, drugs, food, cigarettes and pesticides. The CPSC recalls about 200 products a year, ranging from kettles and hairdryers to snowmobiles and compressed gas cylinders. About half the recalls involve violations of CPSC standards, such as the health and safety rules for toys. CPSC epidemiologists estimate that around 25,000 deaths a year result from accidents involving products under the Commission's jurisdiction.

Even though the Commission has the authority to order a recall, replacement or refund of consumer products, such an order would be the result of a Commission investigation. This is costly and time-consuming and usually the Commission works with a company to obtain a voluntary recall, as opposed to a Commission order. Voluntary recalls account for over 95 per cent of those undertaken by the agency.

Generally, a product presents a substantial hazard when consumers are exposed to a significant number of units or if the possible injury is serious or likely to occur. Section 15 of the Act lists the statutory criteria for determining a substantial product hazard:

- *Pattern of defect.* The defect may be due to a failure of design, composition, content, construction, finish, packaging or the warnings and/or instructions accompanying the product.
- *Number of defective products distributed in commerce.* A single defective product could be the basis for a substantial product hazard determination if an injury is likely or could be serious. By contrast, a few defective products giving no risk or serious injury and having little chance of causing even minor injury would not be considered ordinarily to present a substantial product hazard.
- *Severity of risk.* A risk is considered severe if the injury that might occur is serious or likely to occur. Likelihood of injury is determined by considering the number of injuries that have occurred, the intended reasonably foreseeable use or misuse of the product, and the population group exposed to the product such as children, the elderly and the handicapped.

A company should report to the Commission, under Section 15 of the Act, within 24 hours of obtaining information which reasonably supports the conclusion that a product does not comply with a product safety rule or contains a defect which possibly could create a substantial risk of injury to the public. If a company elects to conduct its own investigation to decide whether it has reportable information, the Commission deems that such an evaluation should not normally exceed ten days.

When the Commission receives a report about a possible product defect its Division of Corrective Action undertakes the same product hazard analysis as that required of companies. First, a preliminary decision is made as to the presence of a defect in the product. If this is positive, the Division assesses the substantial product risk presented to the public and applies hazard priority standards to classify the severity of the problem. This provides guidance as to the level and intensity of the corrective action programme that the company will be asked to undertake.

The Hazard Priority System has three classes, each of which presents a substantial product hazard which requires corrective action to reduce the risk of injury.

Class A Hazard

This exists when a risk of death or grievous injury or illness is likely or very likely, or serious injury or illness is very likely.

These hazards warrant the highest level of company and CPSC attention. They call for immediate, comprehensive, and imaginative corrective action measures by the company, such as identifying consumers having the defective product and advising them of what steps to take to remedy the problem. Such corrective action measures would include, but are not limited to:

- maximum direct notice to the product distribution network;
- maximum direct notice to consumers or groups who have or use the product.

This notice could include one or more of the following communication channels:

- a joint news release issued by the CPSC and the company;
- purchase of mailing lists of suspected product owners;

- use of 'bill stuffer' enclosures;
- paid advertisements in nationally and/or regionally distributed newspapers and magazines reaching suspected owners of the product;
- installation of a toll-free telephone line to receive calls from consumers who have the defective product;
- using incentives such as 'bounty' money, gifts and premiums to prompt consumers, distributors and retailers to return the product;
- point-of-sale posters at retail outlets and service centres to alert consumers to a product recall;
- use of product warranty cards or other owner information, such as rebate return cards or service contract names, to identify users of the product;
- using product catalogues, marketing newsletters or sales materials to publicise the product recall;
- notification to groups and trade associations for whom the product recall may have particular concern.

Class B Hazard

This exists when a risk of death or grievous injury or illness is not likely to occur, but is possible, or when serious injury or illness is likely, or moderate injury or illness is very likely.

This hazard priority warrants the second highest level of product recall. Efforts should be made to reach owners and users of defective products through one or more of the following:

- a joint new release from the CPSC and the company;
- if available, direct notice to consumers owning the product by means of warranty cards, catalogue names, etc;
- paid notices in newspapers and specialist magazines to reach targeted users of the product;
- point-of-sale posters in retail outlets and service centres to alert consumers who may have the product;

- incentives for consumers, distributors and retailers to return the product;
- installation of a toll-free telephone line to receive calls from consumers with the product.

Class C Hazard

This exists when a risk of serious injury or illness is not likely, but is possible, or when moderate injury or illness is or is not likely but is possible.

This level of hazard concerns products that present a less serious risk of injury than products in the previous two categories, but still warrants a recall. Since a substantial risk of injury is presented, the following resources are among those that should be used to reach consumers having such products:

- a joint news release from the CPSC and the company;
- if available, direct notice to consumers owning the product by means of warranty cards, catalogue names, etc;
- point-of-sale posters in retail outlets and service centres to alert consumers who may have the product;
- notice to distributors and retailers about the product recall;
- installation of a toll-free telephone line to receive calls from consumers with the product.

For recalls of products presenting Class A, B and C priority hazards, these elements serve as guidelines for companies to use in communicating information to owners and users of the defective product.

Once the Commission's Division of Corrective Action has determined that there is a substantial risk to consumers from a product defect, it asks the company (manufacturer, importer, own-brander, distributor or retailer) to submit a voluntary corrective action plan. When agreed, the plan then forms the basis for any action taken, which has to address the requirements of the Substantial Product Hazard Report regulations.

All communications concerning a recall have to be agreed in advance by the Division. Unless all the purchasers of a product can be identified, the Commission will seek to issue a press release jointly with the company. Such releases are made available to the national wire services, major metropolitan daily papers, TV and radio networks and agencies on the company's mailing list. If the company issues its own press release, it may conflict with the Commission's press release and confuse the public.

See Figure 2.1 and Figure 2.2 for examples of a Consumer Product Safety Alert issued by the Commission, pp. 36 and 37.

Food and Drug Administration

The Regulatory Procedures Manual has a section on recall which gives an insight into the methods adopted by this agency. Their policy is stated in the following manner:

> Recalls are an appropriate alternative method for removing or correcting marketed consumer products, including their labelling and/or promotional literature, that violate the laws administered by the Food and Drug Administration (FDA). They are generally more efficient and afford equal and more timely consumer protection than formal administrative or civil actions, especially when the product has been widely distributed. Recalls may be undertaken at any time on the initative of manufacturers and distributors to carry out their responsibility to protect the public health and well-being, or in response to a formal request by the FDA.

A recall can be either 'firm initiated' or 'FDA-initiated'. The former is one commenced without a formal request from the FDA, while the latter is one in response to a formal request. A request by the FDA that a company recalls a product is usually concerned with the most serious cases and is addressed to the company with the primary responsibility for the manufacture or marketing of the product. This happens when the company concerned has not undertaken a recall on its own initiative and is usually classified as a Class I (see p.39). Before requesting a recall the FDA will usually have evidence capable of supporting legal action.

Consumer Product SAFETY ALERT

FROM THE U.S. CONSUMER PRODUCT SAFETY COMMISSION, WASHINGTON, D.C. 20207

June 1990

HEALTH HAZARD!

Do Not Use Indoors Any Water Sealers Intended For Outdoor Use

The U.S. Consumer Product Safety Commission has reports of 19 incidents in which consumers suffered health problems after being exposed to water sealers. In some cases, consumers reported they had to leave their homes because of fumes. Two people died after exposure to water sealers.

Some of the symptoms reported by consumers after exposure to water sealers were headaches, nausea, dizziness, and breathing difficulties. The chemicals identified in these incidents included petroleum distillates, mineral spirits, xylene, toluene, and naphtha. Many of these water sealers have labels warning not to use them inside. Use solvent-based water sealers outside unless labels give specific directions on how to use them safely indoors. If a water sealer is labeled for indoor use but does not have instructions for ventilation, open all windows and doors and use a fan to exhaust the air outside during application and drying. Be sure the air moves throughout the area in which the product is used. Observe all flammability warnings on the product label.

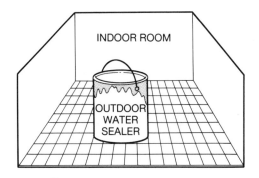

INDOOR ROOM

OUTDOOR WATER SEALER

Do not use indoors any solvent-based water sealers intended for outdoor use because the fumes can cause health problems.

Figure 2.1

Consumer Product SAFETY ALERT

FROM THE U.S. CONSUMER PRODUCT SAFETY COMMISSION, WASHINGTON, D.C. 20207

June 1990

Household Batteries Can Cause Chemical Burns

Since 1988, the U.S. Consumer Product Safety Commission has received over 100 reports of household batteries leaking, overheating, and rupturing. This permits corrosive liquid to leak, which can cause chemical burns. About ⅓ of the incidents involved injuries, a number of which were chemical burns to children from the leaking battery liquid.

Household batteries can overheat and rupture in several ways:

1. RE-CHARGING THE WRONG BATTERY OR USING THE WRONG CHARGER.

If you ry to re-charge a battery not intended to be re-charged, the battery can overheat and rupture. *If you have a re-chargeable battery, be sure to use the proper battery charger intended for the size and type of battery you have.* Do not use an automobile battery charger to recharge flashlight batteries because the batteries could rupture.

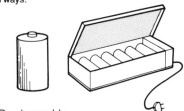

Re-chargeable

Battery charger

2. MIXING BATTERIES.

If you use alkaline and carbon-zinc batteries together in the same appliance or if you mix old batteries with new freshly-charged ones in the same appliance, the batteries can overheat and rupture. *Always use a complete set of new batteries of the same type when replacing batteries.*

3. PUTTING BATTERIES IN BACKWARDS.

If a battery is reversed (positive end where the negative end belongs and vice versa), it can overheat and rupture. This has happened when young children install batteries backwards. Warn children not to take out batteries or install them. *Parents should install batteries in household appliances and children's toys.*

Battery compartment

Figure 2.2

Once a company has commenced a recall it must conduct effectiveness checks to verify that the consignees have received the notification and taken appropriate action. The FDA recognises that in certain cases it may not be possible to check the effectiveness of a recall because it extends down to consumer level or to parts of the distribution chain which refuse to co-operate. In these cases the FDA will provide direct assistance and seek the help of other state agencies. As part of its responsibilities the FDA will separately audit the effectiveness checks of the recalling company.

The FDA will review the company's recall strategy while developing a strategy for its own audit programme; the factors involved will include the need for publicity, the depth of the recall and the level of effectiveness and audit checks.

The agency's weekly Enforcement Report contains information on all recall actions. In addition, notices or warnings may be published to the general public and specialist groups, such as health professionals and trade associations, to warn them of serious health hazards.

The FDA makes a distinction between a recall, a correction, a market withdrawal and a stock recovery. A *recall* concerns a product or its promotional material which is in violation of the laws administered by the agency and against which legal action could be initiated. A *correction* is the repair, modification, adjustment, relabelling, destruction or inspection of a product without its physical removal. A *market withdrawal* involves a minor violation for which the agency would not take legal action and which incurs no violation; removal of products from the market because of malicious product tamper are considered to be a market withdrawal. *Stock recovery* occurs when a company corrects a product that is still under its control and has not been put on the market.

The regulations in the United Kingdom concerning the recall of medical products (see the Medicines Act 1968, p.46) use different definitions from those adopted by the FDA for the classes of recall.

The assessment of the threat to health presented by a product is carried out by a health hazard evaluation, which takes into account the following:

1 Deaths, diseases, injuries or other adverse reactions that have already occurred from the use of the product.
2 Existing conditions that might contribute to a clinical situation that could expose humans or animals to a health hazard.
3 Assessment of population who may be at greatest risk (age, physical condition).
4 Assessment of degree of seriousness of the health hazard to the population at greatest risk (e.g. a product intended for use in emergency room situations).
5 Assessment of the likelihood of the occurrence of the health hazard.
6 Assessment of long-term or immediate consequences of the hazard.

The FDA assigns a classification to a recall to indicate the degree of health hazard presented by the product:

- Class I is a situation in which there is a strong likelihood that the use of, or exposure to, a violative product will cause serious, adverse health consequences or death.
- Class II is a situation in which the use of, or exposure to, a violative product may cause temporary or medically reversible adverse health consequences, or where the probability of serious adverse health consequences is remote.
- Class III is a situation in which the use of, or exposure to, a violative product is not likely to cause adverse health consequences.

In Class I and Class II recalls the agency will carry out audit checks to verify that the consignees at specified levels have received the notification and taken appropriate action. Class III recalls are not normally audited.

The level in the distribution chain which the recall is to reach is called 'the depth of recall'. This is the consumer or user level, which includes individuals, doctors, restaurants and hospitals; the retail level, which includes groceries, pharmacies and nursing homes; and the wholesale level, which can be all levels between the wholesaler and the retailer.

The recall notification has clearly to identify the:

product, potency, dosage, type, model and/or number(s), contain a concise statement of the reason for the recall, and instructions for consignees to follow in handling the recall. The possible necessity for bilingual or multilingual notifications should be explored with the firm's marketing offices.

The recall envelope, letter, mailgram, telegram or other type of message should be flagged URGENT DRUG (or FOOD, BIOLOGIC, DEVICE, etc.) RECALL (or CORRECTION). Letters should be sent first class and, where appropriate, by certified mail. The notification should be brief and to the point.

The FDA's Regulatory Procedures set out a comprehensive reporting system for the recalling company to follow, including the officials concerned and the forms which must be used; for instance, all recall classifications must have the agreement of the Center Compliance Director and all recall audit checks have to be on Form FDA 3177 Recall Audit Check Report.

European Community and United Nations

A Council Resolution of 14 April 1975 stated the Preliminary Programme of the European Economic Community for a Consumer Protection and Information Policy. It was this document that set out one of the priorities as the harmonisation of 'the law on product liability so as to provide better protection for the consumer'. Ten years later the appropriate Directive was approved, (see below).

In the 1975 Policy, consumers were seen as having five basic rights:

1 Right to protection of health and safety.
2 Right to protection of economic interests.
3 Right of redress.
4 Right to information and education.
5 Right of representation (the right to be heard).

The aim of the Policy towards consumers was to secure:

- effective protection against hazards to consumer health and safety;
- effective protection against damage to consumers' economic interests;
- adequate facilities for advice, help and redress;
- consumer information and education;
- consultation with and representation of consumers in the framing of decisions affecting their interests.

The first measures for achieving the objectives were given in the following principles:

- Goods and services offered to consumers must be such that, under normal or foreseeable conditions of use, they present no risk to the health or safety of consumers. There should be quick and simple procedures for withdrawing them from the market in the event of their presenting such risks.
- In general, consumers should be informed in an appropriate manner of any risk liable to result from a foreseeable use of goods and services, taking account of the nature of the goods and services and of the persons for whom they are intended.
- The consumer must be protected against the consequences of physical injury caused by defective products and services supplied by manufacturers of goods and providers of services.

Here was the mention of a 'quick and simple procedure for withdrawing' defective products. There is, of course, no quick and simple procedure, as the case histories in Part III demonstrate, and the wording of the 1975 Policy shows how little the EC lawyers understood the problems of industry.

Second Council Directive on proprietary medicinal products (75/317). The first Directive of 1965 (65/65) laid down the principles for government authorisation and the basic conditions required. The second Directive was another step towards the free movement of proprietary medicinal products. Our interest is concerned with Article 28 which says:

1 Notwithstanding the measures provided for in Article 11 of Directive 65/65/EEC, member states shall take all appropriate measures to ensure that the supply of the proprietary medicinal product shall be prohibited and the proprietary medicinal product withdrawn from the market if:
   (a) the proprietary medicinal product proves to be harmful under normal conditions of use;
   (b) it is lacking in therapeutic efficacy;
   (c) its qualitative and quantitative composition is not as declared;
   (d) the controls on the finished product and/or on the ingredients and the controls at an intermediate state of the manufacturing process have not been carried out or if some other requirement or obligation relating to the grant of the authorisation referred to in Article 16 has not been fulfilled.

2 The competent authority may limit the prohibition to supply the product, or its withdrawal from the market, to those batches which are the subject of dispute.

The 'appropriate measures' to withdraw a defective product in the UK are included below under the Medicines Act 1968 (see p.46). The Code of Practice for the Recall of Pharmaceutical Products is in Appendix 4 (see p.262); and the Tylenol case history is in Part III (see p.199).

The EC Directive on Liability for Defective Products (85/374) says in its first Article: 'A producer shall be liable for damage caused by a defect in his product'. In simple terms, this means that anyone who is harmed by a defective product can recover damages without having to prove negligence. It is the absence of negligence that is important, for it has introduced strict liability in tort. In the UK the provisions of the Directive were brought to the statute book by the Consumer Protection Act 1987 Part I (see p.49).

The Directive was approved in 1985 and the twelve member states had until 1988 to incorporate its provisions in their own legislation. Only the UK, Italy and Greece did so and the remaining nine states adopted the provisions at a variety of dates subsequently.

The EC Draft General Product Safety Directive 1989 introduces a general safety duty for all products; there are no exceptions. A safe product is defined as one that does not present an unacceptable risk for the safety and health of persons. Those affected are manufacturers, first importers into the EC, distributors and other professionals in the supply chain. Member states have to establish legal and enforcement mechanisms to ensure that the general safety duty is observed. There is provision for the setting-up of a Product Safety Emergencies Committee drawn from the member states to help the EC Commission investigate serious hazards and impose corrective measures throughout the Community. However, until the Directive is finally approved its provisions will not be known for certain.

The Directive on Liability for Defective Products is concerned with compensating people who suffer damage, and is a responsibility towards individuals who make a specific claim. The Draft General Product Safety Directive is concerned with prevention of damage occurring in the first place and is a responsibility towards the general public. It would have been more logical to have produced the general product safety provisions before those dealing with product liability – to have a statement of the crime before its punishment as it were.

New Approach Directives give the 'essential requirements' for the safety of specific products (such as toys, construction products and simple pressure vessels) written in general terms, which must be satisfied before the nominated products can be sold anywhere in the Community. The essential requirements can be satisfied in a number of ways. The usual method will be by conforming to an appropriate European standard or by demonstrating conformity with the essential requirements themselves. This attestation can be a declaration by the manufacturer supported by his own or independent test results, the certificate of an independent body, or the test results of an independent body. Products which conform have to carry the C€ mark.

The **United Nations General Assembly** adopted guidelines for consumer protection by consensus on 9 April 1985 for use in elaborating and strengthening consumer protection policies and legislation, and encouraging international co-operation in this field.

The **Guidelines for Consumer Protection**, published by the United Nations Department of International Economic and Social Affairs in 1986, ran to 46 paragraphs. In the section on physical safety governments are advised to:

> ... adopt or encourage the adoption of appropriate measures, including legal systems, safety regulations, national or international standards, voluntary standards and the maintenance of safety records to ensure that products are safe for intended or normally foreseeable use.

In support of these measures the following are included:

11   Appropriate policies should ensure that if manufacturers or distributors become aware of unforeseen hazards after products are placed on the market, they should notify the relevant authorities and, as appropriate, the public without delay. Governments should also consider ways of ensuring that consumers are properly informed of such hazards.

12 Governments should, where appropriate, adopt policies under which, if a product is found to be seriously defective and/or to constitute a substantial and severe hazard even when properly used, manufacturers and/or distributors should recall it and replace or modify it, or substitute another product for it; if it is not possible to do this within a reasonable period of time, the consumer should be adequately compensated.

United Kingdom

Contract and tort

Goods sold in the course of business have to be of merchantable quality and fit for their purpose, under the provisions of the Sale of Goods Act 1979, see p.48, which apply to the contractual relationship between the buyer and the seller.

The law of tort is concerned with the rights that one person has against other persons generally, whereas the law of contract is concerned with the rights and liabilities established between two parties. A manufacturer owes a duty of care to those he can reasonably foresee could be liable to suffer loss or injury because of a defect in his product; if he fails in his duty he could be liable under the tort of negligence (see the *Walton* v *British Leyland* case history in Part III, p.210).

A manufacturer with responsibility for a defective product could initiate a recall for reasons of contract or tort, although there is no 'product recall' law. However, certain legislation imposes liabilities on some transactions that make the need to be able to recall a very advisable management skill. The following is a brief review of the more important Acts. Some of the legislation 'imposes' criminal liability on companies which fail to supply safe products, such as the Medicines Act 1968, Health and Safety at Work Act 1974, Consumer Protection Act Part II 1987, and the Food Act 1990.

Medicines Act 1968

Every country has legislation of varying degrees of complexity, covering all stages of the supply of medicine, from production to the point where it is handed to the eventual user, the patient. In the UK the principal legal restrictions were applied at the point of contact with the public, the retail pharmacy, through the Pharmacy and Poisons Act 1933. The situation was changed by the Medicines Act 1968, which superceded the Pharmacy and Poisons Act 1933 and extended control of medicines by legislation, from the point where the manufacturer wishes to institute clinical trials on a newly developed product, to the point where the patient receives the medicine.

Licences and certificates are required by manufacturers, and the whole process from clinical trials to distribution is regulated by a number of official or semi-official bodies. Many products used in medicine do not have a medical purpose and the Act defines a medicinal product as one used for any one or more of the following: treating or preventing disease; diagnosing disease; contraception; inducing anaesthesia; and otherwise preventing or interfering with the normal operation of a physiological function.

Regulations made under the Medicines Act impose certain obligations on licence holders with regard to withdrawal and recall from sale. A distinction is made between withdrawal from sale, which means the total removal of the product from the market, and recall, which means the removal from the market of a specified batch or batches. In the case of a withdrawal the licence holder is required to notify the licensing authority of such a decision, but this requirement does not extend to the recall of a batch.

The following extract is taken from Part 1, Schedule 1 to the Medicines (Standard Provisions for Licences and Certificates) Regulations 1971 made under the Medicines Act 1968:

para 6 The licence holder shall keep such documents as will facilitate the withdrawal or recall from sale, supply or exportation of any medicinal product to which the licence relates.

para 7 When the licence holder has been informed by the licensing authority that any batch of any medicinal product to which the licence relates has been found not to conform with the specification of the product as regards strength, quality or purity or with the provisions of the Act or of any regulations under the Act that are applicable to the medicinal product, he shall, if so directed, withhold such batch from sale, supply or exportation, so far as may be specified by the licensing authority.

para 8 The licence holder shall notify the licensing authority forthwith of any decision to withdraw from sale, supply or exportation any medicinal product to which the licence relates, and shall state the reason for that decision.

The regulations concerning the recall of medical products by the Food and Drug Administration in the United States have different definitions for recall and withdrawal (see p.38).

Employers' Liability (Defective Equipment) Act 1969

If an employee suffers death or personal injury through a defect in equipment supplied, his employer is deemed to have been negligent. The liability is strict and it is not possible to exclude or limit any liability imposed by the Act. The word 'equipment' includes any parts and machinery, vehicles, aircraft and clothing. To come under the umbrella of the Act the employee must show that a defect in equipment caused the accident. The defect must be attributable wholly or partly to a fault of a third party by which is meant negligence, breach of statutory duty or other act or omission which gives rise to liability in tort. 'Injury' includes loss of life, any impairment of a person's physical or mental condition and any disease.

Health and Safety at Work etc. Act 1974

This provides a legislative framework for the protection of people at work and others affected by work processes. Every employer has the duty to ensure, so far as is reasonably practicable, the health, safety and welfare at work of all his employees. He must, so far as is reasonably practicable, make sure that the plant and systems are safe and without risk to health; that the use, handling, storage and transport of articles and substances are safe and without risk; that the necessary information, instruction, training and supervision are provided; and that there are no risks involved with ingress to or egress from the working environment.

One of the principles of the Act is that industry should take responsibility for the health and safety of those people likely to be affected by its activities. The first link in this chain is Section 6, which aims to ensure that acceptable levels of health and safety are incorporated at the design and manufacturing stage. It is the duty of any person who designs, manufactures, imports or supplies any articles for use at work, or any article of fairground equipment, to ensure, so far as is reasonably practicable, that the article is so designed and constructed that it will be safe and without risk to health at all times when it is being set, used, cleaned or maintained by a person at work. Failure to comply can result in a criminal prosecution.

Sale of Goods Act 1979

Certain duties are assigned to the seller, such as those concerned with the delivery and ownership of goods. From a product safety point of view, specific interest is directed at the goods, which must be of merchantable quality if they are sold in the course of business. They must be reasonably fit for their purpose. In a consumer sale, the seller cannot exclude his liability to supply goods that are of merchantable quality and are fit for their purpose. In a non-consumer sale, the seller must prove that any clause excluding these liabilities is reasonable.

The law on the sale of goods was codified by an Act passed in 1893 which was re-enacted as the Sale of Goods Act 1979. This provides for strict liability in contract, which means that the seller of goods is strictly liable to the purchaser of those goods. But this strict liability is restricted to the seller and the buyer as they have privity of contract.

Consumer Protection Act 1987

Part I introduced the provisions of the EC Directive on Liability for Defective Products. Part II brought to the statute book a general safety requirement for all consumer goods, enforced by criminal sanctions.

The chief provision of Part I is that a person who produces a defective product will be liable for any damage that it causes; it will not be necessary to prove negligence in order to recover compensation; and it is in addition to all existing remedies in contract and tort. It is known as strict liability in tort, which is a civil injury or wrong for which the appropriate remedy is an action for damages.

A product is defined as any goods, electricity, components that are part of a finished product and raw materials.

Liability is assigned to four groups of people. Usually it will be the manufacturer who will be liable or, in the case of raw materials, the person who won or mined the product. Processors are only liable if they modify the essential characteristics of a product, although they may be liable as a supplier. Importers are liable if they are the first to import a product into the Community in the course of their business and supply it to someone else. Own-branders may be liable and are defined as persons who have held themselves out to be the producer of a product, by putting their name on the product, or using a trademark or other distinguishing mark in relation to a product. Apart from manufacturers, processors, importers and own-branders, a person who supplies a product will only be liable if he fails to identify the person who supplied him with the product.

A product is held to be defective if its safety is not such as persons generally are entitled to expect. In determining the defectiveness of a product, the following are taken into account: its marketing, instructions, warnings and get-up; what might reasonably be expected would be done with or in relation to the product; and the time the product was supplied by its producer to another.

There are six defences available but the burden of proof lies on the producer (see below).

The six defences available under the Consumer Protection Act Part I

1 The defect was caused by compliance with legal requirements.
2 The person proceeded against did not supply the product to another.
3 The product was not supplied in the course of business.
4 The defect did not exist in the product when it was originally supplied.
5 The producer could not have discovered the defect given the state of the art at the time he supplied the product.
6 The defect was due to the design of a subsequent product or the instructions given by its manufacturer.

The introduction of strict liability will probably do more than any other measure to increase the need to be able to recall a defective product. This is because, although a product recall could be expensive, it would be less expensive than a product liability incident, with unlimited damages available under the Act.

Consumer safety is dealt with in Part II of the Act. It says that a person is guilty of an offence if he supplies consumer goods which fail to comply with the general safety requirement, which means that they are not reasonably safe having regard to all the circumstances. Safe in relation to goods means that there is no risk (or no risk apart from one reduced to a minimum) that death or injury will occur to any person because of the goods. Certain goods are excluded from the provision.

A person guilty of an offence is liable to imprisonment, a fine or both. Part II consolidates the Consumer Safety Act 1978 and the Consumer Safety (Amendment) Act 1986. This includes powers to make regulations, which have been widened, and retains the power of the Secretary of State to issue prohibition notices and notices to warn, and empowers enforcement authorities to serve suspension notices.

Under s13 the Secretary of State can prohibit a person '... from supplying, or from offering to supply, agreeing to supply, exposing for supply or possessing for supply, any relevant goods which the Secretary of State considers are unsafe and which are described in the notice.' A notice to warn requires '... that a person at his own expense publishes a notice about any relevant goods that the Secretary of State considers are unsafe.'

The provisions of s13 do not actually give the Secretary of State the power to order a recall but could virtually have the effect of forcing a manufacturer to initiate one.

Food Safety Act 1990

The Act tightens the controls on food (which includes drink and ingredients used in the preparation of food) that fails to meet the new food safety requirement by:

- the addition of any article or substance to the food;
- the use of any article or substance as an ingredient in the preparation of the food;
- the extraction of any constituent from the food; and
- the subjection of the food to any other process or treatment.

From a recall point of view s8(3) is very important:

Where any food which fails to comply with food safety requirements is part of a batch, lot or consignment of food of the same class or description, it shall be presumed for the purposes of this section and section 9 below, until the contrary is proved, that all the food in the batch, lot or consignment fails to comply with those safety requirements.

Section 9 deals with the inspection and seizure of suspected food by an authorised officer of a food authority.

The Act introduces into the food industry the defence of 'due diligence' for the first time, although it is to be found in other legislation such as the Trade Description Act 1968 and the Consumer Protection Act 1987. It means that a trader is likely to be convicted unless he can show that the offence arose because of someone else's mistake and that he took all reasonable precautions and exercised all due diligence to avoid committing the offence.

The Act makes provision for improvement notices, prohibition orders and emergency control orders. Under s13(5) the Minister:

(a) may give such directions as appear to him to be necessary or expedient for the purpose of preventing the carrying out of commercial operations with respect to any food, food sources or contact materials which he believes, on reasonable grounds, to be food, food sources or contact materials to which an emergency control order applies; and

(b) may do anything which appears to him to be necessary or expedient for that purpose.

The Act runs to 54 pages and contains powers for EC Directives to be implemented in the UK by regulations. Regulations and codes of practice will support the Act and detail certain areas, for example enforcement responsibilities, the qualifications required for a statutory food examiner, factory inspection teams and the registration of food premises. One code of practice provides guidance on an enforcement officer's powers in connection with s8(3).

PART TWO

Product recall planning

3 *The product recall plan*

Making executive decisions

Devising a product recall plan can be likened to a menu that has to be able to provide for a banquet or a snack. No two recalls are identical, and such a plan must cater for the worst situation (a national recall on the Sunday afternoon of a Bank Holiday weekend) and a minor marketing exposure (an organoleptic defect in food). The plan has to enable the company to select the set of options which will best meet a particular product defect, and it has to give the company the opportunity to match its response to the risk.

To be effective the plan must not only have the backing of the board and the chief executive officer (CEO) but also be seen to have such support. The motivation has to come from the top, for the top people have to become involved and not merely be rubber stamps. It is not satisfactory to tell the quality manager to write a plan and for the CEO to sign it – along with other documents – one Tuesday afternoon. The following pages offer 15 steps which could help towards establishing a product recall plan.

In the United States a valuable survey[1] of the product recall practices of 529 consumer product companies revealed a startling disparity between what the respondents said they did and

1   Harrington E, Kamlet K S, 'Risk Avoidance and Product Recall Preparedness in the Consumer Products Industry', A T Kearney Inc 1989. Presentation to the Practising Law Institute.

the conclusions of the survey. Among the key survey findings were the following:

- There is widespread awareness of the product liability problem.
- Nearly one in four (120) of the respondents had experienced product recalls.
- Seventy-five per cent of the companies had some form of recall procedure in place, but the procedures tended to be unsophisticated.
- Seven per cent of the companies said they were in the process of developing recall policies or procedures.
- Eighteen per cent had no recall policy and no plans to develop one.
- Relatively few companies have thoroughly reviewed their safety procedures to prevent defective products.
- Few companies have established a quick, thorough means of repairing, replacing or recalling potentially defective products from the marketplace if a problem were to occur.
- Most companies have not gone beyond the most rudimentary steps in managing risks and are not adequately prepared for the liabilities they may face.
- Food, pharmaceutical and automotive companies, whose products, if defective, can do great harm, were among those who have the most comprehensive plans to manage product liability and recall issues.
- Without exception, company executives emphasised concern for safety and product or company reputation as the key factor motivating a recall action. Regulatory action, consumer pressure and potential liability were cited as secondary concerns. They disclaimed any appreciable consideration for the costs of a product recall. They indicated that their goal was a comprehensive and effective effort to correct the problem.

Harrington and Kamlet go on to say:

> However, the conclusions of the survey present a different
> picture, for they suggest that product liability and recall pre-
> paredness are fundamentally management rather than legal
> issues – although there will always be a critical role for
> lawyers in the process. Where management breaks down,
> legal problems begin. It is critical that companies do not wait
> for disaster to strike, and then call their lawyers to try to bail
> them out. Rather, the prudent company will develop a pro-
> active advance plan to minimise product risks and manage
> them if they do occur.
>
> The data also suggests that, despite the almost universally
> recognised major business impacts of inadequately managed
> product liability risks, the majority of consumer products
> companies fail to do an effective job in managing these risks.
> Indeed, it appears in many instances that major corporations,
> rather than attempting to manage their risks, decide to simply
> walk away from them; choosing to abandon product lines,
> close plants, and forego promising opportunities – viewing the
> certainty of lost profits as preferable to the uncertainty of
> potential litigation, recalls, and bad publicity.

The survey prompted the development of a four-stage model of
a company's preparedness to deal with faulty products,
providing a measure of a company's sophistication in managing
product liability risks and promoting effective recalls:

Stage I [Achieved by 272 companies in the survey or 51 per
cent.] The least sophisticated stage, characterised by informal
planning, limited policies for evaluating and reacting to
potential product hazards. No focused organisational responsibility, authority or accountability below the CEO. Limited or
no recall experience. Low level of knowledge or understanding of regulatory requirements, product risks/liabilities or
logistical demands of recalls.

Stage II [233 or 44 per cent.] Companies which have a formal, but unsophisticated, corrective action plan. Part-time safety co-ordinator. Sporadic and informal evaluation of corrective action preparedness. Routine regulatory compliance. Limited working relationship with regulatory authorities. Moderate level of product tracking techniques.

Stage III [24 or 5 per cent.] Companies which have a formal, comprehensive program for applying corrective action and some integration with risk management efforts. Safety committee. Corrective action preparedness through regular unscheduled audits and mock recalls, sound understanding of pertinent regulations, effective communication with regulatory authorities, proactive use of media for communicating with consumers, and sophisticated product tracking system.

Stage IV [One company] Companies with formal risk management plans that emphasise proactive quality control, a detailed, systematic and tested corrective action program, and senior management involvement. Safety committee with clearly defined duties and sufficient authority to perform them. Regular mock recalls and unscheduled audits, with implementation of necessary modifications. Finely honed understanding of pertinent regulations. Interact well with regulatory authorities. Proactive use of the media to alert consumers to corrective action and to help shape product and company image. Trained company spokespersons. State-of-the-art, on-line product tracking system.

A product recall plan should be an authoritative document which provides as much or as little information required as succinctly as possible. It is not uncommon to find senior managers well satisfied that they have a plan without having actually studied it in any detail. These situations can be dangerous because reliance may be placed on a document whose inadequacies would become only too apparent in an emergency. One major company's 'plan' was four pages of notes while, in the case of a multinational it was a collection of case histories and some vague directions. Plans that have more substance than these examples may have been used successfully in practice, but only for products still under the company's control in its own distribution system. This can lead to a false sense of confidence because the real test only comes when a product under recall has passed out of the company's hands.

A good Product Recall Plan (PRP) should include certain categories of information and these are considered below.

Chairman's Message

It adds weight to the importance of the plan if it is introduced by a statement from the chairman. This can include words to the effect that the requirements of a recall will take precedence over other responsibilities and that the resources of the company will be at the disposal of the recall team.

Objectives

The plan must start with a statement of its objectives, approved by the CEO and agreed by the board. More than one large company has stated the objectives in an unacceptable order, in that the first objective has been to protect the assets of the company. *The first objective of a product recall must be to prevent users and others suffering harm.*

Corporate morality

The issue of corporate morality arises and this needs to be examined carefully so that the board are quite sure of their commitment. The objectives of the PRP can be stated as:

- **To prevent customers and others suffering harm**. The legal sanction (if it is needed) is in the EC Directive on Liability for Defective Products Article 1: 'The producer shall be liable for damage caused by a defect in his product.' In other words, the company will be liable to pay unlimited (in the UK) compensation for the harm caused by a defective product, without the need for negligence to be proved.
- **To comply with all laws and regulations**. One example is the requirement of the Sale of Goods Act 1979 that goods

must be of merchantable quality and reasonably fit for their purpose.

- **To protect the assets of the company**. In many cases a prime asset will be a brand name, which may well not have a value in the balance sheet. The responsibility of the board in this regard is to the shareholders, who will not be on hand to approve the directors' stewardship but may well have strong views subsequently.

The dilemma which occurs when a company is driven to examining its corporate conscience is illustrated in having to decide which of the objectives takes precedence. One potential scenario can be put aside in this context: a product can be recalled which presents no danger to users (see the Kodak recall case history in Part III, p.189); in this situation the first objective does not apply. But a single product company, or one with a restricted range, has all its eggs in one basket and a recall could lead to collapse. In the ultimate, the company may try to balance the possibility of causing harm to users against the probability of making employees redundant and worse. The judgement can depend on weighing those two weasel words 'possibility' and 'probability'.

The problems that can affect a single-product company are illustrated by the Perrier recall of 1990 (see the case history in Part III, p.165). Although Perrier had other products, its mineral water was the flagship, and the company name, the brand and product were all one in 'Perrier'. The contamination found in the US was not a hazard so the first aim of recall did not apply, as the health of consumers was not at risk. However, the need to protect the company's greatest asset – Perrier – was critical and an international recall was initiated.

A different set of circumstances applied to a company that had diversified into a product outside its experience. Reports of six incidents in the marketplace had been confirmed by salesmen and, although no one had been hurt so far, there was a possibility that someone could be. There was no recall plan. The fault had been identified and the design modified to prevent any further incidents. The risk was limited to the units already in the field and an expensive promotion was underway. The board met to decide on what action to take.

At first there was complete agreement that the product should be recalled and replaced with stock incorporating the modified design. The cost of a recall was estimated and the figures put on a flip chart, as each director forecast what his expenditure would be. As the number of noughts on the flip chart increased, the initial moral fervour to recall decreased. It was a conflict between the objectives; no recall was initiated as the first objective slipped from first place. Subsequently, a handful of further incidents did not cause any injuries.

A third example concerned a company supplying a domestic product. The product used both water and electricity and had been on sale for a number of years without incident. Two second-hand reports of electric shock to users were received but, despite determined efforts, first-hand evidence could not be obtained. The approvals body put great pressure on the company to initiate a recall. The board met in continuous session over several days as it sought to reach a decision and balance the demands of the objectives. A major marketing promotion was in hand in the run-up to the biggest selling period of the year. The directors had insufficient information and inadequate time but nevertheless had to come to a conclusion.

In the event a recall was initiated in support of the first objective, with a hastily improvised 'plan' which had been thrown together while the board were in session. A post-mortem revealed a defect in a bought-in component, whose design had been changed without notification, which confined the risk to a limited production run. Unfortunately the batch coding could only be read with the greatest of difficulty by people unfamiliar with its position. No one was seriously hurt but the cost of the incident ran into seven figures; although the company did learn much from the experience it was a very expensive exercise.

The US Consumer Product Safety Commission is a regulatory body and as such its objectives are not the same as those of a manufacturer. The Commission gives the objectives for a recall as being to:

- locate as quickly as possible all defective products;
- to remove defective products from the distribution chain and to retrieve them from the possession of consumers; and
- communicate accurate and understandable information to the public about the product defect, the consumer hazards and the corrective action plan.

Legal

A statement of the legal responsibilities of the company, prepared by the company's lawyer, must set the background against which the recall actions are taken. Part I of this book sketches in some of the general requirements, but each company should detail those that affect it specifically. The EC Directives should not be overlooked and be regularly updated.

Preparation

Product recall plans written by one manager sitting in an office are easily recognisable and are of little use operationally. They usually consist of a catalogue of instructions to other managers, who rapidly forget their content as they put the PRP in the bookcase alongside last year's diary. What is needed is commitment. This commitment can be obtained by getting those who will manage a recall to have the plan written. In the event they should be following the management practices which they have established and are familiar with. The recall co-ordinator and the product recall committee should have this responsibility. As it may take six months or a year to prepare, and a variety of different managers will be making contributions, the format adopted is critical.

Format

A suitable design is one that provides information at different levels, always bearing in mind that in a recall time is often at a premium. One successful format uses a ring binder with tabbed dividers, for ease of reference, with the majority of the pages appearing in an appendix as a back-up. Pages of a different colour for each section make for ease of reference. The plan starts with a simple flow chart marked with references to the appropriate sections, so the sequence of events can be seen at a glance. Alternatively the information can be presented in the form of a table, again with references to the appropriate sections. Examples of both follow. The next part will deal with some of the subjects that follow in this book, but selected and fashioned to suit the company concerned; authorities and responsibilities will be spelled out, with reference to supporting detail in the final section. The appendix is the place for the detail: contact lists, examples of notifications, instructions for telephone operators, advice on dealing with the media, the path of the distribution chain, and so on.

The copies of the plan should be numbered and each allocated to specific individuals. The senior secretary on the product recall committee can be made responsible for issuing the copies and also the replacement pages that inevitably will be necessary, especially the contact list.

Recall co-ordinator and product recall committee

Step 2

The co-ordinator's responsibility is to establish the product recall plan and take charge of the management of a recall. He may recommend that a recall is initiated, but the actual decision should be made by a different manager. The first break-point in the chain (see Figure 3.1) comes if the co-ordinator decides not to recommend a recall; this could happen, for example, in a malicious product tamper where a recall could be counterproductive.

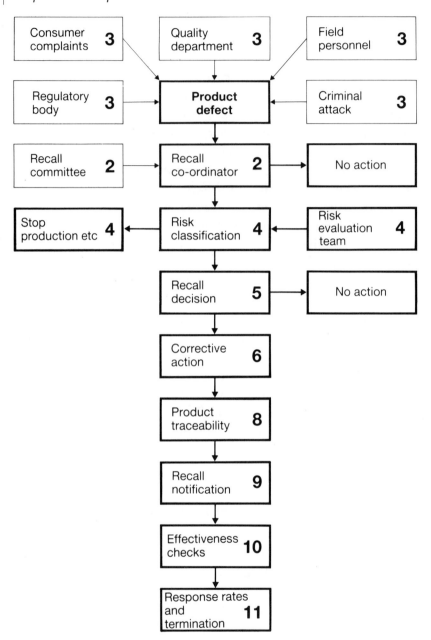

Figure 3.1 *Product Recall flow chart. The numbers refer to the 'steps' in the text*

If he is to be effective, the co-ordinator should be a seasoned professional with experience and management muscle. In a major recall physical and emotional demands are heavy, especially during the initial period, and this should be considered when making the appointment. The co-ordinator may come from any one of a number of functions: marketing, technical, research and development, etc. In some companies the task of co-ordinator will be undertaken by the managing director; in large companies it may be a divisional director or a country manager. The disadvantage of such appointments is that during a recall the co-ordinator will have no time for his normal responsibilities; managing the company or a division. The business of a company has to continue, even if it is managing a product recall at the same time. Further, it is always useful for a senior manager to be able to stand back from the day-to-day or hour-to-hour events so that he can take in a wider perspective.

A product recall committee should be formed to help the co-ordinator establish the plan and support him in an actual recall. It should be the responsibility of the co-ordinator and the committee to have the plan written but not necessarily to write it themselves. The committee should be small in number, four or five at the most, so that it is action-orientated and not merely a forum for an exchange of views. During a major recall the committee will be in virtually continuous session, at least in the initial stages. In these circumstances committee members' deputies will have to carry out their normal management functions. Additional managers can be co-opted on to the committee for limited periods when their expertise is required.

The committee should be formed from senior managers and it is useful to have a senior secretary present to take the minutes. Later, she can carry out vital functions during a recall and maintain the contact list (see Step 13). The product recall plan appendix must contain names and titles of the recall co-ordinator, the members of the committee and their alternates, together with their location details and telephone numbers.

Early warning system

The sooner a potential recall situation is detected the better, so that action can be taken to manage the risks and prevent them from getting out of hand. A company receives information about the performance of its products from a variety of sources, any one of which could be a pointer to something untoward. These should be arranged so that warning signals are directed not only to the manager responsible but also the recall co-ordinator to alert him to possible action.

Broadly speaking there are two main sources: internal and external. A method should be established so that the information from both can be gathered together; the overall effect being greater than the sum of the parts. This can be done by collating the information into a regular review and analysis with a limited circulation, including the recall co-ordinator. A suitable manager to carry this out would be an information scientist or a technical information officer.

Internal Sources

Quality

The quality function is often in the best position to detect trends, but may only store raw data without seeking to discover what this could reveal. In some companies quality control is more a data-gathering operation reporting to production, while quality assurance in its monitoring role may overlook the mine of information readily available. The use of statistical techniques can provide a valuable insight into trends not easily found otherwise.

Incoming components, sub-assemblies and defective ingredients can lead to an end-product manufacturer having to initiate a recall. Vendor certification and certification of conformance of incoming goods may not always be the best vehicles for revealing movements away from the acceptable. Working close to extremes of tolerance levels, while within laid down limits, may be an indication of potential problems which routine approvals may mask.

Modern methods of production, such as statistical process control (SPC) and computer aided manufacture (CAM), will generate important data that can be so arranged that warnings are given if predetermined levels of acceptability are exceeded. The standard for quality management, BS 5750, should ensure that adequate data are recorded, but action points for potential recall situations should be built into the system.

Even when all these checks and balances are in place, goods may be despatched unless they are blocked by the quality department. This is a negative release system and can allow defective products onto the market before action can be taken to check this. A positive release system provides a final check by allowing the despatch of goods only when specifically cleared by means of a sticker or a method that can be recorded.

The part that can be played by a professional quality system in a recall is shown in the Remington electric shaver case history in Part III, p.182. The company had a roving quality assurance audit team in Europe reporting directly to the parent company's headquarters in Connecticut. It was this team that picked up a potentially dangerous defect, which originated in France, when it was auditing a German warehouse. A recall was initiated as a result.

Spares and replacement parts

An unusually high demand for safety-critical items could be a warning of serious consequences. If a 'normal' level of call-off is designated, any requirement above it should trigger a warning that problems may be arising in the field. Computerised systems enable this to occur automatically and a predetermined series of actions taken to alert responsible managers, including the recall co-ordinator.

Warranty claims

An analysis of product returned because it did not meet its per-formance claims, or under a product guarantee system, may provide valuable information that could lead to a recall. In these instances a recall may be the best way of protecting the manufacturers' good name, even though the product presents no danger.

Insurance claims

The company's insurance manager or insurance broker will be familiar with claims made on product liability or product guarantee policies if they are in place. When these are small they will probably be dealt with as a matter of course and the details not known to other managers. A regular analysis of claims circulated to senior executives can be a valuable addition to more technical information, because it provides data on defects from a different source.

However, indemnification of claimants may be the tip of an iceberg of unknown size, for there is a danger that the safety of a company's products may only be judged by the number of claims paid. A history of a low number of claims is not in itself the guarantee of blameless products that it is sometimes thought to be; nor is it a guarantee that the future will be the same as the past. While information from insurance sources can be valuable, it must be put into a wider perspective and not used as the sole measure of safety.

Field personnel

Company employees in direct contact with end-users include sales representatives, service engineers, merchandisers and custtomer service personnel. They have access to valuable informaation without being aware of the fact. A minor defect detected by one source may not be reported because it is not thought to be significant, but if the same minor defect is reported from a num ber of sources a different picture may emerge.

The reporting system adopted for the activities of field personnel should ensure that they do not make value judgements on safety-related failures. Strong central management will be required when field personnel are not employed by the manufacturer, as the turnover can be high among installers, franchisees and commission salesmen. Any information concerned with a product safety failure should be sent to a central point for analysis.

External sources

Complaints

Some 43 per cent of consumers said that they had a cause for complaint about goods or services during the previous 12 months, according to an Office of Fair Trading Survey[2]. Of those with cause for complaint who had a choice, 43 per cent would not buy the same goods or services from the same source again; 34 per cent would not buy the same brand again; 52 per cent would not recommend the source or brand to a friend; and 67 per cent had told friends about the unsatisfactory goods or service. Approximate estimates of the total number of lost customers are 6.5 million lost to suppliers and 5.6 million lost to branded names.

In the US, research by the Technical Assistance Research Programme (TARP) showed that for every consumer complaint received there are 50 customers who do not complain. When a consumer was dissatisfied with a product or a response, eight or ten others were told about the problem. The accepted average complaint level in the food industry was about seven per million units sold.

Complaints are an important source of information but they are not always used in the most productive manner, bearing in mind the above figure which shows that the number actually received are only the tip of the iceberg.

All complaints received by a company should be channelled through one department before being sent to the manager most suitable for taking action. It sometimes happens that a complaint is dealt with by the department that initially receives it, such as quality, marketing, sales, customer service or even the managing

2 'Consumer loyalty. A report on a research survey', May 1990, Office of Fair Trading, London.

director himself. This prevents an overall assessment being drawn up.

The method of collation and analysis of complaints needs careful thought and consideration if it is to provide the most valuable information. For an early warning system detection of trends is of first importance. Typical is the monthly analysis of complaints which consists of columns of figures or wordy descriptions without any attempt at comparative data.

The use of relevant indexes can be a great aid in pointing to shifts in emphasis. Examples are foreign bodies per 100,000 units, breakages per tonne, electrical failures per month, returns per £1 million sales, and so on. Individual indexes can be broken down further into categories. For example, foreign bodies in a vegetable pack can be divided into natural (extraneous vegetable matter such as weed seeds, stalk, pod, grass) and alien (glass, wire, wood, plastic); breakages can be divided into those that resulted in danger to a user or handler and those that presented no danger; and electrical failures can be divided into non-performance issues, (failure to operate, slow to respond, malfunction) or potentially dangerous issues, (cross-wiring, insulation failure, thermal cut-out failure).

Another method of presenting this type of information is by graphs for products or product groups. A rolling one-year graph can be marked with a 'normal' upper limit for a particular category of complaint. If the curve for the current position rises above the limit, this triggers a series of actions, including notification of the recall co-ordinator. For product recall, some categories of complaint will be of little interest, such as problems with payment, incivility of salesmen, restricted product range and delays in delivery.

Medical sources

Requests for product information from hospitals or doctors, to help in the treatment of a patient who has become ill apparently after using the product, need to be noted with great care. Such requests may be answered by technical managers who are familiar with the scientific aspects of a product. It will be important to keep the recall co-ordinator informed of these enquiries as they could be significant pointers to future difficulties.

Regulatory bodies

Today a complainant is virtually encouraged to approach his local regulatory body, such as the Trading Standards Department. It is important to maintain a close relationship with such bodies so that they are familiar with the product safety strategy of the company and its responsible attitude to genuine complaints.

Consumer associations

The national consumer associations publish information about products which are potentially dangerous. In the UK the Consumers' Association magazine *Which?* has carried a number of reports, as well as a feature on product recall itself.

Internationally there is the Community Rapid Information Exchange of the EC, the Bureau des Unions de Consommateurs (BEUC) and the International Organisation of Consumer Unions (IOCU). In the United Kingdom there is the Food Hazard Warning System, through which the Department of Health and Social Security can warn all environmental health officers of a hazard within two hours. The Consumer Safety Unit of the Department of Trade and Industry has established HAZPRO (Hazardous Products Data Base) with the Local Authorities Co-ordination Body on Trading Standards (LACOTS) and the Institute of Trading Standards. It is based on a computer which stores data on products that are either dangerous or are potentially dangerous.

Suppliers

Advice about a defect in raw materials, ingredients or components may come from a third-party supplier anticipating its discovery by the manufacturer's own quality procedures. Such information could be serious with just-in-time operations if finished product is despatched without delay.

Criminal attack

Product extortion and malicious product tamper describe circumstances in which a person deliberately contaminates a product for financial gain or to settle a grudge. The attacks can sometimes, although not always, lead to a product recall.

A recall initiated in response to a criminal attack on a product has a fundamental difference from one which responds to an accidental defect in a particular batch. The first is a random contamination so that a recall would probably have to be a blanket operation. The second is specific and related to a design defect, a manufacturing error or a failure of product information, and can be limited in its application. A criminal attack may or may not be repeated, whereas an accidental product defect can be prevented from recurring once its source has been identified. There have been occasions when a product under attack has been recalled more for the public relations effect than to eliminate any danger to consumers. This is a very difficult decision to make and one which can find strong arguments both for and against.

Crisis management plans are established to deal with these attacks. Management should realise that a crisis management plan and a product recall plan are separate documents which are complementary to each other. It is possible to have a product crisis without a product recall and to have a product recall without a product crisis. Examples are given in product extortion and malicious product tamper case histories in Part III (see p.213).

Step 4 Risk classification

A mechanism must be established in the product recall plan by which the seriousness of a risk can be categorised. It requires a classification table to give the scale against which risk is measured and the allocation of responsibility for specific managers to carry out the assessment. The classifcation given will have a

Table 3.1 *Summary of major actions by classification*

Risk classification	Recall decision	Recall level	Provide emergency facilities	Recall notification	Effectiveness checks	Activate public relations	Inform insurer	Capture costs
1	Chief Executive	Consumer	Yes	Media	100%	Yes	Yes	Yes
2	Divisional Manager	Retailer	Some	Phone Fax Visit	10% to 100%	On alert	Yes	Yes
3	Unit Manager	Wholesaler	No	Letter	Up to 10%	No	Yes	Yes
4	5	7	13	9	10	14	15	12

The numbers in the bottom line refer to the 'Steps' in the text.

direct impact on the actions that will be required to manage the recall (see Table 3.1, p.73).

The information available on which to base the judgement can come from a variety of sources (see 'Early Warning System' above). On occasion the information will be clear and unambiguous and make the classification a simple and straightforward matter, as when there is evidence of a death attributable to the product. On other occasions, the information available will be second-hand or ambiguous, with little opportunity in the time available to obtain direct on-the-spot reports from experts such as doctors, hospitals, or regulatory officials.

There are four basic reasons why a company will recall a product. Because the product will:

- kill;
- injure;
- damage property;
- cause commercial damage.

Examples of these will be found in the case histories in Part III. The maximum damages awarded in the UK for single person injury is £1.5 million, but the greatest financial exposure for a company, in a product liability incident, will be the commercial damage it could suffer. See Costs, below.

For a brand-driven company the most severe damage will be the harm caused to its brand image. The quantification of this will be a matter for subjective judgement and the ultimate cost of recovery may never be known precisely. Reputation and goodwill are concepts that have a great value and are built up over years of exemplary trading. However, there is a lack of agreement between some sections of industry and those who set accounting standards over how goodwill should appear in the balance sheet. Research into acquired goodwill, as opposed to internally generated goodwill, as a proportion of a bidder's net worth rose from 1 per cent to 44 per cent over the decade to 1987. Companies that have capitalised brand values include Guinness and Rank Hovis MacDougall. The weight put on this exposure is illustrated in the Nova Fritex case history (see p.190), Part III, where it was one of the reasons for postponing a recall.

An unusual example of commercial damage is bar code recalls. When the bar code on a fast-moving consumer good is incorrect the product may have to be withdrawn to prevent economic loss; if the price is wrong, for example. With a short shelf life product the only solution may be to destroy the product, as it may not be possible to take appropriate corrective action in the time available before the product runs out of shelf-life. One supermarket chain rejects incoming goods if the bar code is inaccurate, while another will reject a consignment if the bar code fails four times on a laser scanner. In such circumstances the printer could be responsible for the costs incurred if his error resulted in, say, the wrong price being encoded.

The most difficult area of all is the perceived risk, that is the way in which the public would assess the risk regardless of the views of the experts. One example of this was the Perrier recall (see Part III, p.165) where experts advised that the benzene levels in the drink posed no threat to health but, nevertheless, the company recalled 162 million bottles worldwide. Assessment of perceived risk has to be a matter of subjective judgement by experienced managers because it is difficult to quantify. In a brand-driven company any potential threat to its brand may outweigh all scientific considerations.

Ingredients or components present a difficult recall problem, when a defect can cause the end-product into which they are incorporated to become potentially dangerous. Frequently, ingredient and component suppliers will not necessarily know into which end-products their products have been incorporated. This happens when the ingredient or component passes through third-party merchants, wholesalers or distributors and the track is lost.

However, it is far better to have a product recall plan than none at all if problems do arise. One company producing ingredients found that one of its suppliers had delivered a contaminated product: the ingredient supplier's ingredient supplier in fact. Because the former had introduced a computerised recording system, when it was establishing a PRP, it was able rapidly to identify the customers who had received the suspect consignment. Further, the terms and conditions of purchase ensured that the costs involved were met by the supplier upstream, who was responsible for the incident.

Ideally the facts required to allocate a classication include:

- the source of the defect: design, manufacturing or product information;
- number of units involved, which may have to be an estimate;
- date the defect was discovered;
- production dates;
- location of suspect units;
- the degree to which the contamination will be obvious to the consumer or user.

Unfortunately we do not live in an ideal world and in some cases only inadequate answers will be available to these questions.

One of the most difficult things to define can be a defect. In the US the Consumer Product Safety Commission uses the following examples[3] to help companies understand its concept of a defect:

(a) An electric appliance presents a shock hazard because, through a manufacturing error, its casing can be electrically charged by full-line voltage. This product contains a defect as a result of manufacturing or production error.

(b) Shoes labelled and marketed for long-distance running are so designed that they might cause or contribute to the causing of muscle or tendon injury if used for long-distance running. The shoes are defective due to the labelling and marketing.

3 Code of Federal Regulations 1989 16 CFR 1115.4 US.

(c) A kite made of electrically conductive material presents a risk of electrocution if it is long enough to allow it to become entangled in power lines and be within reach from the ground. The electrically conductive material contributes both to the beauty of the kite and the hazard it presents. The kite contains a design defect.

(d) A power tool is not accompanied by adequate instructions and safety warnings. Reasonably foreseeable consumer use or misuse, based in part on the lack of adequate instructions and safety warnings, could result in injury. Although there are no reports of injury, the product contains a defect because of the inadequate warnings and instructions.

(e) An exhaust fan for home garages is advertised as activating when carbon monoxide fumes reach a dangerous level but does not exhaust when fumes have reached the dangerous level. Although the cause of the failure to exhaust is not known, the exhaust fan is defective because users rely on the fan to remove the fumes and the fan does not do so. However, not all products which present a risk of injury are defective. For example, a knife has a sharp blade and is capable of seriously injuring someone. This very sharpness, however, is necessary if the knife is to function adequately. The knife does not contain a defect insofar as the sharpness of its blade is concerned, despite its potential for causing injury, because the risk of injury is outweighed by the usefulness of the product, which is made possible by the same aspect that presents the risk of injury.

These examples show how this US regulatory agency views product defects. In reaching a decision on a recall, the Commission would take into account a number of factors: the utility of the product; the nature of the risk of injury; the need for the product; the population exposed to the risk; case law and statutes. They hold the view that a consumer product may be defective even if it is designed, manufactured and marketed exactly as the company intended.

Generally, to assess a risk and allocate a classification to it, two questions have to be answered:

- at what frequency will the hazard present itself? In other words, what is the probability of the dangerous defect arising?
- how severe will be the effects of the harm when it does occur? In other words, just how serious will the damage be?

There have been incidents where it was known that contamination was present in a product but the source could not be identified, despite the attention of the best experts. An example was the Spanish cooking oil 'toxic syndrome' which resulted in 600 deaths in 1981. Originally, strawberries and caged birds were among the causes named but expert scientific evidence, at a trial six years later, was unable to pinpoint the exact reason for the contamination. Another example occurred in Michigan where 90 per cent of the nine million inhabitants were found to have polybrominated biphenyl in their bodies in 1978. The highly toxic chemical was not identified for eight months but the cause was eventually traced to a packaging mix-up at a plant making cattle feed; 40,000 animals and 1.5 million chickens had to be destroyed.

The reverse has also happened when the source of a contamination has been identified but could not be found in the product at the time its recall was initiated. The Farley baby food recall was an example of this. A high statistical association of illness among infants pointed to Farley baby food as the source, although intensive bacteriological analyses failed to find the causative organism in the product. It was found at a later stage (see Farley's baby food case history in Part III, p.151).

An example of a risk classification is:

Class I where there is a reasonable probability that the use or exposure to the defective product will cause serious, adverse health consequences or death. Examples are:

- *Clostridium botulinum* toxin in food;
- label mix-up of a potent drug;
- electrical leakage in a device sufficient to cause death or serious injury;
- excessive exposure to radiation.

Class II where the use of, or exposure to, a defective product may cause temporary or medically reversible adverse health consequences or where the probability of serious adverse consequences is remote. Examples are:

- pathogenic microorganisms in food, apart from *Clostridium botulinum*;
- sub- or super-potent drugs, not life-saving in nature;
- shock hazard of small consequence, not life-threatening;
- improperly calibrated thermometers.

Class III is a situation in which the use of, or exposure to, a defective product is not likely to cause adverse health consequences. Examples are:

- organoleptic fault in food or drink;
- malfunction not affecting safety;
- filth in food relating to aesthetic qualities;
- labelling violations.

Class IV A *market withdrawal* of a distributed product for a minor violation which would not be subject to action by a regulatory body. A *stock recovery* of a product which has not left the company's direct control and has not been released for sale. Examples are:

- wrong colour or style of an appliance;
- incorrect pricing;
- out-of-life product with no safety consequences;
- incorrect attachments.

Another example of risk classification is one used by a supermarket chain:

Class I There is a reasonable probability that use of the product will cause serious health consequences or death. A recall in this category will not be initiated when the defect is in a proprietary line carried by other retailers; in such cases the supplier should be asked to carry out the recall.
Class II There is a risk of serious defects in the product, but serious health consequences are remote or there is a risk of minor injury from the product.
Stock withdrawal Removal of stock from sale for reasons other than those justifying a Class I or Class II recall.

The US Department of Agriculture (USDA) has statutory authority to seize or condemn a product which does not comply with statutory requirements; if a company refuses to initiate a 'voluntary' recall it can institute seizure or condemnation proceedings. The Department recognises only two classes of recall:

Class A. The product presents a health hazard, either actual or potential.
Class B. The product does not present a health hazard.

The USDA treats contaminated products with the slightest health implications as Class A.

Food presents a special problem for risk classification as biological matters are not always susceptible to accurate measurement. In 1980, the US Food Safety Council[4] proposed the following definition:

A substance is regarded as safe it is does not exceed a socially acceptable risk of an unfavourable effect at levels of

4 'Proposed System for Food Safety Assessment', Final Report of the Scientific Committee of the Food Safety Council, Washington, June 1980.

consumption that are experienced by high consumers of food in which the substance occurs.

It was suggested that, generally speaking, there were six classes of hazard associated with food. In order of decreasing importance these were:

1 Food-borne disease of micro-biological origin which acts through chemically defined toxins. There are three important types: enterotoxin, botulinum and aflatoxin.
2 Malnutrition.
3 Environmental contaminants, such as the trace elements arsenic, cadmium, copper, iron, lead, tin and zinc.
4 Natural toxicants which are toxic normal constituents of foods, such as the pesticides synthesised by plants which are as harmful to man as those from a chemical factory.
5 Pesticide residues.
6 Food additives.

The US Consumer Product Safety Commission and the Food and Drug Administration both have classification systems, and these are to be found on pp.32 and 39.

A company has to establish its own classification system and make sure that all responsible management are familiar with its significance. Much of the subsequent emphasis in the recall will depend on the classification allocated to it (see Figure 3.1 p.64 and Table 3.1 p.73 above).

Usually it is the end-user who will be at risk and this is the most frequent way of examining a recall situation. But there are other classes of people who could be at risk in some circumstances. For example, the following could be exposed to danger from a defective product. Those who:

- produce, test and sell;
- distribute and store;
- use, assemble and process;

- install, maintain, service, repair and dispose of the product;
- are third parties, such as bystanders; or
- are exposed to harmful waste products.

The product recall plan has to establish who will carry out the risk classification. A risk evaluation team should be available for this purpose, comprising probably not more than three managers, with alternates provided for emergencies (see Figure 3.1 p.64). The risk evaluation team will need a scientific or engineering member to assess the technical problems and a representative to judge the marketing impact on customers and consumers. In addition, a manager from the operations side can provide an input on the effect on purchasing, production, distribution and so on.

The team should have access to outside experts when necessary and these should be identified and named in the recall plan. For example, an independent laboratory with specialised equipment, on call 365 days a year, could be valuable if the contamination of a food was deliberate. Most company laboratories are not set up to determine paraquat, a contaminant used by criminals, which requires high performance liquid chomotography, or drugs of abuse which need a reference standard that can only be obtained on a licence from the Home Office. If the nature of the contamination is unknown there is no substitute for experience; for instance microscopy may give a quicker answer than chemistry when time is at a premium. Company laboratories have no requirement for the capability to determine such contaminants as 'Weedol' or slug pellets and consequently need the back-up of an outside expert should the occasion demand it. In the same way, expert medical advice on the effect of certain contaminants could be required at short notice, when a product extortion or a malicious product tamper is involved. A company doctor may not be able to give a quick answer and support from an outside expert, such as a poisons unit, should be immediately available. Contact with the poisons unit should be established and telephone numbers obtained for inclusion in the plan.

On occasion neither outside experts nor scientists are required to determine the source of a contamination, in what can be called a misidentified domestic contamination such as when crystals of sugar are thought to be glass or clear plastic. One elderly lady complained about the two pickled onions she found in her jar of instant coffee. Investigation showed that the jar of coffee and the jar of onions were kept side by side in the pantry and, as the lady was short-sighted, she accidentally returned the onions to the wrong jar.

It is vital for the risk evaluation team to identify the source of the defect when this is accidental. All product defects can be traced back ultimately to one of three reasons: a design or formulation defect, a manufacturing error, or a failure of product information. The actions necessary to correct the situation are different in each case, as are the implications. A design or formulation defect will have a widespread impact, whereas a manufacturing error will be limited to a batch or production run. A failure of product information may be more difficult to pin down, but a mistake in one word can have serious consequences, as the Renault case history in Part III (p.233) shows. A mis- take in one number was the cause of a tyre recall. The sidewall was moulded with 'Max load 1980 lbs' when it should have been 'Max load 1680 lbs' because someone had got the 6 upside- down. With a possible overloading of 300lbs the company initiated a costly recall.

Apart from its contribution to the recall decision, the conclusion of the risk evaluation team will trigger a series of actions outside the scope of this book. One likely result will be to halt production and distribution for a period until the source of the defect has been eliminated; this may involve postponing the delivery of incoming ingredients or components and packaging, and possibly laying-off employees. Customers and consumers may have to be offered alternative supplies while advertising and marketing promotions may be affected. One drinks company has reached an agreement with a distant competitor that each would supply the other if a recall temporarily interrupted either's supply of product.

Step 5 Recall decision (See Table 3.1 p.73)

The responsibilities of the recall co-ordinator and the product recall committee should be separated from the action of the prime decision maker. The former establish the recall plan and take charge of the day-to-day management of a recall; the recall co-ordinator may recommend the initiation of a recall. The executive decision to recall should be taken by a separate manager. This provides the second break-point in the series of actions shown in Figure 3.1.

The prime decision maker in some companies will be the chief executive, and it should be well known that no recall can be instituted without his specific agreement. An alternative should be nominated to act in the event of sickness, holidays or travel.

However, in larger companies it may be an advantage to adopt a different system based on the principle that the more serious the defect, or the closer the recall level gets to the public, the more senior should be the prime decision maker. For example:

Risk classifcation	Prime decision maker
1	Chief Executive
2	Divisional General Manager
3	Unit General Manager

In some divisionalised companies the individual operating units make the recall decision, whereas others tend to centralise all decisions that could affect the image of the corporation. Multinationals often delegate recall decisions to national managements, although for some companies the supranational product divisions take the decision.

In larger companies it is often a requirement that all recall decisions have to be reported to corporate level. Where international branding is practised such a method is essential, as bad publicity in one country can rapidly be reported in the media of others. There seems to be a trend to remove the recall decision from the individual operating units and centralise it for a group as a whole, especially when a recall has to reach the consumer level.

The executives who make the decision to initiate a recall should be trained, which itself can be a sensitive issue on occasion. The blacks and whites are easy enough, from a decision-making point of view, but it is the grey area that can be difficult. This is true where an assessment of the perceived risk is involved (see under Risk classification, above).

For example, the options that a probability presents can be less than clear-cut. Statistical examination can seemingly reduce a risk to a proportion on which a decision can be taken. In one case intensive investigations had determined that there was a risk of glass contamination in a bottled drink of three in a million: but the risk was not straightforward. In each million it was forecast that three bottles would have 'birdcages', a fault well-known in the glass-bottle industry and which could result in fragments of glass inside the bottle if they were struck by the filler tube on the bottling line. The question for the prime decision maker was whether to recall or not. To recall may have reduced the risk but certainly not eliminated it, as not all the suspect batch would be recovered. Not to recall meant a chance, however remote, that a customer would be put at risk – and it was a major national brand.

The difficulty facing the drinks company was that, until the incident related above, it did not know what its usual defect rate was. So that the three in a million forecast could not be put in perspective. In the event, the decision was taken at the highest level not to recall. There were no reports of injury.

Consider a claim by an engineering company that an audit of its products showed that they were 99.999 per cent safe and according to specification. On the face of it, this sounds admirable. But turn the figure around; it is the same thing as saying that one in 100,000 is defective, which is 10 in a million. If these were cardiac pacemakers, parachutes or a car's braking system, would it be acceptable? Or would a recall be necessary?

The US electronics company, Motorola, advertised in 1990 that its aim for 1992 was to reduce the number of defective pieces to 3.4 in a million. This was the latest in a serious company initiative to improve the quality of its products to match the best of the Japanese competition. To those who understood the programme the target was praiseworthy and acceptable, and there was no suggestion that a defect was associated with product safety. However, the advertisement publicly acknowledged that some defects were inevitable, just as they are in any manufacturing process. A fact demonstrated by the engineering company's figure of 99.999 per cent.

Some senior executives in a bout of moral fervour may initiate a recall more in a spirit of corporate martyrdom than commercial reality. Without training there can be a desire to throw money (the shareholders' money) at the problem in the belief that it will go away. Simulation exercises (see Chapter 5, p.131) should include sessions not only on risk classification but also on risk decision-making.

Step 6 Corrective action

The method of dealing with a defective product will often be strongly influenced by the product itself. There are four basic methods:

Refund. A can of fish exchanged for reimbursement of its purchase price.

Replace. A small electrical appliance exchanged for one from a sound batch.

Repair. A car's defect rectified at a garage.
Retrofit. A fault in an item of heavy equipment rectified *in situ*.

Some research in the US reviewed the product recall practices of 529 consumer product companies.[5] For corrective actions they found that for products which are inherently defective or potentially dangerous, the most appropriate action is repair or redesign. Twenty per cent of the companies with recall experience said they took this action. If repair was not feasible, the next level of response is to provide consumers with a safe replacement. Thirty-seven per cent of the companies with recall experience took this action. Replacement can be less time consuming and less burdensome from a practical standpoint, although generally more costly, than repairing a product. Repairs may require meticulous and often confusing directions or close supervision; and repairs may themselves create safety concerns if not performed properly.

The most dramatic action, reserved for the most serious safety risks, is a total withdrawal of the product from distribution together with action to reclaim it from consumers.

The recall co-ordinator will set up the procedures to support the corrective action before issuing the recall notification (see p.95). For a refund the relevant points of sale will need instructions, documentation and possibly payment; for a replacement approved stocks must be in place, together with the means of retrieving the defective units; for a repair the necessary personnel, instructions and parts must be available; and for a retrofit similar arrangements will be required and an appointed time to carry out the work.

Returned product should not be placed in the recalling company's warehouse because mistakes do happen and it could be sent out again. It is preferable to store returned product in a third-party warehouse or one that is remote from the main recall activity.

5   Harrington E, Kamlet K S, 'Risk Avoidance and Product Recall
Preparedness in the Consumer Products Industry', A T Kearney Inc 1989.
Presentation to the Practising Law Institute.

Some returned products can be repaired or re-worked but others will have to be destroyed or sold-off. The disposal of returned product needs close supervision to ensure that it is not re-labelled or re-packed and put back on the market, or exported to another country and sold there. Disposal by landfill requires monitoring and it is advisable to employ a specialist company for this type of operation, as inexperienced operators can cause inappropriate publicity.

The product recall plan should record the options available for corrective action and spell out the actions to accomplish them. For example, it may be advisable to contact a field selling company to examine ways in which they could help uplift product from retailers. To do this, the administrative arrangements will need to be established (see the Remington electric shaver case history in Part III, p.182). If an engineering service company is to be used to repair or retrofit a domestic appliance it will require briefing in advance.

Step 7 Recall level

The level or depth to which a recall must penetrate will be influenced by the classification it has been given (see Table 3.1). This will assist in answering the question: How far down the distribution chain must the defective product be pursued?

It is an advantage to include in the recall plan a flow diagram showing the routes by which a product can travel from the factory gate to the end-user. Along each route there will be a point at which the company no longer has control of the product, and it is from here on that the difficulties can arise. Some companies can integrate their record-keeping with that of their customers' so that there is no break in traceability (see below) when the control passes from one to another. Third-party haulage con- tractors and warehouses usually mean that authority and control are lost, especially when order picking is in operation at the warehouses. Major customers may have their own distribution systems into which a manufacturer has to feed his products as instructed. Fast-moving consumer goods frequently have a multiplicity of outlets to the end-user, not all of which will be known to the manufacturer: in such a situation the way to reach right down the distribution chain will be to go public.

Often there are three possible recall levels which can be tied directly into the classification, for example:

Risk classification	Recall level
1	Consumer
2	Retailer
3	Wholesaler

The consumer or user level will vary with the product and include any intermediate wholesale or retail level. The retail level immediately precedes the consumer or user level and would include shops and food service establishments. The wholesale level includes all distribution levels between a manufacturer and a retailer and will not be encountered in every recall situation.

Generally speaking, the closer a recall level gets to the consumer and thus the greater the publicity, the more will be the expense and the lower the response rate. Conversely, the closer a recall level is kept to the manufacturer, the greater the chance of a silent recall without publicity, and the exposure will be less and the response rate higher.

Product traceability

Step
8

Once a serious product defect has been confirmed the units involved must be identified and located. To do this an effective system of product traceability must have been in force for some time. Such a system forms the core of the product recall plan, and it is not something that can be done retrospectively. Different products have different requirements, and how product traceability is established will depend on individual circumstances. Recalls can range from major items of equipment and plant sold directly to the end-user to fast-moving consumer products, which find their way to the end-user via distributors, wholesalers, agents and retailers. Industrial products with direct or short channels of distribution are easier to trace than consumer products with longer or indirect channels of distribution.

Product traceability, or the 'fingerprinting' of products, has to be effective in two directions from the coding point: upstream to supplier and downstream to the end-user. How far along these lines traceability is maintained is a matter for managerial judgement (see Figure 3.1 p.64). Incoming goods can make an end-product defective and a link into suppliers' records could be crucial for safety-critical components. The further down-stream traceability is sought usually the more difficult it becomes to achieve, given the complexity of some distribution chains.

In this context it is worth remembering that in some cases product traceability may be important to enable a company to show that it did *not* make a product. This can arise with high-volume multi-sourced parts in the plastics industry, for example, when the provenance of a batch may decide where the liability for a defective product and its recall will lie. Fasteners provide another example; the same type may be purchased from several different suppliers, with no identifying features, marks or means of batch identification when all are mixed together. If such a product has a defect which could result in a serious hazard, then the problem of traceability could be acute. An incident involving 1½ inch bolts occurred in June 1990 when the cockpit window of a British Airways BAC 1–11 blew out over Oxfordshire. The pilot was blown half-way through the hole left by the window as a result of the decompression within the aircraft; only the crew prevented him from falling out completely and the plane landed safely. The bolts were later discovered to be one thirty-second of an inch smaller than they should have been. The incident demonstrates the importance of commonplace items.

For companies where counterfeiting, passing-off, lookalikes and parallel trading are practised traceability can be important. A defence under the EC Directive on liability for defective products is 'that the person proceeded against did not at any time supply the product to another' (Section 4(1)(b)).

This underlines the importance of being able to prove a negative, especially as it has been estimated that between 3 per cent and 6 per cent of world trade is represented by counter-feiting. Products involved include coffee, perfumes, fungicides, matches, jeans, ball-bearings and helicopter parts. Drugs present a special problem as copies can be sold legitimately by distribu-tors under the system of parallel imports; but drugs are also the subject of counterfeit attack.

For example, the world's best-selling drug is Glaxo's anti-stomach ulcer 'Zantac', which earned £1,291 million in a recent financial year. A prescription for a pack of 60 tablets costs the National Health Service £30. Three men in Athens were arrested with the raw materials to make the drug, equipment to print fake packaging and 6,000 packs of the drug itself.

The key to any product traceability system is record-keeping. The records must be immediately available to reveal the identity and location of suspect units. Frequently it is assumed that traceability would be possible if it became essential – without running a trial to ensure all links in the chain are actually in place. A complete trace may be possible but only by searching numbers of different records and making manual links; this can take considerable time and many people, when time is at a pre-mium and staff with the necessary skills and knowledge are not available.

The Department of Trade encourages companies to achieve approval to BS 5750. This is a standard for the quality management system of a company; it is not a standard for a product. The standard includes the following:

4.7 Product identification and traceability.
Where appropriate, the supplier shall establish and maintain procedures for identifying the product from applicable drawings, specifications or other documents, during all stages of production, delivery and installation. Where, and to the extent that, traceability is a specified requirement, individual product or batches shall have a unique identification. This identification shall be recorded (see 4.15).

To develop these 50 odd words to fit a particular industry a Quality System Supplement or Technical Schedule is prepared by the certification body. The degree to which an individual company complies with BS 5750 in this area will depend on how the certification body interprets section 4.7. Furthermore, there are certainly variations in the commitment by companies which do gain approval.

From this it follows that a company with BS 5750, dedicated to its principles, will generate information significantly to help in effective product traceability. Just how far that reaches upstream and downstream will depend on the Technical Schedule. The standard was written by engineers for engineers, and this shows when it is applied to non-engineering industries such as food, distribution, financial services and hotels. British Standard 5750 is equivalent to ISO 9000 (the International Organisation for Standardisation, which is a worldwide federation of national standards bodies) and to EN 29000 (the European standard).

The use of computers has radically changed the ability of producers to trace products, and this is especially true for computer integrated manufacturing (CIM). A CIM system involves the application of computers, telecommunications and automation throughout the business. It is made up of a number of application modules, which can stand alone on one site or be part located on other sites, linked via computer communications and formed into a completed integrated system. The archiving of historical information can give full traceability so that a product recall can be a surgical operation rather than a blanket withdrawal.

The records required to find a suspect batch could include:

- incoming goods specification and quality checks;
- design review log;
- end-product specifications, including instructions, warnings, packaging and marketing literature;
- quality control, quality assurance and statistical process control data;
- records of retained samples;
- warehousing and distribution records;
- end-user records, if available.

For consumer durables a good warranty card system is valuable. It should use cards that are precoded with the critical information that will enable an adequate trace to be obtained. Customers should be encouraged to return the cards by adopting an attractive design and providing prepaid postage.

Few companies have a rule regarding the length of time records should be kept, apart from those statutory periods which company secretaries follow. The Companies Act 1985 has many provisions for the creation and retention of records and this is supplemented by the Financial Services Act 1986. There is a British Standard, 6498, on the 'Preparation of microfilm and other microforms that may be required as evidence'. The Consumer Protection Act 1987, the Health and Safety at Work etc, Act, and the Data Protection Act all have an influence on record retention.

The period of record retention is critical for product traceability because it cannot be fully established without also fixing retention periods. The factors that must be borne in mind are:

- design (or formulation) and development phase;
- period of manufacture;

- warehousing and distribution delays;
- the life of the product;
- Limitation Act 1980.

A complete set of records must be retained for a longer period than the life of the product, because defects on occasion only appear after extended periods of use.

The EC Directive 'on indications or marks identifying the lot to which a foodstuff belongs' (89/396/EEC) is usually known as the Lot Marketing Directive and could have a direct application to product recall. The 'lot' means a batch of sales units produced, manufactured or packaged under practically the same conditions, and the identifying mark has to be preceded by the letter L. Minimum durability or 'use by' dates can serve as a means of lot identification. Sophisticated systems provide sequentially numbered cases or real-time coding where this can be justified.

Automatic identification, or auto ID, has bar coding as the dominant technology. The essential parts are a means of encoding the identifying information and applying it to a product, a machine to read the code and software to feed the data into a computer for analysis. Manufacturing offers the greatest scope for bar coding as it can tell the computer the location of everything in the factory at any moment. It has become the technology used for tracking goods and documents in a broad spectrum of industries. US car makers require their parts and materials suppliers to use bar coded containers. Bar codes are also a requirement on safety-related parts as they enable the manufacturer to trace cars with potentially faulty parts exactly. Electronic data interchange (EDI) or computer-to-computer transmission of data is extensively used by Ford's Common Manufacturing Management System, which links 57 of Ford's manufacturing units to more than 3,000 suppliers.

Retail outlets may not take the time to identify a specific code on recall, if there has been publicity concerning a defect. Often they will merely remove the brand from sale, regardless of the code it bears, and replace it with a competitive brand. If a supermarket chain has removed a brand to its warehouse it may sort it there by code, at a charge to the manufacturer.

One supermarket chain has the following in its recall plan: 'All stock in storerooms and shelf stock, irrespective of code, shall be immediately withdrawn from sale/distribution and securely held in an isolated area where it cannot be mistakenly put on show/distribution.' A food manufacturer's recall plan includes: 'Retail removal from shelves to be covert and routine unless there has been a press leak.' This suggests that speed would be important and the niceties of code identification disregarded. Incidentally the word leak, rather than report, implies that the company has not come to terms with how to handle the media.

The manner in which a code is applied can also influence the actions taken by retailers. One company used the method by which the edge of the pack labels has a number of small cuts, which could only be read by means of a plastic card printed with the key. This takes time and requires a card, neither of which may be available in an emergency and could result in the wholesale removal of a brand.

The recall of one domestic electrical product had to be for products bought between two dates because the code could not be read by the public. The company had good traceability and could isolate the suspect batch but the code was very difficult to read by the uninitiated, as it was very small and inset in the plastic base. Consequently a wide range of product had to be recalled instead of a narrow one.

Recall notification (see Table 3.1, p.73)   Step **9**

This is the communication to those who hold the product which is being recalled. The recall level will determine the different types of notification required. Wholesalers, retailers and end-users will each require different instructions and reporting requirements; national accounts and major customers may need special treatment and probably personal contact by a senior manager. The notification can take several forms but should include:

- a means of attracting attention. 'Safety Warning' is more effective than 'Important Notice';
- identification of the supplier;
- a clear description of the product: an illustration is more informative than words;
- a serial or code number to identify the suspect lot;
- a simple statement of the defect and the risk;
- any limitations of use or storage;
- specific instructions on what to do with the product;
- a free telephone number for enquiries;
- a ready means for the consignee to report on stocks held of the suspect product.

Great care is needed in the wording of a recall notification: it would be an advantage to include examples in the product recall plan (PRP). Unless the source of the defect is known with certainty it is wise to avoid admitting liability in the notification. The reason is that the cause of the defect could be the responsibility of a third party, such as a component supplier, and the legal liabilities may take time to establish.

The managers who approve a notification before publication should appear in the PRP. The means of communicating the notification are discussed below.

Letter

It will be necessary to know the names and addresses of the end-users; this is obvious, but to have a completely up-to-date list to hand in an emergency needs forward planning. Agents and distributors may need to be involved; and in one case a mail order company had to be paid for a computer run to identify relevant consignees. A great advantage of the post is that it provides a means of documenting the fact that the notification has been received if recorded delivery is used. A specialist direct mail company may be able to provide a more efficient, and cheaper, service than an in-house operation.

In some circumstances postcodes can be used to divide up the country into convenient areas if a team of engineers has to be used to retrofit. This method was used in the recall of 3,000 tyres by a manufacturer where suspect tyres had to be inspected by the manufacturer's own engineers and changed on the spot if they were defective. There were not enough qualified personnel to man all the service centres on any one day, so the country was broken down by postcode, which enabled the optimum use to be made of the limited resources.

A record of letters sent out must be maintained for the subsequent effectiveness checks (see below).

Advertising

The amount of advertising necessary for a recall will depend on the risk the defective product presents to the public. To place advertisements in the national press is an expensive operation and they must be integrated with the logistics of the recall. Considering the importance and consequences of a recall advertisement, it is surprising how elementary some of the mistakes are: one advertisement did not mention the product so that the reader was unaware of what was actually being recalled; another got the serial numbers wrong and had to publish a correction the next day; a number have had headlines more associated with a sale than a warning.

The layout of an advertisement is important as this affects the success or otherwise of communicating information. The clean uncluttered look with the basic information, preferably accompanied by a line drawing, is more attractive than a layout overloaded with excess detail.

A review of recall advertisements shows that the most popular headline is either 'Important Notice' or 'Important Announcement', followed a long way behind by 'Warning'. To the casual reader the first two could be more concerned with a marketing promotion than a safety message, while 'Warning' ought to catch the attention more readily. The amount of copy in some advertisements is quite daunting and the order in which the information is given appears to be completely random. A few short sentences using simple words, with a clear logical sequence is the most effective way of communicating. The size of recall advertisements varies from a single column to half a page.

In appropriate circumstances the recall notification can be used to reflect credit on the company, if it is presented well. Indeed, with skill it can almost be turned into a positive advantage. For example, a Marks & Spencer recall of canned ham was followed later by an announcement with the headline: 'thank you to all our customers who responded to our appeal concerning . . .'. Another instance is in the copy of an advertisement by Tefal for the recall of a food processor: 'We apologise for any inconvenience. There are 88 Authorised Tefal agents throughout the country. So you can rest assured that whichever Tefal products you buy, we have a national network ready to give you a fast and efficient service. You may never need our service, but isn't it nice to know we're there.'

Point-of-sale posters

The use of display signs at the stores from which the product had been purchased is a good way of communicating if they are strategically placed and eye-catching.

Fax and telex

These have the advantage of immediacy, provide a record and are not confined to office hours. They can be valuable for contacting consignees abroad at short notice.

Telephone

Instructions must be given to the people making the call so that they fully understand their objective. A record must be made of each call. If the consignee asks for additional information, outside the competence of the caller, this can be accommodated by having a knowledgeable manager available either to take over the call or to 'phone the consignee back as soon as possible.

Companies which specialise in telephone interviewing for market research or telephone selling will have personnel already trained in relevant techniques. They can be used to notify consignees of a recall and thus relieve the recalling company's personnel of this task.

Personal visit

A company with appropriate people in the field, such as salesmen or representatives, can use them to inform the consignees in their area of the recall. Instructions must be given to the field personnel to ensure that the message gets across accurately and a record of each call must be made. This has the advantage of personal contact to provide a report on the reactions of the consignees in judging the effect of the recall on the company's reputation.

Press release

If a product has a defect that gives it a Class I risk (see above), then a press release may be essential. Such a major step has to be handled with great care by professionals (see public relations, p.117). A press release will escalate the impact of a recall but may also significantly increase the damage to the company's reputation unless skilfully presented.

There have been occasions when a press release about a potentially dangerous product has been put out by a government department or the police. In one instance, subsequent investigations showed that the named product was in fact not defective. In another case the first the managing director of a company knew that a press release had been issued was when he saw it in the *Financial Times*, in spite of the fact that he was in discussion about initiating a recall with the government department which issued it (see the Remington electric shaver case history in Part III, p.182).

The product recall plan should include not only those holding the product on recall, but also those outside organisations and individuals who expect to and should receive the notification. These can include the local Trading Standards Department, the

Department of Transport, the Ministry of Health, the company's insurance broker and legal adviser, union representatives and trade associations. In multinationals, it may be necessary to inform the corporate or divisional headquarters: for internationally branded products, brand managers in other countries should also be named, so that they too can be alerted to the possibility of knock-on effects (see the Formula Shell petrol case history in Part III, p.207).

The compilation of this list requires thought and care because of the implications of some of the actions taken. Details of the individuals should appear in the contact list so that they can be reached rapidly.

The US Consumer Product Safety Commission has the following advice about recall notifications:

Notices to Consumers, Distributors, and Retailers:

Letters or other forms of communication should be specific and concise. The words 'Important Safety Notice' or a heading such as 'Recall Notice' should appear in the lower left-hand corner of the envelope and at the beginning of each letter.

The letter or communiqué should state that the recall is for safety reasons.

The nature of the product defect or hazard, as well as the recommended action for the consumer, distributor, or retailer, should be contained in the letter.

The letter should be individualised for the target audience (one letter for consumers, a different letter for distributors, yet another for retailers).

Point-of-Sale Posters

Posters and counter cards should be printed in colours that contrast with the background of the poster or counter card.

Posters and counter cards should be readily visible and not blocked from consumers' view by other signs or products being sold. The message should also be easily understandable for consumers.

Posters and counter cards should be readily displayed in several conspicuous locations throughout the store. Locations include: on the shelf where the product was routinely sold, at checkout counters and customer services desks, and at the entrance and exit to the store.

Posters may fit standard display holders. Ideally, posters should be no less than 22 by 28 inches to be most visible to shoppers.

Counter cards may also fit standard display holders. Ideally, cards should be no less than 11 by 19 inches.

In some countries there is a legal requirement to inform the regulatory body of a recall. For example, in Australia the Trade Practices Act provides that the Minister for Consumer Affairs must be notified within two days. The Act says that the notification must state that the goods are subject to recall and provide details of the nature of any defect in the goods. As many consumers in Australia either do not communicate well in English or do not read English language newspapers, the Minister would expect companies to publish a recall notification in the ethnic language press.

Effectiveness checks (see Table 3.1, p.73)

Step

10

Once a recall has been initiated the company will need to have immediately available the means of checking its effectiveness. The product recall plan must contain the method by which this can be achieved.

The purpose of effectiveness checks is to verify that all known consignees have received the recall notification and have taken action accordingly. Basically it is essential to know two figures:

- the number of units out in the field;
- the number of units returned or corrected.

If the latter is taken as a percentage of the former the effectiveness of the recall is determined. Unfortunately it is not always easy to obtain the necessary data, and the further the recall is pursued from the factory gate the more difficult becomes the gathering of the data. With a small number of consignees, checking the effectiveness is fairly straightforward, but with many fast-moving consumer goods the task becomes one of judgement: to what extent should the effectiveness checks be carried out? In other words, what proportion of consignees should be audited? This is the effectiveness check level.

The greater the proportion of consignees contacted the greater the cost but also the greater will be the confidence in the result. The more serious the risk then the higher the proportion of consignees who will have to be contacted.

The US Food & Drug Administration have established the following effectiveness check levels:

Level A 100 per cent of the customers at the recall depth decided upon.

Level B Between 10 per cent and 100 per cent of the customers depending on the individual circumstances of the recall.

Level C 10 per cent of the customers at the recall depth decided upon.

Level D 2 per cent of the customers at the recall depth decided upon.

Level E No effectiveness checks.

The elements of an effectiveness check can be summarised as:

1 *Consignee list.* These are the people who have received the product on recall and each one has to be a candidate for an effectiveness check. The depth to which this is done (wholesale, retail, consumer, for example) will depend on the classification given to the risk and the distribution chain. An important factor is the ability to link a suspect product code to an up-to-date list of consignees. The product recall plan should establish that this is possible and set out the way in which it can be obtained. Each consignee should be allocated a unique number to enable

swift and accurate identification to be made; in some cases it may be an advantage to use all or part of the postcode for this purpose or the consignee's account reference number.

2 *Questionnaire.* For each consignee contacted a series of questions will require answering. For instance, details will be needed in response to such questions as:

- Was the recall notification received?
- Was the product handled as instructed?
- Was the product further distributed before the notification was received?
- If so, were the downstream consignees notified of the recall?
- How many units have you removed from circulation?
- Where are they now?

The product recall plan should include the questions appropriate to the company's products and market.

3 *Recording the replies.* This key activity has to be well planned and executed if it is to have any value. No one method will be suitable for all recalls but an example will indicate the type of system that can be adopted. Labels are prepared for each consignee carrying the name, address and a unique identifying number. One label can be placed on an index card to become part of a control file, a second can be used for the completed questionnaire. Others can be used for mailings and to help record telephone calls and personal visits. Completed questionnaires can be put with the relevant control card for record purposes and the subsequent establishment of a master file. The use of a computer will eliminate such a tedious manual method. But computers are not always a practicable solution when staff, unfamiliar with the business in hand, are used in an emergency situation.

The choice of contact method for effectiveness checks was investigated in a study carried out in the United States in the late 1970s[6]. Although the material is old it demonstrates the principles that need to be considered. Seven recalls were studied involving over 600,000 consignees from which nearly 30,000 provided the sample. The results of this contact method study are given in Table 3.2.

Table 3.2 *Contact method effectiveness*

Contact method	Contact rate	Cost/Attempted contact
	%	$
Mail	69–78	1.51
Mailgram[7]	50–76	4.89
Telephone	80–93	7.06
Personal visit	93–100	18.29
Mail and phone	89–95	3.20
Mailgram and phone	79–96	7.85

The letter and telephone follow-up method was the most efficient as it had the second lowest cost and one of the highest contact rates – the proportion of the attempted contacts where the consignee was successfully contacted. Today, fax would have to be included in the equation.

Step 11 Response rates and termination

One measure of the success of a recall is the proportion of defective products returned out of the total number in the market. An important factor is that manufacturers do not always know how many units are in circulation and potentially available for recall. Apart from the inadequacy of the manufacturers' own records, this may be due to units being out of life and discarded, and to consumers who throw away the offending product without notifying the manufacturer.

6 Soviero C A, *Checking the effectiveness of recalls: a cost-effectiveness study*, US Food and Drug Administration Report No. FDA/ACPE-78/35 1978.
7 A document that looks like a telegram but is delivered by mail.

With fast-moving consumer goods the manufacturer may not know with accuracy how many sales outlets actually sell his product, let alone the quantity available for sale. One tobacco company, for example, thought it had about 220,000 outlets but had no way of confirming this, because of the manner in which its products were distributed.

Some of the figures quoted for response rates have to be treated with reserve because of the reasons given above and the lack of any independent audit. Indeed, the chance of a 100 per cent response is so remote that it can be discounted altogether, except in highly specialised circumstances. Vehicle recalls in the UK have very high response rates which are associated with the unique situation created by the Driver and Vehicle Licensing Agency at Swansea, which stores the names and addresses of registered keepers on its computers (see Vehicles case history in Part III, p.217).

The form of the recall notification may influence the response rate. It seems that when consignees are notified directly – by letter, fax, telephone or personal visit – a recall is more effective than if an indirect method is used – by advertisement or press release. Support for this view is given by vehicle recalls which can include a recorded delivery letter and which contributes to the high response rates achieved.

The recall of components and ingredients poses particular problems, because it may be difficult to discover the location of the finished product into which they have been incorporated. Close co-operation between the component or ingredient supplier and the finished product manufacturer is the solution here. Such a relationship can be developed when just-in-time deliveries are made or single-sourcing practised.

The effectiveness checks will provide information on how the response rate is progressing: generally it will peak in the two or three weeks after the recall notification and then tail off. Flagging results may point to the need for a further notification to stimulate the response (see Nova Fritex case history in Part III, p.190). A formalised reporting system can be an advantage in larger companies, especially if the hazard is serious and a number of senior executives have to be kept informed of progress.

Regular status reports with a restricted circulation can meet this requirement. The chief headings should include:

- number of consignees notified, with date and method;
- number of consignees responding, with quantity held;
- number of consignees who did not respond;
- number and results of effectiveness checks;
- amount of product returned and accounted for.

The frequency with which the status reports are circulated will depend on individual circumstances but will be daily at the start of a recall. A pro forma for a status report should be included in the recall plan.

Usually the response to a recall notification will run down rather than come to a stop, accepting that a 100 per cent response is unattainable. A decision will need to be taken on dismantling the special arrangements established to manage the recall and allow the staff involved to return to their normal jobs. This decision should be taken on the recommendation of the recall co-ordinator, by the manager who initiated the recall in the first place. Responsibility for handling the final responses can be allocated to managers as part of their regular jobs, using the experience and knowledge already gained.

An analysis of the most important factors which influenced recall success rates examined 128 recalls initiated by the US Consumer Product Safety Commission from 1978 to 1983[8]. The average correction rate was 54.4 per cent, with a third of the recall success rates being either less 29 per cent or more than 89 per cent. A number of variables were examined to seek an explanation for this large variance.

8   Murphy R D and Rubin P H, 'Determinants of Recall Success Rates', *Journal of Products Liability* (US) Vol 11 1988.

The product life had a positive and significant effect. There was an inverse relationship between recall success and the number of months a product was in distribution before the start of the recall. There was a similar relationship between success and the lag between the end of distribution and the start of the recall.

The percentage of recalled items in the hands of retailers and consumers were significant determinants of recall effectiveness. Products in the hands of retailers had a success rate 10 per cent below that for recalls where the products were with producers. Correction rates for items in the hands of consumers were on average 87 per cent below the levels for inventory held by producers. From this it follows that higher success rates were obtained when no products had reached retailers or consumers. The most significant variable in recall success rates was the proportion of the product held by consumers.

Other factors being equal, correction rates for scuba diving and mountain climbing equipment was 14 per cent points higher than for other consumer products. No correlation was found between the severity of the safety hazard and success rates; nor was there one between the benefit of complying and the cost of the product, to test the assumption that success rates would be found for recalls employing a refund or exchange remedy. Correction rates were higher for those recalls that offered in-home repairs rather than other forms of repair or replacement.

The analysis showed that it was possible to construct a simple model of the determinants of recall effectiveness that could account for a high percentage of the variation in recall rates. The predictive equation derived from the model was claimed to be able to forecast Consumer Product Safety Commission recall success rates with considerable precision.

The most salutary conclusion from this work is that 'for a product entirely in the hands of consumers, with no lag between distribution and recall, no notice, no home repair and which is not a "sports product", the success rate is only 7 per cent, so that low rates of return for products should not be surprising.'

Step **Costs (see Table 3.1, p.73)**

12

It is probably true to say that a company involved in a major recall will never know its true cost. The published figures for recall costs can run into millions but these can be no more than estimates. For a branded product it will be very difficult to calculate the long-term effect on sales and the company image, which may be the company's most valuable asset even though it does not appear in the balance sheet.

Broadly speaking the costs can be divided into those that are borne by the company and those which society has to bear.

The product recall plan must contain a means of capturing the relevant company costs that can be activated very quickly. Some forward planning regarding costs can ensure that, in selected areas, the most cost-effective choice is made. For example, there are a number of different ways in which effectiveness checks can be carried out and a forecast of the different costs involved, included in the plan, would enable the most cost-effective choice to be made.

There are two main divisions into which recall costs can be placed. Direct costs such as:

- inventory write-off;
- contacting customers, printing, advertising;
- transport, travel, warehousing;
- corrective action: repair, refund, replacement, retrofit;
- administration: extra personnel, telephones, fax, telex, accommodation, overtime.

Indirect costs such as:

- loss of sales, brand share;
- loss of production;
- redesign or redevelopment of the product;
- damage to the company's image.

In a serious recall far-reaching decisions will have to be taken at an early stage and the need for speed can overwhelm an unprepared company, with the expenses racing away out of sight. The problem can raise thorny, moral and ethical arguments when the board has to weigh the cost of recalling against the seriousness of the hazard presented to its customers. It has been known for the influence of the moral and ethical view to wane as the size of the financial consideration waxed.

The real cost to a recalling company gains perspective if it is seen as the amount of sales it would be necessary to generate to provide the sum involved. It is the impact on the bottom line that counts in the end. For example, if the cost was £100,000 (which is a very modest figure when a full-page advertisement in a national newspaper can cost over £20,000) and the return on sales was 5 per cent, then it would require £2 million of sales to produce the £100,000. This rule-of-thumb approach is set out in Table 3.3.

Table 3.3

Recall cost	Sales required at 5% return
£	£
10,000	200,000
100,000	2,000,000
1,000,000	20,000,000
5,000,000	100,000,000

A product recall insurance policy will respond to some, but by no means all, of the expenses incurred, and adequate records will need to be available for the insurer to examine before indemnification will be forthcoming.

If we now look at the economic loss caused by a recall, the costs that society has to bear, then the division between directs and indirects can be categorised differently.

Direct costs can be accurately determined, such as:

- industry costs;
- hospitalisation costs;

- loss of income;
- investigation costs by government departments.

Indirect costs are those given an arbitrary value by economists, such as:

- loss of victims' productivity;
- loss of victims' leisure time;
- value of pain, grief and suffering;
- death.

A Canadian study[9] examined the economic loss caused by 20 recalls between 1963 and 1982 in eight countries. The costs ranged from $36,000 to $164 million (in US dollars as at 1983), as shown in Table 3.4, p.111.

The story of the canned salmon recall is related chronologically in Part III, see p.144. The Canadian study examined it from a cost point of view and the figures are reproduced in Table 3.5, see p.112. A total of 60 million cans were recalled in many countries, including the United Kingdom, Australia, New Zealand and Canada. It is a poignant commentary on the way in which we manage our affairs that the value of the two deaths in England accounted for only 5.8 per cent of the total costs, while the value of the life of the Belgian who died was just over 1 per cent of the total.

The response of the stock market to a recall is another measure of the cost. A study of 48 recalls by 31 companies between 1977 and 1981 in the United States compared the market value of the companies 40 days before the recall announcement to 40 days afterwards.[10] The average loss in equity value was 6.9 per cent. In another study on drug recalls a 6 per cent loss in equity was revealed, while automobile recalls resulted in a 1.4 per cent loss. The aggregate net loss from the 48 recalls was $7 billion.

9   Todd E C D, 'Economic loss from Foodborne Disease and Non-illness Related Recalls Because of Mishandling by Food Processors', *Journal of Food Protection*, Vol 48 July 1985, pp 621–33.
10   Rubin P H, Murphy R D, Jarnell G, 'Risky Products, Risky Stocks', AEI Journal on Government & Society, *Regulation* 1988 Number 1.

(*Source: Journal of Food Protection Vol. 48 July 1985*)

Food	Date	Country	Etiologic agent	Number Ill	Number Dead	Total direct costs	Average direct cost/case	Indirect costs	Total costs	Average total costs/case
Raw milk	1981	Scotland	*Salmonella*	654	2	$152,800	$234	$1,226,100	$1,378,900	$2,108
Cheese	1965	U.S.	*S. aureus*	42	–	$490,400	$11,676	–	$490,400	$11,676
	1977	Canada	*S. aureus*	15	–	$653,400	$43,560	$1,600	$655,000	$43,667
	1976	U.S.	*Salmonella*	234	–	$251,000	$1,073	–	$251,000	$1,073
Cakes	1977	Canada	*Salmonella*	44	–	$36,400	$827	–	$36,400	$827
	1978	Canada	*Salmonella*	264	1	$345,430	$1,308	$3,020,800	$3,366,230	$12,750
Cocoa	1970–1971	Sweden	*Salmonella*	110	–	$83,000	$755	–	$83,000	$755
Chocolate	1973–1974	Canada, U.S.	*Salmonella*	200	–	$62,063,300	$310,317	–	$62,063,300	$30,317
	1982	England	*Salmonella*	245	–	$248,000	$1,012	–	$248,000	$1,012
Diet drink	1982	U.S.	*Salmonella*	N.A.[a]	N.A.	$2,434,000	N.A.	–	$2,434,000	N.A.
Canned corned beef	1964	Scotland	*Salmonella typhi*	507	3	$163,485,268	$322,456	$871,060	$164,356,320	$324,174
	1979	England	*S. aureus*	80	–	$2,747,700	$34,346	–	$2,747,700	$34,362
	1973	England	Bacteria	N.A.	N.A.	$4,933,000	N.A.	–	$4,933,000	N.A.
	1979	England	Bacteria	N.A.	N.A.	$686,000	N.A.	–	$686,000	N.A.
Canned salmon	1978	England	*C. botulinum*	4	2	$5,802,000	$1,450,500	$358,600	$6,160,600	$1,540,150
	1982	Belgium	*C. botulinum*	2	1	$148,246,650	$74,123,325	$1,585,000	$149,831,650	$74,915,825
Canned tuna	1963	U.S.	*C. botulinum*	3	2	$162,658,000	$54,219,333	$1,529,000	$164,187,000	$54,729,000
Bean salad	1978	U.S.	*C. botulinum*	34	2	$8,203,000	$241,265	$164,800	$8,367,800	$246,112
Chicken	1979	Australia	*Salmonella*	450	–	$1,757,000	$3,904	–	$1,757,000	$3,904
Fried rice	1980	Netherlands	Nitrite	2	2	$11,592,000	$5,796,000	$2,127,400	$12,719,400	$6,359,700
12 foods	1963–1982	8 Countries	4 Agents	2890	15	$576,868,348	Mean[b] $196,822 Median[b] $34,346	$9,884,360	$586,752,708	Mean[b] $200,242 Median[b] $43,667

[a]N.A., not applicable for recalls without illness
[b]Costs for recalls without illness have not been used to determine costs per case.

Table 3.5 *Cost of two botulism outbreaks involving canned salmon.*

	1978 botulism outbreak in England		1982 botulism outbreak in Belgium	
Direct costs				
1. Loss to the United Kingdom importer for recall of 400,000 cans and loss of business	$5,600,000	96.5%		
1. a) Cost to the United Kingdom for recall and screening of 20 million U.S. and Canadian cans by importers and government officials			$825,000	
b) Cost to the United States				
i) Reflected by a loan from the State of Alaska to finance 1982 salmon purchase			$120,500,000	
ii) Purchase of equipment to detect loss of vacuum in cans at $100,000 each for 57 canneries			$5,700,000	
iii) Promotion of salmon sales by the State of Alaska			$4,100,00	
iv) Food and Drug Administration cost of ensuring 60 million cans recalled, including 312,000 retail store visits			$11,100,000	
Total			$141,400,000	95.3%
c) Cost to Canada for Canadian salmon recall				
i) Unsold product			$4,285,000	
ii) Storage			$1,540,000	
iii) Inspection costs (excluding salaries)			$86,000	
iv) Promotion of salmon sales			$860,000	
Total			$6,771,000	4.6%

2. Hospitalization costs
   a) For the 4 patients in intensive care for a total of 110 d at $370/d — $40,700
   b) For a further 80 d for the 2 patients who recovered at $185/d — $14,800
      Total — $55,500 — 1.0%
3. Investigational, laboratory and administrative costs (central and local health departments, public health laboratories, meetings with the industry and representatives of exporting countries) — $146,500 — 2.5%
4. Total costs — $5,802,000
5. Average cost per case — $1,450,500 — 100.0%

Indirect costs

1. Value of the 2 deaths
   a) 64-year-old man — $196,100
   a) 66-year-old woman — $162,500
      Total — $358,600

Total direct and indirect costs

1 Total direct costs — $5,802,00 — 94.2%
2 Total indirect costs — $358,600 — 5.8%
   Total — $6,160,600 — 100.0%
3. Average total per case — $1,540,150

---

2. Hospitalization costs
   a) For the two Belgium patients in intensive care — Not determined
   b) For a woman with botulism in Connecticut who probably ate the salmon (85 d in hospital) — $67,700 — 0.1%
3. Investigational costs for the Connecticut case (4 persons for a total of 21 d) — $1,650 — 0.0%
4. Laboratory costs for the
   a) Analysis in Belgium — $4,000
   b) Analysis in Connecticut and Atlanta (Centers for Disease Control) — $2,300 — 0.0%
      Total — $6,300
5. Total costs — $148,246,650
6. Average cost per case — $74,123,325

Indirect costs

1. Value of life of the 27-year-old man who died — $1,585,000

Total direct and indirect costs

1. Total direct costs — $148,246,650 — 98.9%
2. Total indirect costs — $1,585,000 — 1.1%
   Total — $149,381,650 — 100.0%
3. Average total per case — $74,915,825

**Accommodation, facilities, contact lists, security
(see Table 3.1, p.73)**

Preparations to deal with the considerable extra demands of a recall will depend on individual circumstances and available resources. Some factors that require consideration are discussed below.

Incident room

The recall co-ordinator (RC) and the product recall committee need a place in which they can assemble to manage the recall, should the classification demand it. It is better not to use the board room as that will be required by the board who still have a company to run, in spite of the recall. The incident room needs essential facilities and these should be identified, located and listed in the product recall plan (PRP). Thought should be given to providing the following:

Telephones

The number that may be needed can often be greater than that forecast. It may be necessary to provide lines restricted to outgoing or incoming calls, tie-lines to other company locations, internal lines and so on. The possibility of being able to use recording equipment may be important.

Fax and telex

These have the advantage of supplying a record, not being limited to office hours and being convenient for communicating with foreign contacts.

Copier

A recall can generate a surprising amount of paperwork to ensure that instructions are correctly communicated.

Secretarial staff

The senior secretary, who works with the product recall committee, should ensure that adequate secretarial support is available, in terms of people, stationery and hardware.

Flip chart

A means of temporarily fixing the sheets to the walls of the incident room will ensure an effective method of informing visiting senior executives of the situation, without interrupting the business of managing the recall.

Logbook

A chronological record of events is critical for a review of a recall, which should follow at a subsequent date so that the lessons learned can be applied to the PRP.

Refreshments

A liberal supply of tea and coffee and soft drinks is essential.

Sleeping bags

If local conditions demand, it may be wise to provide emergency overnight facilities for key personnel.

Access

It will be important to be able to control access to the incident room to prevent the merely curious and bystanders from interfering with the action.

Warehouse space

It is always advisable to keep the returned defective product isolated to prevent the chance of any mix-up with sound products. If the company cannot allocate one of its own warehouses for this purpose, it should consider hiring one.

Waste disposal

When thousands of items are returned, the disposal of the associated packaging can present a problem, unless plans have been made for its removal and disposal. In some cases the disposal of the returned product itself will need careful managing.

Contact lists

The first few hours of a potential recall are often the most critical, when major decisions will have to be made. Key personnel must be available with the minimum delay and up-to-date lists of where they can be contacted are essential. The appendix of the PRP should contain this information, which needs regular revision if it is to remain viable. This is a task that can be assigned to the senior secretary who works with the recall committee in establishing the plan. The list can include details of the following, together with their alternates:

Recall co-ordinator	Risk evaluation team
Product recall committee	Directors
Senior managers	Company doctor
Legal adviser	Insurance broker
Public relations agency	Specialist outside agencies
Trading Standards Department	Corporate executives
Independent laboratory	Union representatives
Government bodies	Trade association

Movements of personnel, as well as holidays, sickness and so on, make names by themselves of limited value. Titles should appear alongside names so that responsibilities can be easily determined: in large companies this is essential as individuals may not always know each other by name.

It will be an advantage for members of the recall team to carry with them the more important elements of the contact list, so that it is always available. This list can be held in a briefcase, a personal computer or on a plastic card – similar to credit cards and included with them.

The means by which in-house contacts can be reached quickly will need consideration. The telephone is the most obvious method, and where numbers require it a cascade list is valuable. An example will illustrate its use. A supermarket chain has a small number of key store contact numbers which are contacted by head office in the event of a recall. Each of these then has a designated list of stores to contact with the message. This process is repeated so that all the several hundred stores can be reached within an hour. The original message has to be passed on word-for-word and is followed up with hard copy as soon as possible. One result of this system is a silent recall when circumstances justify it. Other means to help rapid contact are 24-hour radio pagers and car phones, both of which may need care in their allocation as they can convey status or rank. Electronic mail can speed the process where the installation and timing allows it.

Security

The beginning of a recall can involve very long hours for the recall team. To ensure that access to the company's site is controlled in a responsible manner additional security measures may be needed. This will be more important if the recall becomes public knowledge.

A number of people who are not employees may be involved and they can require access at any time of the day or night. The merely curious and inquisitive will have to be kept away and the media directed to a nominated point where they can be properly accommodated.

Step 4 **Public relations (see Table 3.1)**

The ideal recall is one in which public relations plays no part and the product is recovered without any harm being done: a silent recall in fact. This situation occurs more often than may be realised, but of course no one hears about it. For example, a supermarket can recall one of its own brands through its in-house system without the public being aware, or being in any danger.

If the media are likely to comment on a recall, the company will require public relations professionals to handle its response to protect its most valuable asset, which is consumer loyalty. Recalling companies will do their best to avoid media attention unless it is necessary to go public to reach possible end-users. Even so, word-of-mouth stories can travel fast, be picked up by local stringers and then be passed on to national newspapers. Thus it has to be a matter of judgement when to involve public relations, but sooner rather than later is a good general rule, coupled with a restriction that can only be lifted by a senior executive.

The product recall plan must spell out very closely the responsibilities and authorities in connection with public relations. Importantly, the manager responsible for communicating with the media, and the alternate, should be named, while at the same time the company in general must know that all contact with the media can only pass through him; company sites remote from the scene of the action must be informed as well.

The speed with which a product recall can propel senior executives into the news (see the John West and Farley case histories in Part III, pp. 144 and 151) means that they must have the requisite skills available at a moment's notice. It is no good imagining that it will be all right when the occasion arises. Successfully handling an adversarial interview on TV requires training and this should be carried out for a selected number of executives on a regular basis.

In a serious case the first 24 hours of a recall are often the most critical for public relations. A company which resolutely maintains silence, or keeps repeating 'No comment', cannot expect a good press just when it certainly needs it. On the other hand, there may not be any time for lengthy discussions or obtaining legal clearance when the media are at the door requesting information to help their readers/viewers/listeners. On such occasions the professional agency with a proven track record in recall situations is valuable in helping to co-ordinate response to media questioning. When contradictions arise the press comment will be unfavourable (see the Perrier case history in Part III, p.165).

Some public relations agencies will claim that they could handle a recall; but it is worthwhile examining their actual experience in this field. There is a vast difference between arranging press conferences, product launches and getting editorial mentions, and organising a national recall. A company's agency may be excellent at its normal tasks but need support in an emergency such as a major recall. For these reasons, it would be as well to establish who could provide that support and include the details in the product recall plan, especially the 24 hour contact points.

The experienced agency will be able to allocate a telephone answering service to deal with enquiries: a hot-line. This will prevent the company's switchboard becoming jammed with calls and at the same time provide a record and analysis of the callers. The provision of accommodation for press conferences can be handled by the agency, and if this can be remote from the company's premises so much the better.

Apart from the media there are other aspects of public relations that require attention. The company's employees and their families will need information on what is happening and this should be provided by the company and not the media. The employees may be concerned about the future of their jobs if production is stopped and sales suffer. Recalls have resulted in factory closures (see the Farley case history in Part III, p.165).

Unions may require special attention, as their responsibility is to protect the interests of their members. Where a company is a significant employer in its area the local community must be included in the coverage, as well as the local authority and opinion formers.

Shareholders and the City may need reassurance to prevent a fall in share values, from which recovery can be lengthy.

Regulatory bodies and the police have their own press departments which put out press releases on matters of public concern. Suitable liaison with them is advisable so that the company's announcements are not at variance with theirs (see the Remington Electic Shaver case history in Part III, p.182).

Step 15 Recall insurance (see Table 3.1, p.73)

When insurers refer to 'risk' they mean the subject matter of insurance, such as a building, a car, legal liability or the cost of a product recall. For product safety management 'risk' has two elements – probability and severity – which measure the chance of a hazard becoming a reality and the severity of its consequences if it does.

Product recall insurance is not easily obtainable and needs expert advice if it is to be worthwhile. The aim of this section is simply to show that a product recall plan should set out in clear terms just what is covered and what is not covered, and the actions that are required by the recalling company to ensure that a policy would respond.

Although the concept of insurance goes back to the ancient Phoenecians it is more valuable to examine it in the light of today. An insurable risk must satisfy certain criteria: for instance it must be capable of financial measurement, homogeneous, fortuitous and in accordance with public policy; the proposer must have an interest in the risk which is legally enforceable and by which he stands to lose if loss or damage occurs.

Insurance provides compensation after a loss and its position in product recall management is a consequence of this. The first management action is to reduce the risk of a recall and then be able to manage it if it does occur, which is the contribution of the recall plan. Insurance comes at the end of the line and provides compensation for certain specified losses that have been incurred. As insurance is usually claims-driven it has a strong cyclical nature which makes long-term planning for premiums difficult. A poor claims experience will affect insurers' profit and could ultimately result in a reduction in the market's capacity for underwriting risk.

Product recall falls into the 'liability and casualty' class of insurances, which include employers' liability, public liability, product liability, product guarantee, product contamination and product extortion. Contamination and extortion are regarded as specialist policies because of the potentially high exposure to loss associated with them and their sensitive and criminal aspects.

As few insurers offer product recall cover, the total market capacity in this respect is consequently small. In addition, premium rates for product recall insurance are comparatively high so there is not a great demand for it. As a result there are no available underwriting statistics which insurers can use as a guide to premiums. The effect is a restricted market capacity, which in its turn leads to less dynamic policy wordings. If on the other hand there were a large demand and strong market capacity, then premium rates would be more stable and there would be a wider choice of policy wordings. About 25 companies, including Lloyd's underwriters, are known to underwrite product recall insurance with only a small number being prepared to lead such cover.

There is a limited market for pure product recall insurance and a separate market for recalls related to product extortion and malicious product tamper. Product recall can be under-written by an insured's own captive insurance company. The limit of indemnity is often £1 million or £2 million, with up to £5 million obtainable on occasion, and even higher with product extortion and malicious product tamper. Premium rates are very variable and do not necessarily have a linear relationship with the limits of indemnity, so that as the latter increases the former may increase disproportionately. Some insurers impose min-imum premiums and insurance buyers consider product recall insurance poor value for money.

In summary, product recall insurance is regarded by both insurers and buyers as a secondary class of business compared to other liability covers. This is because of the circle of low market capacity, few insurers, high rates, restrictive wordings and poor demand.

An insurance policy is very much an example of give and take. The actual cover which is provided is the difference between what the insurer gives in the operative clause and what he takes away in the exclusions; a policy will be administered by the conditions it contains. The operative clause sets out the circumstances in which the indemnity would operate. Where product recall is offered as an extension to a primary policy the operative clause may not refer to it, but use an endorsement instead to give the cover.

Because the market for product recall insurance is fragmented, wordings vary. In many cases any differences that do emerge will be the result of the broker's or proposer's bargaining position. It is very much a niche market.

An example of an *operative clause* in a product recall policy is that of Willis Wrightson's wording:

> Notwithstanding anything contained herein to the contrary this Policy is to provide reimbursement of expenditure incurred for Recall Expenses of products manufactured and/or distributed by the Assured and/or the Assured's Agent as a result of a decision by the Assured taken with the agreement of the Insurers that it is necessary to recall any such products because their use or consumption may cause the Assured to incur a legal liability as defined in the operative clause of this Policy.

The fundamental features which affect the actions of the insured are:

- indemnification of the costs incurred in recalling a product;
- the recall must be necessary to avoid a legal liability; and
- the insurers must agree to the recall.

The first point means that compensation is only available for the costs of the recall, which does not include the cost of the product itself. Further, if a third party made a claim for damages due to the recalled product causing injury or damage, this policy would not respond, although a product liability policy would do so. Just what is included in recall costs is explained in the section headed Definitions:

Expenses shall mean:
1 the reasonable and necessary expenses including the costs of correspondence, newspaper and magazine advertising, radio or television announcements and transportation costs incurred in arranging for the return of the products or any part thereof to the manufacturer or his nominated agent.
2 the cost of examination and where necessary replacement or re-working of the products or work or any part whether incurred by the Assured or his nominated Agent including any costs incurred in delivering the same to the nominated Agent arising out of a recall as described above.

The second feature restricts the insured to when a recall can be implemented and also limits the circumstances under which it can be initiated. For the policy to respond there has to be potential legal liability for injury or damage to third parties, which the recall is designed to avoid. A recall initiated because the product was not performing as claimed would not be included in this policy nor would one launched because of a competitor's product.

The third point could turn on the relationship between the insured, the insurer and the part played by the broker. The product recall plan should have the relevant 24-hour contact telephone numbers so that agreement can be sought out of office hours if required.

The following are the *exclusions* in a Willis Wrightson combined product liability, product guarantee and product recall policy:

The recall extension excludes expenditure arising from a decision to recall any products:

1 forced upon the Assured by any Government or Public Authority and which the Assured would not have made but for the intervention of the said Government or Public Authority.

2 which would not have been distributed by the Assured and which remain in the care and custody and control of the Assured or his parent or subsidiary or associated company.

3 solely as a result of their having been misdelivered or mis-directed by or on behalf of the Assured.

4 where recall is brought about solely due to the exposure to weather or due to external loss or damage or gradual deterioration. This exclusion shall not however apply where a defect in the product supplied is merely exacerbated by exposure to weather or the passage of time.

The first exclusion needs to be fully appreciated. It means that if a regulatory body forces a recalcitrant company into a recall the policy will not meet the resulting expenses. In some countries certain regulatory bodies have the power of mandatory recall – the United States, France, Australia and Japan for instance. In many other countries, the powers available to public authorities can amount to indirect coercion which could force a recall by ordering the company to publish, in a specified manner, a warning notice about the danger its product presents, for example. In a difficult situation, the importance of this exclusion should be in the product recall plan and well understood by the recall co-ordinator and his team.

The second exclusion refers to products which are still under the control of the company, usually called a silent recall because media publicity will not accompany the action. This would apply to a vertically integrated company with a chain of retail outlets.

Product recall cover includes certain *conditions* which govern the policy and which may, for example, refer to arbitration and the provision of written notice. An example of two other conditions is:

1 The Assured shall as soon as is reasonable give to the Underwriters full particulars in writing of any material increase in the risk and shall pay such reasonable additional premium, if any, as may be required by the Underwriters.

2 The Assured shall do and concur in doing all things reasonably practicable in order:

(a) to avoid the happening of any circumstances to which this extension applies and

(b) to minimise to the best of their ability, in the event of a recall becoming necessary, the expenses of such recall.

The first condition may seem obvious enough but there have been occasions when a company has diversified away from its declared product lines, which has materially increased the risk without informing the insurer. Such an action could well lead to difficulties if one of the 'new' products was involved in a recall.

The second condition is capable of wide interpretation and turns on that word so beloved of lawyers 'reasonably'. An example would be the existence of a product recall plan which would minimise the exposures of a recall, although it is more than possible in practice that an insurer would not provide cover unless he was satisfied that such a plan was in place. The adequacy of the plan in practice may be another matter, for that will depend on keeping it up-to-date and regularly tested.

Contract conditions

The chief method of transferring to third parties the residual risks of a product recall is by insurance. Another method is by contract conditions.

A finished-product manufacturer may have to recall one of his products through no fault of his own. A supplier may deliver a defective component or ingredient which consequently makes the finished product potentially dangerous; this is particularly worrying if the defect only comes to light after a period of use: a latent defect. Recalls in the vehicle industry can be occasioned by a bought-in-part, such as a seat belt or a cruise control.

A third party downstream of a finished product manufacturer can cause a defect which results in a recall. This can arise through unauthorised modification, inadequate storage conditions (for temperature-sensitive products for instance), failure of stock rotation, and inadequate assembly or inspection. In these cases the finished product manufacturer will look either upstream or downstream for indemnification. However, it will be the terms and conditions of purchase or the terms and conditions of sale which will determine where the liability will lie, with the former probably being the most important in this respect.

There are companies which are quite surprised to discover that they do not have any terms and conditions of purchase at all and that they buy on their suppliers' terms. These may limit liability to the value of the goods concerned, or to a multiplier thereof, which would not meet the cost of a recall caused by a defect in the goods.

Where terms and conditions of purchase do exist they do not always address liability in a way that is in keeping with a regime of strict liability. Alternatively they may seek to make a supplier liable in such a way that it would be made void by the Unfair Contract Terms Act 1977.

There is a move towards including a clause to the effect that the supplier will be liable for any recall costs that arise due to a defect in his goods. Another approach is a clause that would make the supplier indemnify the manufacturer for any loss he suffers due to contraventions of the Consumer Protection Act 1987, caused by a defect in the goods supplied.

During the establishment of the product recall plan it is advisable to review contract conditions. It will have to be borne in mind, however, that commercial considerations can outweigh legal preferences and that the realities of the marketplace may make acceptance of less than favourable contract conditions a necessity.

4 *Market research and relaunch*

In a major product recall some of the management effort has to be directed towards finding out what impact it is having on the public, rather than concentrating exclusively on retrieving the defective product. Further, plans needs to be set in motion at the earliest opportunity for the relaunch of the product.

An important brand may not appear in the balance sheet as an asset, but asset it is nevertheless. The Perrier recall was initiated to protect its brand, for there was no danger from the product itself. Once the public are aware that all may not be as well as they imagined, they draw on the company's bank of goodwill, which may have taken years of exemplary trading to accumulate.

The recalling company needs to know as soon as possible how much goodwill it has left in the bank.

Farley carried out market research twice a week for four weeks, and then once a week for six weeks, to find out how the public were reacting to the news of the recall. Within ten days of the announcement of the Perrier recall in the UK, the company knew that 98 per cent of London restaurants would restock the water when it was available. Johnson & Johnson had daily telephone research carried out during the Tylenol recall and also filmed many interviews with people to discover their feelings towards the company. See the case histories in Part III.

The product recall plan should address the question of market research, especially who will be responsible for having it carried out and who will do it. Experience and knowledge are prerequisites for the individual manager given the responsibility, while it may well be an advantage to use a professional agency to carry out the actual research itself. Telephone interviewing gives a rapid response but needs trained operators, who will be available at one of the agencies.

Market research will modify recall activities on occasions. Nova used it to advantage when they found that a second advertising campaign was needed. Farley stopped a second advertisement for their products not on recall when they discovered it was reviving memories associated with the product on recall. Shell announced the withdrawal of Formula Shell petrol because 'the confidence of the public in Shell petrol could be affected'.

It is never too early to think about the relaunch of a product being recalled. Obviously the timing and method are going to depend on individual circumstances, but it is an area that the plan should include, to ensure it is not overlooked in the pressure of events. For example, Farley established a special team concerned with the relaunch while other managers got on with the recall and handling the media. The Tylenol case history graphically illustrates the decisions and actions taken by the chief executive officer to relaunch the product and recapture its market share. Similarly Perrier planned the relaunch of its brand by some adroit public relations activities, while the world-wide recall was going on.

Reassurance can be provided to the public by a number of means. Advertisements were used by John West, Perrier and Tylenol to tell the public the problem had been solved. Personal calls, letters, faxes and visits, especially to large customers, can be part of the programme. Editorial mentions and publicity in the news columns are more difficult to obtain; the Tylenol 30-city news conference, using satellite links, is a classic example of this approach but is a one-off.

It is advisable to make the relaunched product demonstrably different from the one that has been recalled. Tylenol had triple-sealed tamper-evident packaging. Perrier had a 750ml bottle instead of the previous 1 litre size and 'New Production' on the label. Farley's packs carried 'We're Back for Good'.

A major recall will generate negative publicity which has, unfortunately, been defined as 'the non-compensated dissemination of potentially damaging information'. For marketers negative publicity can pose a new type of threat which is different from that presented by the competition. In many cases the initiation of a socially responsible response may be advantageous; while diverting the focus of blame can also pay dividends. The best example of this occurred in the Tylenol case when Johnson & Johnson pointed out that the incident was not an attack on the company but on the American health care system, and that they were very socially responsible in recalling the product.

When a company suffers from production line sabotage and the media report the situation, its sales will fall and the competition will move in. This is a particularly difficult marketing task. In 1989 HP was forced to recall 300,000 cans of baked beans because of factory sabotage, whereupon Heinz increased its advertising spend by $1 million on its brand. Heinz's baby food had glass problems and the company responded with advertising, a public relations campaign in hospitals and clinics, and replaced the recalled jars with those having tamper-evident seals.

How successful companies are in recovery from a recall is very difficult to measure. The value of publicity about market share has to be judged on its source and weighed against the cost of the operation. As there can never be a control against which an objective measurement can be made, the degree of success has to remain unknown to some extent.

5 *Testing the plan*

A product recall plan (PRP) is not established unless it has been tested, in the same way that fire drills and lifeboat drills prove the effectiveness of their emergency planning. The test can take a number of different forms, but it is better to learn to walk before attempting to run.

Individual elements of the PRP can be tested to check the more sensitive areas. For example:

1 Run a risk classification exercise based on one of the company's products. The allocation of a risk category will be the responsibility of the risk evaluation team using their specialised knowledge, which takes into account the way in which the public would perceive the risk, using outside experts when necessary. The exercise should present the team with information that does not enable a clear-cut answer to be given. Further, the source of the hazard causing the risk should be identified as a design or formulation defect, or a manufacturing error; the consequences and the remedial action are very different.

2 Physically check the traceability of randomly chosen products from points of sale back upstream to incoming ingredients or components. While it may be estimated that this would be possible, the reality can discover unknown problems in making an accurate trace. Time can be of the essence in a serious incident and this factor should be measured in the check. An alternative is to start the check at the coding point, working back upstream to suppliers and downstream to

customers and consumers, to reveal just how far a trace can be maintained.

3 Locate and summon the recall co-ordinator, product recall committee and risk evaluation team out of normal office hours. A severe test is to call out the managers at a weekend or a holiday period: this may result in voluble complaints, but nevertheless a surprising number of emergencies seem to arise at such times or late on a Friday afternoon. A call-out could be tied into one of the other tests discussed here to make it more fruitful.

4 Have recall notifications and press releases prepared and cleared for publication against a time constraint. Succinct, comprehensive and accurate statements do not come easily under pressure. It is an advantage to have the releases challenged and further information demanded, because of the publication of a damaging claim from a former employee, for example.

5 Test the methods of conducting effectiveness checks, especially the detailed documentation. The organisation of the paperwork or the use of computers by personnel unfamiliar with a recall situation can cause delays. Effectiveness checks are the key to determining response rates, which is one measure of success.

6 Activate the specialised accommodation and individual facilities earmarked for the recall co-ordinator and product recall committee. Although this is a question of logistics, the actual assembly of equipment in the designated place should be carried out. It would be an advantage to combine this test with a call-out of the entire recall team. In one major recall all were assembled and operating – except that no one could use the telex to reply to an urgent request from a far distant country that had heard of the incident via the media; and it was the weekend!

To test the plan as a whole needs simulation. This is a realistic exercise designed to identify any weaknesses, so that they can be removed, and to expose managers to the difficulties they would encounter in a real recall.

The first step is to prepare a credible scenario, based on one of the company's products, including a degree of uncertainty; this is because in practice decisions often have to be made on inadequate or secondhand information. The scenario unfolds through a series of documents, supported by telephone calls and faxes. Specific questions have to be answered at specific times and a score given for the risk that faces the company.

The product recall team, including the alternates, gather in a hotel and divide into two or three small syndicates. If the company's own facilities are used they are always susceptible to interruption. Each syndicate has the same information at the same time, so they run in parallel.

At the end the syndicates make presentations on how they have answered the questions, to enable direct comparisons to be made. Importantly, a comparison of the scores for risk at various stages is often very illuminating. As the managers taking part work for the same company, and all are members of the product recall team, the actions of the syndicates should be very similar. If they are not, then a serious review will be required. It is an advantage to have neutral observers present who can give an impartial assessment at the post-mortem, which should take place a week or so after the simulation to allow time for considered views to be formulated.

The scenario can be dramatised by using actors and journalists – to inject an element of surprise – demanding immediate recompense for damage suffered or an instant media interview. Telephone calls, faxes and tapes of 'news' broadcasts are possible ways of conveying urgency. Care is needed, however, not to overdo this type of dramatisation as it can be self-defeating; the scenario must be kept within the bounds of credibility.

A more sophisticated simulation is one that takes place in the normal working environment, without the participants being aware beforehand that it is a simulation. There are companies with well-proven PRPs which adopt this method, but it does require accurate forward planning to prevent it getting out of control. A senior executive acts as a referee and calls a halt to the action at an appropriate time. This type of simulation provides the most effective test as it has to accommodate the everyday occurrences that can clog the best organisations, such as travel delays, communication failures, strikes and the misunderstandings that happen under pressure.

Reviewing the plan

A product recall plan has to be reviewed after:

- it has been used in a recall from the market;
- a simulation or the test of an element of the plan;
- a period without a recall or a simulation.

A post-mortem on the operation of a plan in a recall is essential if the greatest benefit is to be obtained. Under a board member, the recall team and other appropriate managers should be required to give their mature comments and recommendations on how the plan can be improved.

If a product has had to be recalled then obviously something must have gone seriously wrong either with its design or formulation, or during manufacture. The source of the error must be discovered and the management reasons for it revealed. It is not sufficient to be able to pinpoint a failure in a safety-critical component or contamination of a bought-in ingredient, for instance; the management reasons for the failure have to be identified and corrected. After all, it is people who make products unsafe and therefore it is the way in which the people are organised that will ensure that a safer product is the result of their endeavours in future.

The review must examine each element of the operation of the PRP. How accurate was the risk classification? Did product traceability function properly? Was the recall notification effective enough? Should insurance cover be modified? Was the contact list sufficiently comprehensive and up-to-date? And so on.

After the review, the recall co-ordinator should revise the plan in accordance with the comments and ask the senior secretary on the product recall committee to issue replacement pages. To ensure that these have been received and incorporated in the individual copies, the discarded pages should be returned and checked-off against the distribution list.

Simulation will reveal weaknesses in the plan and these should be corrected in a similar manner to that given above. Contributions should be sought not only from those who took part in the simulation but also from the neutral observers who monitored its progress.

A PRP should be reviewed every six or twelve months if there has not been a recall or a simulation. The task should be carried out by the recall co-ordinator and the product recall committee, aided by an independent consultant.

Unless a plan undergoes review it will become stagnant and fail to reflect changes that take place in every company. An established plan will languish without regular critical input.

6 *Product recall plan checklist*

A checklist is not a substitute for thinking. All it can hope to do is to stimulate action. Answering 'yes' to all the questions does not mean that there is an effective product recall plan, because each company has its own unique exposure which no general checklist can cover. Answering 'no' will indicate a possible weakness that needs to be investigated.

The number at the end of the questions refers to the 'Steps' and chapters that deal with the subject they contain.

1 Has the plan been established with board involvement? Step 1
2 Are the plan's objectives approved and signed by the chief executive? Step 1
3 Does the plan have a succinct statement of the major actions on one page? Step 1
4 Have all functions made a contribution during the preparation of the plan? Step 1
5 Does the plan include a statement of the company's legal responsibilities in a recall?   Chapter 2
6 Can you name the recall co-ordinator and his alternate? Step 2
7 Who are the members of the product recall committee and their alternates? Step 2
8 Is there a regular analysis of information that could point to a potential recall situation? Step 3

9   Are quality data examined for trends away from acceptable norms and the results circulated? Step 3

10   Are data on complaints comprehensively collated and an analysis circulated? Step 3

11   Are field personnel required to report any safety-related defects for collation and analysis? Step 3

12   Does the plan have a risk classification system? With examples for each category? Step 4

13   Who are the members of the risk evaluation team and their alternates? Step 4

14   Which outside organisations have been retained to advise the risk evaluation team? Step 4

15   What are the two elements of risk that have to be assessed in determining to which category of the classification a defect is allocated? Step 4

16   Who makes the decision on whether to initiate a recall or not and the alternate? Step 5

17   Does the plan contain the corrective action that would be most suitable for the company's products? Step 6

18   Are the methods for the chosen corrective action fully documented in the plan? Step 6

19   Has a separate warehouse been identified to hold returned product in quarantine and do the details appear in the plan? Step 6

20   How would returned product be securely disposed of? Do the details appear in the plan? Step 6

21   Does the plan include details of the distribution system or indicate where they can be found? Step 7

22   Does the plan show the possible levels to which a recall could pursue a product? Step 7

23   Are the recall levels linked to the risk classifications? Step 7

24   How far back upstream from the coding point to suppliers could traceability be ensured? Step 8

25   How far downstream from the coding point to end-users could traceability be ensured? Step 8

26 Is product traceability physically tested both upstream and downstream at regular intervals? Step 8

27 Is there a company policy on the period of time that product records are retained? Step 8

28 Are the product records that enable traceability to be achieved classified and retained for fixed periods of time? Step 8

29 Does the plan state the essential elements that a recall notification must contain? Step 9

30 Does the plan include approved examples of recall notifications suitable for the company's products? Step 9

31 What are the most effective methods of communicating a recall notification to the company's customers and consumers? Step 9

32 Apart from customers and consumers, does the plan list the outside organisations that should receive the recall notification? Step 9

33 Does the plan contain the details of effectiveness check methods? Including the choice of levels? Step 10

34 Where can a current, complete consignee list be found? Step 10

35 Does the plan contain a pro forma questionnaire for use with effectiveness checking? Step 10

36 Does the plan give details of the information that status reports should contain and to whom they should be circulated? Step 11

37 Does the plan nominate the manager with the authority to terminate a recall and his alternate? Step 11

38 Does the plan have information on a cost control system that can be rapidly activated in a recall? Step 12

39 Does the plan list the facilities that the incident room must provide, and are they always readily available? Step 13

40 Does the plan contain an up-to-date contact list? Is it revised every six months? Step 13

41 Are the means of rapidly reaching the people on the contact list always available? Step 13

42 Does the plan provide information on how security cover can be increased if necessary? Step 13

43 Can you name who would be the sole media contact for a recall; and his alternate? Step 14

44 Are the company spokesmen fully trained in dealing with the media? Step 14

45 Is the company's public relations agency capable of handling a recall? Have they an acceptable track record in this field? Step 14

46 Could the company's public relations agency provide a telephone answering service for a recall? Step 14

47 Does the company have product recall insurance cover? Step 15

48 Are details of the cover included in the plan? Step 15

49 Does the contact list include the company's insurance broker and insurer? Step 15

50 Do the company's terms and conditions of purchase adequately indemnify it for a supplier's fault that leads to a recall? Step 15

51 Do the company's terms and conditions of sale adequately indemnify it for a customer's fault that leads to a recall? Step 15

52 Who is the manager responsible for having market research carried out on the impact of the recall on the customers and the public? Chapter 4

53 Is a team nominated to concentrate on the relaunch of the recalled product? Chapter 4

54 Have the elements of the plan been fully tested in the past year? Chapter 5

55 Has the plan been tested by a simulation involving the product recall team and the alternates? Chapter 5

56 Is the plan reviewed at regular intervals by the recall co-ordinator and the product recall committee? Chapter 5

PART THREE

Product recall case histories

7 *Product recall case histories*

Introduction

Recall case histories are hard to come by. Understandably companies are reluctant to allow the details of what went wrong to be publicised. As one marketing director said of a recall in which his company had received wide media attention, 'That's all behind us now, there is no point in talking about it any more.'

Nevertheless, much can be learned from other people's mistakes and the lessons could prevent other companies following their example. The following case histories have been compiled from information in the public domain, obtained from the newspapers, magazines, radio, television, conference papers, press releases and company announcements.

The three causes of a product defect leading to a recall are illustrated by the cases. A *design* defect was the reason for the recall of the Nova Fritex, Formula Shell petrol and Snecma aeroengines. A *manufacturing* error caused the recall by John West, Farley and Remington. Failure of *product information* initiated the recalls by Wall's, Renault and Larousse.

The chronological sequence is particularly revealing in terms of the speed at which very significant events can occur. The John West, Farley, Perrier and Remington cases all illustrate this in different ways, with the message that the one thing that will not be available is time.

The Kodak recall is unusual because it had nothing to do with product safety but was the result of a patent action in the United

States. The landmark case of *Walton* v *British Leyland* has great importance for any company hesitant about making a decision on whether to recall or not.

A product which has to be recalled because of extortion or malicious product tamper is in a class of its own. The review of this crime and the Tylenol case are included to demonstrate the unique problems that can arise.

Two very special cases are vehicles and medical products. Each has an industry code of practice (see Appendix 3 and Appendix 4) and a government department which takes a particularly close interest in recall activities. Further, every single vehicle is unique because of its Vehicle Identity Number, and medical products have a narrow, closely controlled distribution chain.

The arsenic in beer case history relates the events of 1900 to show that product recall is by no means a modern phenomenon.

The 17 case histories include some famous names. It should not be imagined for a moment that they are alone, for they could easily be joined by many, many more. No company can afford to be complacent and think that it could not happen to them. It could. Tomorrow.

John West canned salmon

The speed with which a major crisis can hit a company is well illustrated by the story of the recall of John West canned salmon in 1978. At the time it was the biggest food recall in the UK and made frequent headlines in the newspapers, led the BBC TV and radio news and its repercussions were still being felt years later. In total it was said to cost Unilever, John West's parent company, £2 million. The detailed cost is examined in Part II (see Step 12: Costs, p.112).

Tinned fish sales in the UK were £100 million a year before the incident and John West had about half the market. The company had been selling canned red salmon for 100 years but only since

1964 under the John West name. The packer of the batch which contained the can that killed two people was the Peter Pan Seafood Company of Seattle, according to the *Sunday Times* of 6 August 1978. It was produced at its 60-year-old cannery at False Pass, Alaska. The plant was inspected and passed by the Alaskan State Health Department before the 1977 season started in June. In April the US Food & Drug Administration checked the processing logs for the season and found nothing amiss.

The *Sunday Times* said that the parts of the can which contained the contaminated salmon were made by Continental Can in Portland, Oregon. The cannery made up the can on site, rather than merely applying one end and sealing it after filling. The defective can was examined by experts from Metal Box (a major competitor of Continental's) on the decision of the Department of Health. They found a pinhole. The source of the hole could not be established with any certainty.

The source of the *Clostridium botulinum*, the organism which produced the toxin that caused the deaths, could not be determined with accuracy. But the head of the Public Health Laboratory at Colindale, UK, said, 'The pinhole is much more likely to have occurred in the United States. Type E [the particular strain of the bacterium which killed members of the Farmer family] is very rare in the UK. Whereas *Clostridia* isolated from salmon are most always Type E – which is, anyway, almost exclusively associated with marine products' according to the *Sunday Times* of 6 August 1978.

The US Food & Drug Administration called in American Canners (an association which polices the trade) to investigate the plant at False Pass. The FDA said that 'bad practices' occurred which arose from the U-shaped production line which an official described as 'unique'. The cans which had been retorted (cooked) passed alongside the beginning of the line where workers were filleting fish. At the end of the day the workers hung their soiled aprons on the warm cans to dry. Raw fish juice from the aprons could fall on the clean cans and contaminate them, on the outside, with any micro-organisms they contained. It was reported that John West's agents in

Vancouver said that no one from the firm had ever visited the cannery. The story continued on:

Sunday 30 July 1978 That afternoon two married couples in Birmingham had a special tea of a 7½ oz can of John West salmon with a salad of lettuce, cucumber and tomato followed by fresh raspberries and cream. They were Jesse (64) and Betty (66) Farmer and Jesse's brother Leonard (79) and his wife Clara (72).

Monday 31 July 1978 At 2am Betty and Jesse Farmer awoke feeling very ill. At 6am they were being examined in the East Birmingham Hospital in Bordesley Green. By 10am they were unable to breathe and tubes had to be inserted in their windpipes and connected to mechanical respirators. At 11am they were injected with anti-toxin to counteract the botulism which had been diagnosed. To confirm the clinical diagnosis the hospital pathologist injected four mice each with half a cc of the Farmers' blood. The first mouse died at 3pm. Next, the can in which the salmon had been contaminated was rinsed out with 10 ccs of salt solution and two mice were each injected with half a cc. Within 90 minutes one was dead and the other died soon afterwards.

During the evening the Department of Health put out an urgent warning to the public not to eat canned salmon: 'If in doubt avoid all canned salmon.' It was essential for the public not to eat any salmon canned in Canada or the United States.

Tuesday 1 August 1978 BBC Radio 2 news at 9am spoke of 14,000 cans of North American salmon with several brands involved, one of which was John West. The warning was, 'Don't eat tinned salmon'. Half an hour later BBC radio personality Jimmy Young mentioned it during his talk to Terry Wogan and then, in the Jimmy Young Show itself at 10.02, Barry Browning, a director of John West, was interviewed.

Browning gave the code of the suspect batch of 291 cases, each containing 48 cans of 7½ oz: RF7GF7145. He said that the batch had been checked in the United States by the Food & Drug Administration, checked by John West's own people in Vancouver and checked again on arrival in the UK. He said that the sterilisation record of the batch in question was 'impeccable'. There had been no case of botulism in canned salmon in the UK this century and the reason for the defect was a mystery. The company were working on it as fast as they could. The listeners were told that all supermarkets were taking all brands of canned salmon off their shelves.

The main BBC1 TV news at 9pm led with the salmon story and showed shots of canned salmon being taken off supermarket shelves. The code of the suspect batch was given and the chairman of John West was interviewed. Every retail outlet in Birmingham was visited by health and environmental staff to ensure all tinned salmon had been withdrawn. In one warehouse 700 tins of the suspect batch were found.

The morning papers carried the story. The *Guardian* had a full column on its front page headlined 'Botulism warning over canned salmon'. *The Times* had a short piece headlined 'Tinned salmon warning'.

Wednesday 2 August 1978 BBC Radio 2 news at 8am and 9am again led with the canned salmon story. It reported that the North American packer had said that the fish had been tested before it left the factory and that it had been satisfactory. *The Times* had a full column on the front page headlined 'US salmon blamed for food poison outbreak'. The Department of Health's warning that no one should eat tinned salmon from the United States was repeated. All the four pensioners were critically ill.

The *Guardian* carried a piece headlined 'The fish that John West didn't reject' – a reference to the TV advertising line of the previous year.

Friday 4 August 1978 One of the first warnings of the commercial consequences of the poisoning came in *The Times* under 'Effects of a food poisoning scare'. The point was made that, when something goes wrong, mass advertising is a two-edged sword. '. . . it will probably be a long time before the average housewife forgets the red salmon scare and her lingering caution may well do damage to the red salmon industry in general and to this part of John West's business in particular.'

Sunday 6 August 1978 The *Sunday Times* carried a full-page investigation by its Insight team, 'Killer that came to tea', which had a trailer on the front page headlined 'Pinhole clue to salmon poisoning'.

Wednesday 16 August 1978 Jesse Farmer died and became the first victim of *Clostridium botulinum* strain E in Britain.

Friday 18 August 1978 John West were reported to be preparing to resume sales.

Tuesday 22 August 1978 The coroner found that Jesse Farmer had died accidentally and that there had been no criminal negligence. There were 14,273 cans in the suspect batch and 2,311 had been recovered; a total of 454,000 cans were imported from the cannery.

Thursday 24 August 1978 Betty Farmer died.

Friday 25 August 1978 The Department of Health confirmed that the warning against eating tinned salmon from the United States still stood. The coroner found that Betty Farmer died through misadventure and that there was no evidence of criminal neglect.

September 1978 A survey carried out by John West showed that 92 per cent of the population was aware of the scare. Few people knew that the Department of Health had declared most tins safe. The government issued a warning against eating tinned salmon from the False Pass factory in Alaska because of 'deficiencies in hygiene' according to *The Times* of 28 September.

Sunday 15 October week Leonard and Clara Farmer left hospital.

Thursday 19 October 1978 384 tins from the suspect batch were stolen from the Co-op store in Whaley Bridge, near Buxton. *The Times* of 21 October reported that Paul Lambert, aged 21, the manager of the supermarket said, 'I was asked by my head office to return the cans to our warehouse about four weeks ago but I had not got round to doing it'.

Saturday 21 October 1978 BBC Radio 2 news at 9am and 10am and the papers carry the story of the stolen cans.

Thursday 2 November 1978 An £80,000 advertising campaign started telling people that 'Canned Salmon is Cleared' except for that from the False Pass cannery. It was backed by the 'British Association of Canned and Preserved Foods Importers and Distributors in co-operation with the Canned Salmon Industry in the USA and Canada and the Can Making Industry of North America and the United Kingdom'. It had been agreed by the Department of Health and Social Security in the UK. The advertisement said:

CANNED SALMON IS CLEARED!
On 27th September 1978, the Department of Health cleared all canned salmon, except, as a precaution, production from one Alaskan cannery. All responsible retailers will by now have removed such salmon from sale.

You can now buy canned salmon again with confidence. But just check your larder for USA cans which bear the code with the letter F in the second place of the top line ... Return any cans with this code to your retailer.

Canning remains one of the safest forms of food preservation.

April 1979 It was reported that £3,500 compensation had been paid to the relatives of Jesse and Betty Farmer who died. Unilever said that all sales of tinned salmon had been suspended for three months. Sales of canned salmon were 30 per cent down on original levels. The cost to Unilever alone was £2 million in lost profits, according to Sir David Orr, its chairman, reported in the *Daily Telegraph* on 26 April 1979. In a summary of its annual statement Unilever said, 'Whether the Department of Health took the right action may be open to question, in view of the fact that the cause of the problem was a single damaged can'.

June 1979 Sales were reported to be back to three-quarters of what they had been before the Farmers' tragedy, when they were £50 million a year. The British Association of Canned and Preserved Food Importers and Distributors started the Canned Salmon Consumer Bureau which provided recipes and information on the product.

Monday 23 July 1979 *Business Insurance* reported, 'Unilever officials in London, where it runs its own captive insurance company, said, "There was no policy taken out to cover stocks losses". They refused to give more insurance details, on the grounds that various legal and liability positions were still under consideration'. A Unilever statement, given in *Business Insurance*, said, 'The publicity which John West received over the botulism case had far-reaching effects on the canned salmon industry throughout the world'. Announcements from the UK Health Department prompted the withdrawal from sale of all salmon canned in North America from markets in the UK, Ausralia, South Africa and most of Europe. Significantly, no withdrawal of any kind was announced in North America. It was not until almost two months later that the UK ban was confined to production from one Alaskan cannery only. By that time, sales of canned salmon had been badly hit, especially in the UK and not only of John West products but other brands as well. From the beginning the John West Group had adopted a 'very open policy with regard to this tragic incident' and the media were never refused interviews. This maintained a good corporate image, ensuring that its other products kept a steady position in the marketplace. The company could not forecast how long it would take for canned salmon sales to recover.

Sunday 7 February 1982 Two cases of botulism in Belgium caused by eating tinned salmon. One victim dies.

Monday 15 February 1982 UK Department of Health and Social Security informed about Belgian cases.

Tuesday 16 February 1982 Department of Health and Social Security (DHSS) issue a warning to the public not to eat half-pound tins of salmon, of any brand name, packed in the United States because they could be contaminated with botulism. The fault was said to be a tear in a tin, which was usually covered by the label, with about five million tins in circulation. It was emphasised that no faulty cans had been found in the UK but that it was possible that cans in this country could be damaged.

John West admitted that the fatal Belgian can had been one of theirs. According to *Product Liability International* of March 1982, an FDA investigation revealed that some of the cans, packed by American Salmon and packaged by NEFCO-Fidalgo Packing Co of Ketchikan, Alaska, '. . . may have been damaged when they were formed at the canning plant, permitting the formation in the can of botulinum toxin, a poison that can cause botulism'. The fish from that batch was distributed only in Belgium, the Netherlands and South Africa.

Thursday 1 April 1982 In the House of Commons, Mr Kenneth Clarke, Minister of Health, said in a written reply that over 10 million half-pound tins of salmon had either been held back from distribution in this country or returned by the public following a public health warning issued by his department. The risk that some of the cans might be contaminated was slight but could not be ignored. It was understood that the Department of Health was consulting with the trade to agree acceptable screening methods for the ten million cans.

Friday 23 April 1982 The DHSS issued a warning to the public not to eat any 7½ oz tins of Canadian salmon after a Manchester family had become ill after eating some.

Monday 26 April 1982 Talks began between the DHSS and the Canadian Department of Fisheries, after talks the previous week with the British Association of Canned and Preserved Foods Importers and Distributors. John West told traders that it had suspended supplies of salmon from Canada.

September 1982 The checking of the 10 million cans was completed. It was carried out at three checking stations normally used by importers with advice from the British Association of Canned and Preserved Foods Importers and Distributors and the Campden Research Station.

Farley's baby food

This recall was the most expensive in the UK with total costs in the £30–40 million region. It is remarkable for the fact that the recall was initiated because of a high statistical association between illness among infants and Farley products; no contaminated product had been identified at the time of the recall. The difficulty in identifying the source of the contamination was great and led to a false restart of production, followed by a nine-month shut down. Over 300 people in total were made redundant.

1985 The milk-based baby food market in the UK declined between 1980 and 1984 then, as the birth rate picked up in 1985, it grew by 10 per cent. The market leader was Wyeth, a subsidiary of the US drug group American Home Products, with a 41 per cent share (according to the *Financial Times* of 22 January 1986) from its Gold Cap SMA and White Cap SMA brands manufactured at its factory in Havant, Hampshire. Cow & Gate, previously owned by Unigate the dairy group but sold in 1981 to Nutricia the Dutch group, claimed a 30 per cent share and manufactured at Wexford in Ireland. Farley Health Products was number three in the market with a 24 per cent share. The only other manufacturer was Milupa, of West Germany, with a 4 per cent share which was supplied from its factory in France. Another milk-based Farley product was Complan, which claimed 85 per cent of the £10 million liquid meal market, with the remaining 15 per cent held by Carnation Foods Build-up products and Boots Vita Foods. Complan was aimed at older consumers and was in decline, having lost considerable ground in the previous few years. There were plans to relaunch the product aiming it at the health food market.

Farley was acquired by Glaxo in 1968 and merged with its food operations to form Farley Health Products. Farley manufactured 4,000 tonnes a year of Oster Feed, Oster Milk Complete Formula and Oster Milk Two. The Oster products were made at a plant in Kendal, Cumbria, which had originally been founded and owned by Glaxo, and had 320 employees. Farley's rusks and cereals were made at a Plymouth, Devon, plant and a £2 million advertising campaign for Original and Low Sugar Rusks was launched in 1985. Farley had been associated with Plymouth since the 1880s when Edwin Farley, a local baker, started making baby biscuits. Farley made a pre-tax profit of £4 million on a turnover of £40 million in the year ending June 1985, according to the *Financial Times* of 22 January 1986; it had an issued share capital of £750,000 and reserves of £2.5 million. Boots were negotiating to buy Farley from Glaxo for £40 million.

The plant at the Kendal factory was installed in 1970 and the processing methods used were standard for the trade. Batches of dried milk were packed into 25kg bags. After satisfactory chemical and microbiological quality control tests, the bags were despatched as bulk product or reopened; the dried milk from the reopened bags was mixed with additives and packaged for the retail trade. Samples were further microbiologically tested before batches were despatched. Charts recording tempterature, rates of flow and concentration of solids during pasteurisation and spray drying were retained. No *salmonellae* were isolated in 1985.

Early December 1985 In the United Kingdom there is a network of 52 laboratories around the country, either in or closely associated with the National Health Service hospitals, which are part of the Public Health Laboratory Service. In addition there are three special units, one of which is the Central Public Health Laboratory (CPHL) at Colindale, London, which is familiarly known just as Colindale. At Colindale there is a unit which has a particular interest in salmonella and other bacteria that cause infections of the gut: the Division of Enteric Pathogens uses highly sophisticated typing techniques, which can fingerprint individual strains, so that the spread of microorganisms in an outbreak can be traced and controlled.

The CPHL deals with conditions that are very rare in the United Kingdom, such as rabies and Lassa fever and the new infections such as Legionnaire's disease and AIDS. Most of the time the CPHL is concerned with the very ordinary, though important, infections that are with us all the time: common hospital infections, hepatitis, influenza and food poisoning.

Early in December 1985 the Division of Enteric Pathogens at CPHL noticed that there had been a large increase in the number of *S ealing* isolations since the beginning of November, compared with the previous ten months and earlier years (see

Table 7.1, which is taken from a report in *The Lancet*). The proportion of infants infected with this uncommon strain was in excess of the normal distribution pattern and the cases were geographically widespread.

Table 7.1   *Human isolations of S ealing 1964–85*[1]

Years	Total cases	Cases aged under 12 months
1964–80	8	Unknown
1981	23	1
1982	25	3
1983	52	9
1984	19	7
Jan – Oct 1985	16	9
Nov – Dec 1985	41	29

It will be seen that there was a great increase in total cases from 16 in January-October to 41 in November-December, while the cases for babies under 12 months rose from 9 to 29 in the same periods. *S. ealing* is an uncommon serotype and is named after an outbreak of food poisoning in the London suburb in the 1960s. It is frequently isolated from human beings and would not be detected by commonly available diagnostic salmonella antisera; consequently isolates were all referred to the Division of Enteric Pathogens for identification.

Wednesday 11 December 1985   A consultant microbiologist reported to CPHL that two infant cases in his area had both received dried-milk baby food produced by Farley Health Products. Further inquiries implicated the same product and health officials first contacted the company on 11 December.

Farley's Quality Assurance Manager, Ron Cooper, was reported as saying that the call from the department was for 'notification and information only'. There was no suggestion

1   Rowe B *et al.*, 'Salmonella ealing infections associated with the consumption of infant dried milk', *The Lancet*, October 17 1987.

that any action should be taken. The company checked its own test records but saw no reason to do more.

Monday 16 December 1985 Further meetings were held after the initial contact on 11 December; on 16 December Farley management and department officials held a fact-finding meeting. The *Sunday Times* of 22 December reported Ron Cooper as saying that no specific conclusions were drawn and the outcome was 'wishy washy'. 'We were not told to take any measures at all by the DHSS at this stage and we did not want to do anything precipitous. We did not want to carry out our own tests in case we used up materials which the DHSS might want to use in later tests.'

Thursday 19 December 1985 Between 17 December and 19 December a case-control study was conducted by CPHL Controls were selected by asking parents of infant cases to nominate families in the neighbourhood with an infant of the same age. Interviews were conducted by telephone with a structured questionnaire. Detailed infant feeding histories were obtained, as well as family food preference histories for a wide range of food and drink items. The parents of 21 infant cases and 15 controls were interviewed by this method.

All 21 infant cases had been fed with Farley's product whereas only five of the 15 control infants had received the same product. Infection was significantly associated with the consumption of the Farley product and no significant association was demonstrated for other brands of infant dried milk or any other food or drink item. At this stage *S.ealing* had not been isolated from any packs of dried milk or from the factory. On 19 December health officials visited the factory in Kendal, Cumbria, and presented the management with their statistical findings.

Friday 20 December 1985 At an emergency board meeting the directors of Farley decided on a product recall and the closure of the factory on the advice of the DHSS. Alan Macfarlane, Farley's managing director, was reported in the *Sunday Times* of 22 December as saying, 'I would be silly if I did not acknowledge that this is going to damage our sales and our high reputation. This is the sort of nightmare that happens to manufacturers and our progress will depend entirely on public reaction.' The DHSS said that the meetings on and after 11 December were informal and based on preliminary findings. Only on 19 December did the DHSS formally present the company with evidence to withdraw the products. Employees at Kendal were due to start their Christmas holiday on 20 December.

The Farley National Sales Conference was being held at a hotel in Bath. The delegates were told that the company had done well and the Marketing Director had just presented the incentive awards when he was called to the telephone. The Managing Director told him that all milk-based products were being recalled. The Marketing Director then had to return to the sales conference and brief them on the situation and the part they had to play in the coming weeks. At 6pm the recall led the TV news with the Export Director, who was at Plymouth, acting as spokesman.

On the ITN News at Ten Sandy Gall announced that two million packs of Farley's baby food were being recalled. Mothers were warned not to use the products. Film clips were shown of the packs being taken off the shelves in supermarkets.

At Bath the sales team retained some of the hotel rooms so that they could devise a policy, prepare press statements, contact key customers and work out question-and-answer responses. At 9pm a telephone conference was held between Bath and Plymouth. A support team was sent to Plymouth.

The DHSS published a press release headed 'Withdrawal of Osterfeed and Ostermilk Brands and Complan'. It said that Farley's had 'voluntarily withdrawn the products as a pre-cautionary measure after consultation with the Department of Health and Social Security and the Ministry of Agriculture, Fisheries and Food'.

Barney Hayhoe, Minister for Health, paid tribute to the urgent and responsible action taken by the company to minimise the risk to the public. In a DHSS press release of 20 December he said, 'I am most grateful to the company for their responsible attitude which is in keeping with a company of their standing'.

Mothers were advised to stop using the named products until further notice and to contact their doctor, clinic or chemist if they required advice regarding alternative feeding arrangements for infants. Products in use or stored in the home should be emptied into the dustbin. Packet tops with the customer's name and address on the back should be posted to Farley for reim- bursement. Mothers who received the products under the welfare food scheme could claim reimbursement or obtain an exchange product from their local clinic. Mothers who could not afford to buy an alternative straightaway were advised to contact their local social security office. Until mothers could obtain a supply of alternative baby food, as a short-term measure over the weekend, they should make up feeds of Ostermilk and boil before use. The press release ended with a list of alternative brands which mothers were advised to use in place of the Farley products.

Saturday 21 December 1985 The front page headline in the *Daily Telegraph* was 'Oster baby milk warning for mothers'. The story began, 'Mothers should stop giving their babies Oster powdered milk products following several cases of salmonella infection, the Department of Health said yesterday.' Farley's board met during the morning.

Sunday 22 December 1985 Over the weekend Boots the Chemist restocked its 1,204 branches with alternative brands. Cow & Gate set up a 'help line' to give information to local suppliers. Hospitals, nursing homes and chemists were urgently restocking with other brands.

Tuesday 24 December 1985 It was announced that a premature baby had died at Booth Hall Hospital, North Manchester, showing traces of salmonella, although subsequently pneumonia was thought to be the cause of death.

Christmas 1985 Checks were carried out on the plant and machinery at Kendal and samples were taken from the 320 employees for testing at the public health laboratory in Preston, where staff worked through the Christmas holiday. All tests proved negative.

During this time Farley's refined press statements and maintained contact with key customers. Communication channels were developed and arrangements made for someone always to be available to answer questions and speak to the press. Three teams were established with 24-hour rotas: a crisis team to deal with the media and health professionals; a recall team to handle marketing, sales and distribution problems; and a relaunch team to prepare for the resumption of sales. This provided a powerful internal signal to Farley employees that there was a future for the brands.

The crisis management team met twice daily and a daily staff bulletin was published on what was called 'Operation Take Home'. Staff were available over Christmas to deal with any queries. A major public relations agency was retained and the first meeting with them took place on Boxing Day.

Sunday 29 December 1985 Mr Nicholas Winterton, Conservative MP for Macclesfield, accused government scientists of delay over the tests. In a report in *The Times* of 30 December he said, 'I would have thought if there was any bacteria it would have been traced within 72 hours and it is now getting on for a fortnight. It is wrong to delay this, holiday or no holiday.' If no link was found with the infection, he said, the government should compensate Farley for the loss of its finances and its reputation in having to withdraw the brand. The DHSS said, 'These things do take a long time, the machinery has to be opened up and swabs taken all over it.' The question of compensating Farley was 'premature' it said.

Tuesday 31 December 1985 The employees returned to work at Kendal. The South Lakelands chief environmental officer said that no traces of bacteria had been found in the factory, among the staff, or in any products so far returned.

Then, at 4.40pm, it was reported that salmonella had been found in the cleaning system at the Kendal factory. At 4.45 ITN requested an interview, immediately followed by the BBC. Within an hour the Marketing Director was being interviewed by Martyn Lewis live on the ITN 5.45 new bulletin, followed by a report on the factory situation by Sarah Allen, with film clips of the Oster products being removed from supermarket shelves. BBC TV and radio interviews followed.

Thursday 2 January 1986 The *Financial Times* reported that traces of a strain of salmonella had been found in dust from the cleaning system at the Kendal plant. But a joint statement by Farley's and the DHSS said, 'The organism has not yet been found in any Farley milk products and all checks on Farley employees have so far been negative.'

Friday 3 January 1986 A spokesman for Boots said, 'The commercial effects of this salmonella business will be considerable.' Boots had not signed a binding agreement with Glaxo for the purchase of Farley, but both companies said that they hoped to complete the deal 'early this year'. A Glaxo spokesman quoted by *The Times* of 3 January said, 'We must now wait for the situation to clarify. We cannot yet say how long Farley will be affected by this problem.'

Farley carried out market research twice a week for four weeks and then once a week for six weeks to discover the state of goodwill towards the company. A large majority of those questioned thought that Farley had reacted speedily, responsibly and correctly to the crisis.

Saturday 4 January 1986 It was reported that the possibility of a connection between the milk supply and the infection in the baby food had almost been completely ruled out. It was thought that the contamination occurred after the milk had been heat-treated and before it was packed. All the 320 staff were submitting stool samples for the second time. Tests so far had shown no evidence of salmonella, according to *The Times* of 4 January. The chief environmental health officer said, 'We may never know the answer but one sincerely hopes we find it. It is the most mysterious case of food poisoning on a national scale that I have known in 30 years in this type of work.'

Week commencing 14 January 1986 Sixty temporary and part-time staff were made redundant in an effort to reduce the cost of closure and preserve as many jobs as possible. The date for a restart of production was not known, or whether more employees would be laid off.

Sunday 19 January 1986 A full-page advertisement was placed in the Sunday papers which said:

> Farley's would like to thank all their customers for their
> continued support for:
> Farley's Rusks with Wholemeal
> Farley's Original Rusks
> Farley's Low Sugar Rusks
> Farley's Granulated Rusks
> Farley's Breakfast Cereal
> Farley's Farex
> Farley's Fingers
> Osterrusks
> Which are made exclusively at the company's Plymouth,
> Devon factory and have no connection with recent events at
> the milk products factory in Kendal, Cumbria.

This advertisement did not achieve its aim and seemed to resurrect memories of the crisis. It was not repeated the following Sunday as had been originally planned.

Monday 20 January 1986 The cost of the incident was put at £4 million so far; in addition there was the cost of the recall at between £2.5 million and £3 million; the company had refunded £60,000 to consumers who had returned products. Of the 30,000 packs returned only 20 were for rusks. The professional officer of the Royal College of Midwives said that the scare might 'be just one more reason why mothers may decide to breastfeed'.

A decision on the reopening of the plant depended on an independent investigation into its pasteurisation system. Consulting dairy engineers were expected to submit a report by the end of the month. Although several traces of the bacterium had been discovered in parts of the factory's cleaning system, investigators were baffled as to the entry route of the infection.

Tuesday 21 January 1986 Glaxo put Farley Health Products into voluntary liquidation to clear the way for the sale of the business. Farley would be split into two subsidiaries. One would take over the milk products business at Kendal, which had already been shut down, and the other would take over the rusks and cereals business in Plymouth, which was operating normally. According to Michael Jordan, joint liquidator of accountants Cork Gully, separating the two parts of the business would make them easier to sell. Boots said that it was very unlikely it would be interested in the milk products business. A condition of the voluntary liquidation was that Glaxo would pay all creditors in full and also meet the cost of the shutdown. The head of baby food marketing for Wyeth, Tom Wall, said, 'Our output has doubled since the Farley announcement. We have worked every day except Christmas and Boxing Day to fill the gap.'

January 1986 Swabs from the factory equipment and environment, samples of powder, dust, waste products, all additives, packaging materials and water from several storage tanks were tested for salmonella. Public Health Laboratory Service laboratories examined all packaged batches of baby milk powder for the home and overseas retail market and many of the company's other milk and non-milk products produced in the factory, as well as packs of dried milk collected from the homes of infected infants, and tested to exhaustion. All factory employees submitted three stool samples at weekly intervals and specimens were obtained from employees who had left the company's employment during the year. But no retail packs of Farley's baby products had been found which contained *S.ealing*. Further, in a major effort 4,554 samples from 658 batches of the company's dried milk products were examined by 33 Public Health Laboratory Services laboratories. It was not until early January that Bath Public Health Laboratory reported the isolation of *S.ealing* from an opened pack collected from the home of an infected infant. Salmonellae were not isolated from current employees but *S.ealing* was found in a worker who had left the firm three months previously.

S.ealing was isolated from scrapings taken from a silo which was part of an extensive vacuum system used in the factory. But no salmonellae were detected in other samples or from the environmental swabs. Investigation of the vacuum system revealed the presence of *S.ealing* but the primary source of the infection could not be found.

Independent engineers reported that the pasteurising and milk drying processes were all functioning correctly but a major inspection of the inner lining of the spray-dryer revealed an irregular hole measuring 1cm x 3cm. When the outer casing behind the hole was removed the insulation material was found to be stained, and when this was removed a large collection of powder was revealed surrounding the hole. *S.ealing* was isolated from samples of the insulation material and from the powder.

After the investigation the inner skin of the spray-dryer was repaired, the outer skin and insulation material were removed and the fixed vacuum system was dismantled. A major cleaning, disinfection and repainting operation of the whole site was carried out and, after many environmental swabs had been negative for *S.ealing*, a carefully monitored trial run was successful.

Friday 24 January 1986 The DHSS said that the Kendal plant could resume production immediately on the '... basis of a thorough programme of cleaning and refurbishment which had been carried out at the factory.'

Tuesday 28 January 1986 The cost of the recall was estimated at £9 million. This figure was high because the shelf-life of the milk-based products was between one and two years and spread around the world in the hands of wholesalers, retailers and the general public. Farley had to refund not only its factory-gate price but in many cases the full retail price paid by consumers. At the time of the incident Farley had intra-group loans from Glaxo of £10 million which had risen to £12.8 million. The formal statement of affairs lodged by Farley at Companies House gave a grand total of trading losses, loans, ordinary trading liabilities and assumed cost of redundancies – were the business to be discontinued – of £40 million. The statement put the realisable value of the two businesses at £15 million, leaving a shortfall of £25 million. Glaxo said that there had been a surprising number of enquiries from prospective purchasers for both the milk products business and the rusk business. An £8 million spray-drying plant was about to be commissioned at Kendal at the time of the outbreak.

Friday 31 January 1986 Glaxo's spokesman, John Barr, was quoted in *Campaign* of January as saying, 'It took John West about a year to recover from their troubles and Farley's will probably find it will take roughly the same time. It was obviously a terrible blow but everything is not entirely lost. There is a strong possibility that the rusks division will be sold as a going concern, and the plant in Kendal has some value but its future is up in the air at the moment. The liquidators have been brought in and they will do the best possible job.' Barr dismissed the thought that the milk products might be able to advertise their way out of trouble. 'It is a difficult situation where you have been out of production for some time and there are certain World Health Organisation Regulations on baby feeds which would restrict advertising the products.'

Wednesday 12 February 1986 A test production run was started to establish whether the infection had been eliminated. If the test run was successful, there would be further tests on machinery.

Friday 14 February 1986 An unidentified bidder made an offer for the Farley baby food plant at Kendal.

Saturday 8 March 1986 Boots bought the Farley Kendal plant and the Plymouth plant for £18 million. Boots said that they would restore the Kendal brands. Wyeth, the US-owned leader in the milk baby products market, had topped the Boots figure but Cork Gully, Farley's liquidators, ruled it out because of likely opposition on monopoly grounds. Boots said that its own quality control staff were now in charge of the Farley operation and that all employees had been told that they were subject to Boots' rules, which made an employee in breach of standard operating procedures liable to instant dismissal.

Tuesday 16 April 1986 Glaxo's annual group trading profit was £12 million down because of the losses associated with Farley.

Saturday 19 April 1986 The Kendal plant was closed by Boots. They said, according to *The Times* of 19 April, 'Although the product and the process is free from any contamination, we are not yet 100 per cent confident that the old plant can be made to meet the company's exacting standards and we are, therefore, placing all our resources in completing and commissioning an entirely new milk drying plant.'

A spokesman said that it would take between three and six months for the new plant to be ready. The production of all dried milk foods had stopped until the new plant could open, although ready-to-feed production would continue. There would have to be a review of short-term manning levels and discussions would take place in the near future with the unions. The new drying plant cost £8 million and was to have made the factory one of the most modern and efficient milk drying plants in the country. It was to have been completed by the end of 1985, but had yet to be commissioned.

Sunday 15 June 1986 Five families were considering bringing an action to recover compensation from Farley Health Products because of sickness in their children. Farley denied liability but said that they were prepared to negotiate 'some sort of compensation'. Glaxo had set aside £10 million to settle outstanding debts and compensation claims.

Tuesday 26 August 1986 An announcement from Boots said Ostermilk and Osterfeed baby food, Complan and other milk-based products would soon be back in the shops after an absence of nine months. Milk powder bought in from Danish, Dutch and British manufacturers would be available in September. The Kendal plant was expected to reopen in October or November. Most of the workforce had been kept employed packing and shipping suspect products for sale as animal feed. About 100 jobs had gone at the Plymouth rusk factory as payroll, administration, marketing and selling had been taken over by Boots' central organisation. Boots planned a campaign to market its baby food range to health care professionals and also heavily to promote Complan.

Thursday 4 September 1986 The marketing manager of Wyeth, Tom Wall, claimed that its total market share had increased 11 per cent points to 51 per cent since Farley had withdrawn from the market. He said that following departures of Farley's specialist staff Boots was facing an area it was not familiar with. Baby milks were a complex business requiring in-depth knowledge. It would be an enormously difficult task. Milupa claimed that it now had 10 per cent of the market compared to 4 per cent before the Farley withdrawal.

Thursday 18 December 1986 Farley's new £8 million plant at Kendal started production.

Friday 7 April 1989 Boots admitted that Ostermilk had only regained 15 per cent of the market and that sales could not support both the Plymouth and Kendal operations. The Plymouth factory was to be closed with the loss of most of the 295 jobs and the manufacture of baby cereals moved to Kendal; rusk manufacture would be done on contract by Northern Foods. At Kendal £1.5 million would be spent on machinery and a number of jobs would be created.

October and November 1989 One of the difficulties for Farley's in trying to regain their market share was that baby-milk products cannot be advertised direct to the consumer – in fact the mothers who buy the product. This is because of a voluntary code of advertising based on the World Health Organisation's International Code of Marketing Breast-milk Substitutes 1981. Further, the competition had moved in while the Oster products were off the market for nine months.

A video was made for showing to health professionals. The new packaging was tamper-evident and emphasised the Farley Seal of Quality Assurance. The packs carried 'We're Back for Good' and 'Discover how you can rest assured with Farley's'.

Perrier mineral water

This recall was unusual for two reasons. It was more the major international recall of a brand rather than a product and there was no health danger to consumers. In fact, this costly exercise took place to protect the brand's image in the eyes of the public and not to protect them from harm. Essentially it is a public relations story and mistakes certainly happened along the way.

Perhaps the most important lesson to be learned is to get your act together from the very beginning – especially if your company has international operations.

Perrier mineral water was originally launched in 1903. In 1948 it was bought by Gustave Leven who transformed the product into an international brand. In 1988 global sales were $2.6 billion with a 1989 estimate of $3 billion. The British market was worth £130 million in 1988 and Perrier claimed a 60 per cent share. The competition was Cadbury Schweppes' Malvern Water, Nestle's Ashbourne Water and Belgium's Spa; Perrier's other brands were Buxton, Volvic, Vichy, Saint-Yorre and Contrexville.

Perrier moved into the US in the late 1970s, despite advice from experts that America would not buy bottled water. In 1988 US sales were $450 million, after the purchase of Beatrice Foods Arrowhead Drinking Water Company.

Perrier employs 3,300 people and has its headquarters at the source in Vergèze, France, which has a population of 3,100. There are 23 bottling lines producing 120,000 bottles an hour. The company started making its own glass bottles in 1973 and produces a fifth of France's glass; it is said to be the only factory in the world that combines a glassworks with a bottling plant. From sand to bottled Perrier takes five hours and production grew from 20 million bottles in 1948 to 1.2 billion in 1989.

Saturday 10 February 1990. The company recalled 72 million bottles of its mineral water in the United States and Canada following tests which found that bottles in North Carolina had between 12.3 and 19.9 parts per billion of benzene. The US standard for drinking water is 5 parts per billion according to the *Financial Times* of 12 February. The US Food & Drug Administration said that there was no immediate risk to anyone who drank the water.

In London, Perrier said that there were no problems in the UK. The French Ministry of Health certified that there was no contamination at the source at Vergèze. The news arrived in the UK at 6am and by evening the US recall had been announced. Perrier in the UK contacted the Ministry of Agriculture Fisheries and Food (MAFF). The company called together the Crisis

Management Team of four core people in accordance with the plan which had been in existence for five years. The only media mention was on LBC radio.

Sunday 11 February 1990 The BBC 6pm news carried a report of the recall in the US. Analysis of samples of Perrier in the UK was arranged; an MAFF spokesman said it was purely a precautionary measure, while Perrier said they were confident there was no problem. Reports that production had been suspended in France were dismissed as totally untrue, after the company's head office in Paris had said that production would stop until it could be established how the benzene got into the water.

The *Financial Times* of 12 February reported the President of the Perrier Group in the US said that sales would be suspended for two or three months at a cost of about $40 million. He said that the search for the cause was focusing on distribution and packaging in Vergèze. The contamination had been found in bottles filled between June 1989 and January 1990 and it appeared to be human error.

According to *The Times* of 12 February a Manhattan estate agent said, 'What is there left to believe in?' A Washington senator said, 'Personally, I am not going to be satisfied until thousands of rats have consumed millions of bottles of Perrier and survived.' A consultant believed that an entire class of people had just had their weekend ruined. A New York playwright explained, 'This is terrible! It's the end of an era. We'll have to go back to Scotch.' The company established an emergency freephone service to reassure anxious customers.

The Chairman of Perrier, Fredrick Zimmer, said that human error was to blame. He thought that an employee at Vergèze had used a solvent to clean something on the bottling line, although benzene was banned from the plant.

Monday 12 February 1990 Analytical tests on the water were started in the UK with the results expected on Wednesday. The Perrier organisation was put on crisis alert and a communication plan prepared with draft press releases. The Perrier switchboard was told to divert all calls concerning the US recall to Infoplan International Public Relations, the UK agency, which had established ten dedicated lines for the purpose. The first meeting with MAFF took place at 10am.

Perrier put out a statement estimating that the cost of recalling the 72 million bottles in the US would be less than FFr200 million. The press reported that the cause of the problem was a careless employee who splashed the wrong cleaning fluid onto a bottling machine at Vergèze. In the US the company would push its other bottled mineral waters including Arrowhead with 7.7 per cent of the market and Poland Spring with 3.5 per cent against the Perrier share of 5.7 per cent. The *Financial Times* of 13 February reported that the Paris Bourse share dealing in Perrier was suspended after a rush of sell orders but were eventually requoted at FFr1,450. It closed at FFr1,490 down FFr 202, or 12 per cent on the day; 3 per cent of the company's shares changed hands in hectic trading.

Tuesday 13 February 1990 In the UK Perrier were deluged with enquiries. Trade buyers were alerted that tests were in hand and that the results would be known the next day.

Despite fresh assurances that the problem had been solved, and that exports to the US would resume within a week, shares were sold on the Bourse in Paris and the price fell by almost 12 per cent. A Perrier spokesman said: 'The hypothesis of human error being to blame for the presence of benzene in precisely 13 bottles in the US is increasingly likely.'

Wednesday 14 February 1990 Preliminary test results showed low-level benzene contamination in the water in the UK, according to MAFF. Traces of benzene contamination were also found in samples in West Germany, Denmark and the Netherlands.

In Paris, Gustave Leven, President of Source Perrier, announced at the company's first formal press conference the worldwide recall of 160 million bottles (representing three to four months supply) at an estimated cost of £40 million. He said that the 'infinitesimal' traces of benzene did not pose the slightest threat to consumers' health. Perrier blamed faulty maintenance of the filtration system at Vergèze.

The press conference was attended by Jacques Vincent, the vice-president who represented Perrier's biggest shareholder Exor. He refused to give a frustrated questioner a quick answer on the cost of the crisis because he wanted to explain at length how it was calculated. The Chairman of Perrier, Fredrick Zimmer, sharply interrupted him to give the figure: FFr220 million after tax. The press reported, 'They look like men from different worlds.'

The French Stock Exchange launched an enquiry into unusually heavy dealing in Perrier shares. In Paris the shares continued to fall with 269,125 being traded and the price dropping by FFr60 to FFr1,413, or 4 per cent down on the day; and 16.5 per cent down since Friday 11 February. The *Financial Times* of 15 February said that according to Jacques Vincent the cost of the recall would be met from profits. The board said that their decisive action would improve the product's quality image, although commentators were saying that it would present an opportunity for competitors.

It emerged that the US Food & Drink Administration first asked Perrier to check its water in the US on 2 February. It was not until the previous weekend that the full results were received, showing between 12.3 and 12.9 parts per billion of benzene against the FDA's limit of 5 parts per billion.

The Chairman and Chief Executive of Perrier UK, Wenche Marshall Foster, said that while there was the slightest possible doubt about the purity of Perrier, sales could not continue. The full-page advertisements which would appear in tomorrow's newspapers stating that there was no health risk were a precaution, a spokesman said. The MAFF confirmed there was no health risk and set up a hotline to advise consumers on the health implications.

Perrier France asked Perrier UK to delay the recall announcement until 4pm. In the UK key buyers received a hand-delivered statement before the announcement and the trade was alerted by telephone, fax and hand-delivered letter. There was no press conference, because at this time the company would not have been able to answer all the questions which the journalists would ask. However, the media were invited to meet the Chairman of Perrier UK at 6.30pm, with the aim of putting the problem into perspective by telling the truth. Consumers were to be offered their money back and the recycling policy explained. The Friends of the Earth demonstrated about the possible effect on the environment of disposing of 40 million French green glass bottles.

In the event, 20 million bottles were recycled and 20 million crushed and held in stock for recycling over the following 12 months. Originally the company had said that half the bottles would have to be disposed of in landfill sites, as there was not enough recycling capacity within the one month deadline they had set. All the bottles recalled in Europe would be recycled. The Friends of the Earth said that not to have recycled all the bottles would have been a dreadful waste of perfectly good resources. The Chairman of Perrier UK said she was delighted that a solution had been found as they were a highly responsible company.

A leading food retailer, ASDA, said it was clearing its shelves of Perrier mineral water. The UK distributor was HP Bulmer of Hereford who handled 200 million bottles of water, as well as the Perrier-owned Buxton Spring brand.

[Benzene is the simplest aromatic hydrocarbon and is highly inflammable. It is used as a solvent for fats and resins. It is the basis for a range of derivatives used in plastics and detergents. In humans it is suspected of affecting blood-forming tissues and being a carcinogen capable of inducing leukemia.]

Thursday 15 February 1990 Full-page advertisements in the UK national newspapers said:

As a voluntary measure, all supplies of Perrier are being recalled worldwide. This follows tests which have shown very slight traces of impurity in some bottles of Perrier though at levels which represent no hazard to health. There is no impurity in the Perrier spring, which is regularly tested and certified as pure by the French Health authorities. If you would like to know more, 'phone our customer and trade information service on 01–402–4474.

Press reports said that scientists were casting doubts on Perrier's explanation of the cause of the contamination, although there was no health risk to the public. The results of tests in the UK were in line with those in the US, according to MAFF, at between 7 and 22 parts per billion of benzene. The World Health Organisation's level for benzene was 10 parts per billion, although there was not thought to be an immediate risk to health at concentrations below 100 parts per billion. The WHO action level was not the same as the danger level because of the large safety margin.

At Vergèze Perrier had produced six million bottles every 24-hours since Sunday 11 February, when the all-clear had been given that the source was not contaminated.

The insurance press reported that Source Perrier did not carry product guarantee or produce recall insurance cover and so the company itself would have to bear the cost of the benzene contamination as a commercial risk.

Friday 16 February 1990 In the UK Perrier were issuing regular statements to the media and on this day they received 1,700 calls from consumers and the trade, all of which were logged. Over the period of the crisis the following enquiries were received: 5,000 from the media, 7,000 from the trade, 15,000 from consumers, 100 from scientists, engineers, chemists and universities. Within ten days of the start of the crisis, 93 per cent of the UK population knew of the contamination and 98 per cent of London restaurants said they would re-stock Perrier when it was available.

Tuesday 27 February 1990 Full-page advertisements appeared in the newspapers which said:

The cause of the technical problem which led to the withdrawal of Perrier has now been traced. The problem has been solved, new quality control procedures are in place and bottling has started again at the Perrier source. An independent report by the Institute of Hydrology at the

University of Clermont-Ferrand leaves no doubt that the Perrier source is pure. All the international medical experts and regulatory officials consulted have confirmed that there has been no danger to the health of Perrier consumers. New bottles of Perrier will be easy to identify and on sale within weeks. If you would like to know more, phone our consumer and trade information service on 01–402–4474.

In France other mineral waters were in trouble besides Perrier. Hepar water, produced by the Vittel group, had been recalled after a 'technical accident' in January when consumers noticed a petrol-like smell from the product. Another bottled water, Katell-Roc, was withdrawn after pollution with nitrates was suspected.

It was reported that Perrier would announce an ambitious publicity campaign in the next few days. The same green bottle would be used but marked new production and backed up with an extensive newspaper and television advertising programme. Perrier had hired a team from the public relations consultancy Burson-Marsteller and installed them in the Head Office. Leo Burnett, the UK advertising agency, had been working on the new campaign.

Perrier said it had recalled over 90 per cent of its world stock of 160 million bottles and all production has been returned in the UK, North America, Asia and the Far East. Less has been returned in France and neighbouring continental European countries; the best Parisian restaurants continued to offer Perrier throughout the crisis. In the UK Perrier said that the retail chains and trade customers had been enormously supportive and there was no sign of any reluctance to renew stocks, when they became available at the beginning of April.

The *Financial Times* of 27 February reported that in Paris Perrier shares were down FFr52 at FFr1,433 on the day.

Wednesday 28 February 1990 According to a survey by Yamaichi, the Japanese security house, Perrier was likely to recover its full UK market share.

Sunday 4 March 1990 A £4 million relaunch campaign would start by the end of the month, according to Wenche Marshall Foster, the Chairman and Chief Executive of Perrier UK, aiming to recapture its 60 per cent market share within three months. The competition was said to be limited by production capacities and unable fully to exploit the absence of the leader.

Wednesday 7 March 1990 The new production returned to the shelves in France after a three-week absence; Belgium, Luxembourg and Switzerland would receive supplies by the end of the week. West Germany, Spain, Greece, the Netherlands and Italy would follow by the third week in March. The UK, Scandinavia, Canada and the East Coast of the US would receive supplies during the first week in April, but California would have to wait until the third week in April. The bottles would carry a special label marked 'New Production'.

Further explanations of the cause of the contamination were reported.

Perrier hired a British consulting group called Hydrotechnica, a unit of Robertson Group plc, to supervise work and recommend new quality control procedures. They concentrated on what Perrier calls its concrete bunker, where it pumps up the natural carbon dioxide which it adds to its water to boost the gas content. It was in that bunker, Perrier says, that failure to change gas filters allowed tiny amounts of benzene into the water.

Duncan Finlayson, Director of Robertson's Minerals & Water Division, disclosed in an interview that the contamination followed the start-up of a new carbon dioxide pipeline at the Perrier plant. The new pipeline began regular service just over a year ago, replacing previous gas sources. Perrier engineers thought the new gas source was less contaminated with undesirable gases than the old ones, and they intentionally began to change filters less frequently. Finlayson said Perrier engineers then did not test for the presence of benzene. Instead, they tested for a foul-smelling but non-toxic gas called hydrogen sulphide. By filtering out that gas, they assumed they were filtering out other undesirable gases as well. It appears the new gas source did indeed contain less hydrogen sulphide, but the benzene level was not lower.

The *Wall Street Journal* of 7 March said that another Perrier consultant, Professor Denise Pepin of the University of Clermont-Ferrand in France, confirmed that Perrier intentionally reduced the filter-changing frequency. But she said Perrier workers appeared also to have begun erring during that period, changing the filters less frequently than even the new rules required. That, rather than the rule change, caused the benzene contamination, she said.

Up to then, Perrier had been saying that the mishap was due entirely to human error: the failure to change the filters as frequently as required. Perrier officials have said they cannot explain the human error and have attributed it to oversight.

The problem arises from the fact that Perrier is not naturally as bubbly as its manufacturer would like. Perrier officials say it once was as naturally bubbly as it is in the bottle, but heavy production reduced the gas content. Perrier therefore pumps up extra gassy water from deep below its water source, extracts the gas and adds it to the water from the main source. The water that comes up with the extra gas is too full of minerals to drink.

Perrier's consultants say the water from the upper source has never been contaminated with benzene. The extra gas, however, has always had various undesirable gases, including methane, ethane, hydrogen sulphide and benzene. The benzene apparently was filtered out with the hydrogen sulphide until recently.

A telephone poll in France showed that 78 per cent of mineral water drinkers had found the company's attitude to the benzene contamination exemplary and that 88 per cent would be buying the new Perrier. In the UK 81 per cent of Perrier drinkers planned to buy it again. In the US the figure was 84 per cent, while 47 per cent of those who did not drink Perrier previously thought that they might do so now.

Tuesday 13 March 1990 It was reported that Perrier was estimated to have lost £22 million and that only £500,000 was covered by insurance.

Saturday 24 March 1990 A press report picked up the story that some of the gas was added to the water at ground level and that it came from a second underground source. It recalled the first explanation that the cause was the use of the wrong sort of cleaning fluid on bottling equipment, and that it took four days to correct this impression.

It was reported that bottled water sales had not dropped much. Perrier's competition had put their plants on 24-hour shifts to cope with the extra demand. A straw poll of 40 London restaurants and two drinks chains found that only one outlet was not intending to reorder Perrier.

Sunday 25 March 1990 This week three million bottles of Perrier were due to be delivered by train to six warehouses in the UK and within three months the company expected to recapture its 60 per cent market share. A £4 million advertising campaign had preceded the launch with a guaranteed benzene content of less than 1 part per billion.

Jonathan Miller, the opera theatre director, said, 'I can't imagine how anyone could have an opinion about Perrier. It would be like having an opinion about soap or gravel.' Tim Rice the lyricist said, 'I would not say that mineral water was an important part of my life. I don't really notice which one I drink.' Tom Conti the actor said, 'I like Perrier, I love the flavour and the green glass bottles. I have a deep loathing for mineral water in plastic pots.'

In France the TV commercial showed a Gallic lover wooing a bottle of Perrier with, 'I knew you'd come back, that you wouldn't drop me like that. Don't cry, you'll spoil your beautiful new label.' The bottle replies, 'I'm not crying ... it's happiness.'

Monday 26 March 1990 Full-page advertisements in the newspapers said:

Perrier will be on sale again at the beginning of April. For the first time in the UK it will be in 750ml bottles, to make the new production easier to identify. This size of bottle is used internationally which also means that we have been able to resume supplies more quickly. In addition the bottom label will be especially printed as shown [New Production]. If you would like to know more, phone our consumer and trade information service on 01-402-4474.

Tuesday 27 March 1990 A press report said that Perrier was bubbling back with a rip-off as there would be a hidden 10p-a-litre price rise, when the bottles reappeared in a 750ml size against the previous 1 litre size. The new bottles would cost 55p to give a price of 73p a litre against 63p for the old size, a 16 per cent increase. At the American Bar at the Savoy in London, a litre bottle used to cost £2.40 while a new 750ml bottle would cost £1.80. The Savoy said that it was not 'holding its breath' for a complimentary case of the new production as the water had not been missed. Supermarkets were said to be disappointed that Perrier's competitors had done so little to exploit the absence of the market leader. There had been no heavyweight promotion of any other bottled water since Perrier was recalled. A Perrier spokesman said that the 750ml size was standard throughout Europe and it made restocking faster.

The new label would in future list under the official analysis the amount of such chemicals as calcium, magnesium, chloride and bicarbonate. The entry for benzene would be 0.000.

Wednesday 4 April 1990 Perrier returned to the retail shelves in the UK with demand reported to be exceeding supply. The line was 'Hell without Perrier. Helleau!'.

Insurance sources reported a 'dramatic' increase in enquiries for product recall insurance as Perrier confirmed it did not have such cover.

Thursday 12 April 1990 The US relaunch was a week or two behind schedule because of delays in rebuilding inventory and obtaining Food & Drug Administration approval.

Friday 20 April 1990 The words 'naturally sparkling' are to be dropped from Perrier labels in the US because the Food & Drug Administration considers them inaccurate.

Monday 23 April 1990 A limited amount of Perrier was available for sale in the US, but it would now be the end of May before it was available throughout most of the country and then in limited volume.

Press reports said that Perrier's handling of the crisis had deeply disturbed a small number of its most wealthy and influential former fans. They felt Perrier had betrayed a trust by failing to explain properly how small amounts of benzene, a suspected carcinogen, got into its high-priced water.

Some, such as Charles Fisher, a New York caterer for big banks, law firms and securities houses, say they will never sell or drink Perrier again. John Dingell, a powerful Democratic congressman, is threatening to hold hearings next autumn on accusations that bottled-water makers in general, and Perrier in particular, mislead consumers in their labels and advertising. The US Food and Drug Administration required Perrier to modify its label before allowing it back in the US, removing suggestions that Perrier's bubbles occur naturally.

Perrier has become the object of a dozen class-action lawsuits in the US, under which the company is asked to pay damages to entire categories of people who are not even involved in the suit. Because of that kind of worry, the Paris brokerage Sellier SA, which follows Perrier closely, published a study urging clients to sell Perrier shares.

The *Wall Street Journal* of 23 April reported that officials at Perrier Group of America Inc, Perrier's US subsidiary, say they intend to 'aggressively relaunch Perrier throughout the country', as Kim Jeffery, sales and marketing senior vice-president, put it. The aim is to regain Perrier's former US market share of 14 per cent of all sparkling waters, and 6 per cent of all bottled waters. Perrier is tripling its US ad budget to $18 million this year, and will spend an additional $7 million on promotions. That is far more than any competitor will spend.

Jeffery says he believes Perrier advertisements and labels have been fair and accurate. Perrier officials insist that any health hazard from the benzene contamination was minuscule.

After a New York ceremony on 26 April Perrier plans a series of giveaways, television advertisements and talk-show appearances around the country, as its water gradually arrives in

Miami and then Los Angeles and New York. Los Angeles alone accounts for one-third of US sales.

Two trucks decked out like giant Perrier bottles are to dispense free glasses of Perrier. Commuters are to be offered free Perrier at major train stations. For weeks, radio advertisements featuring the imaginary 'Perrier News Network' have urged consumers to wait for the water's return. Now the advertisements will herald the big event.

Wednesday 25 April 1990 Sainsbury's told Perrier that it would not stock the product until the label had been changed from 'naturally carbonated' to 'carbonated natural' mineral water. Sainsbury's technologists had visited the source at Vergèze and suggested changes to the bottling process.

May 1990 Cadbury Schweppes bought the bulk of the soft drinks interests of Source Perrier for £125 million. Perrier said that the deal had nothing to do with the recall earlier in the year.

June 1990 Group sales were running at 60 per cent of their previous level. At Perrier's annual meeting in Paris the Chairman, Gustave Leven, said that the company was finding it particularly difficult to regain its market share in the US.

Gustave Leven, at 76 years of age, was retiring in favour of Jacques Vincent, who was vice-chairman of Exor, a holding company with a 31.8 per cent stake in Perrier. A further FFr400 million (£42 million) provision had been made to meet the recall costs; this was in addition to the previous provision of FFr435 million.

The Financial Director, Marcel Richard, said that output had been rising by 25 per cent since February and that the eventual net cost would be about FFr435 million.

July 1990 In the UK it was reported that 60 per cent of the distribution was back to what it was and that 78 per cent of restaurants and hotels stocked Perrier.

HP Bulmer are the UK distributors of Perrier and their year-end results at £12 million were below City forecasts because of the recall. Although Perrier met the cost of collecting and disposing of the old stock, Bulmer were without supplies for two months and their other mineral waters could not compensate for the loss of sales. These exceptional events cost about £1 million in lost profits.

Saturday 11 August 1990 A report in the *Daily Telegraph* on exposure to benzene from petrol evaporation and car exhausts said that it could be a contributory factor to the risk of leukaemia. The scientist concerned from University College London cited the scare over tiny amounts of benzene in Perrier. 'In reality the amount of benzene people get from walking in urban areas is thousands if not millions of times as much (as from factory exposure estimates).'

Monday 20 August 1990 Perrier claimed it had recovered its position as leader of the British mineral water market. The Chairman and Chief Executive of Perrier UK, Wenche Marshall Foster, said that during the previous three months sales had been running at 75 per cent of the level before the recall. Seventy-six per cent of retail stores sold the product compared with 89 per cent, and 45 per cent of pubs and restaurants sold the water compared with 60 per cent. She said that none of the competition had gained sales because of the absence of Perrier, 'We are twice the size of the nearest brand in the take-home trade, and four times the size of our closest rival in the pub and restaurant sector.' Mrs Marshall Foster replied to criticisms about the price increase by saying 'The 750ml bottle was the standard international size. Converting to that helped ensure quicker and continuous supplies from our bottling plant.' The new price of 55p for 750ml included a 13 per cent premium of the kind normally charged for smaller packages of goods.

The monitoring company, MEAL, estimated that Perrier had spent £2.6 million on television and press advertising since the relaunch in April.

Tuesday 28 August 1990 A News Release from the Ministry of Agriculture, Fisheries and Food (FSD 62/90) said:

RE-LABELLING OF PERRIER WATER
Perrier natural mineral water is to be re-labelled, following moves from the British Government.

The decision was agreed by the European Commission in Brussels and the French Government.

The description of the product will be "Natural Mineral Water Fortified with Gas from the Spring", which is the appropriate description of the product, in the terms of the natural mineral waters directive.

Food Minister David Maclean said today:

"I am pleased that the French authorities have responded positively to our suggestion that Perrier water should be re-labelled to describe it more accurately.

"The production procedures at the source of this water where the natural gas is largely added to the water after it is taken from the ground, mean that it is misleading to consumers to label it as 'naturally carbonated' as has been the case hitherto.

"Similar changes in labelling had already been agreed for the US market and it is right that UK consumers should also have the same treatment."

The changes will be made by 1 November 1990.

Notes for Editors:

1. The exploitation and marketing of natural mineral waters in the European Community is controlled by the Natural Mineral Waters Directive (80/777) and is implemented into UK law in the Natural Mineral Waters Regulations 1985. (SI 1985/71).

2. The Directive and the Regulations provide for two major descriptions of naturally carbonated mineral waters:

'Naturally carbonated natural mineral water' where the gas in the water is as it is when the water is taken from the source.

'Natural mineral water fortified with gas from the spring' when the gas, which is also derived from the source, is added to the water *after* the water has been taken from the source.

At the source of Perrier, the water has some carbonation in it, but the levels of carbonation found in the retail bottles offered for sale are achieved by adding further gas from a different strata level of the source during the bottling process.

Thus Perrier is more accurately described by the second definition above rather than the first which is what has been used hitherto.

3. The information about the production of Perrier only came to the attention of the UK authorities a few months ago. The decision to re-label, taken by the French authorities who are responsible for the application of the Directive in France, results from a request from the UK Government to the Commission in Brussels that the Directive should be followed, in order to avoid UK consumers being misled as to the exact nature of Perrier water compared to the other natural mineral waters on the UK market.

Wednesday 29 August 1990 The *Wall Street Journal* called the announcement of the relabelling 'another blow' to the reputation of Source Perrier SA. Perrier officials said that they still considered their water naturally carbonated, since none of the carbon dioxide was produced artificially. The company's international marketing director, Peter Thomas, estimated that just under half the gas in Perrier was added from the secondary source.

Saturday 1 September 1990 *The Economist* said 'Just as it was forgetting about its troubles with benzene, Source Perrier has been caught out again. The European Commission has insisted that its fizzy water is not 'naturally carbonated'.

Thursday 27 September 1990 Daphne Barrett, chairman of Infoplan, was reported as saying that Perrier had regained 86 per cent of its distribution outlets.

Wednesday 12 December 1990 'Perrier is a brand in deep water, struggling to regain its mystique and its volume, now just 60 per cent of pre-recall levels. Marketing experts say the brand's current plight would probably be less severe had it not been for the evasiveness and strategic blunders of Perrier officials on both sides of the Atlantic,' said the *Wall Street Journal*. Its share of the imported bottled water market had shrunk to 20.7 per cent from 44.8 per cent. Of the competitors who benefited, BSN's Evian has been the most successful.

The paper said that Perrier compounded its troubles by taking a 'bizarrely whimsical' view of the crisis, with Gustave Leven, chairman of Source Perrier, making jokes about the recall at a Paris news conference. The comparison is made with the way in which Tylenol, see p.199, managed a textbook triumph of crisis marketing.

Thursday 13 December 1990 The *Financial Times* reported that H P Bulmer's turnover was down 9 per cent due to the slow recovery of Perrier sales. Although the product had recovered its brand leadership in the sparkling water sector, sales were only 60 per cent of the former level. 'It will be some time before we can recover lost ground' said Mr Esmond Bulmer, the chairman.

Friday 4 January 1991 The new chairman of Source Perrier, Jacques Vincent, said that by the summer he expected Perrier to recover its sales in the US to the level attained before the recall, the *Financial Times* reported. The incident cut Perrier's share of the US market from 44.8 per cent to 20.7 per cent but by July the group had recovered 70 to 75 per cent of its share and this had since improved to 75 to 86 per cent. Mr Vincent did not expect US sales to surpass the 1989 level.

Friday 15 February 1991 Before the recall Perrier had a third of the mineral water market in the UK, which climbed back to 5 per cent within a month of the relaunch and then dropped to 2.5 per cent between January and March 1990, according to the *Daily Telegraph*. It now has 11.6 per cent, with 65 potential rivals including numerous own label products. A Perrier spokesman was quoted as saying that its share of the sparkling mineral water market was now 24 per cent compared to 49.6 per cent in July 1989.

Remington electric shaver

The first the public knew of a possible problem with the Remington M3 shaver was on Friday 6 October 1978. The *Financial Times* carried a restrained and factual piece under the headline 'Remington recalls shavers'. It said that Remington would be launching a nationwide campaign in the electrical trade press on 18 October and in the national press on 20 October. The campaign would tell owners to return their shavers if they had certain markings. The company would send a replacement, fully guaranteed for 12 months. The *Manchester Evening News* had a headline 'Shavers death risk warning' with just 44 words underneath. It merely said that shavers with certain markings should not be used in any circumstances because of a risk of electrocution.

The following week the trade press was more realistic. *Electrical and Radio Trading* used the headline 'French Remingtons faulty' and set out a short summary of the situation. The *Electrical and Electronic Trader* used '"Danger" shavers recalled', the *Electrical Times* 'Recalling M3 shavers' and the *Chemist & Druggist* '"Shocking" problems with Remington's M3.'

The reports had been triggered off by a press release put out by what was then the Department of Prices and Consumer Protection (DPCP) on 5 October. This single sheet of A4 was responsible for considerable problems at Remington's headquarters in New Malden, outside London. It seriously confused the national recall which the company was in the process of setting up. Indeed, the first that Charles Carter knew of the press release was when he read it in his Friday morning *Financial Times*. As he was the managing director of Remington, this had considerable significance.

In 1978 Remington were part of Sperry Remington, a subsidiary of the American Sperry Rand Corporation. They marketed shavers made at factories in France and the United States. The M3, with its triple shaving system, was one of a wide range of shavers for men and women sold across Europe. In the UK the company had been selling electric shavers for 40 years and the French factory had produced over 250,000 M3s without any problems. However, the company was well aware of the need to avoid complacency; to reduce product hazards to a minimum, it operated a comprehensive product safety programme. There were two elements of this programme which are crucial to the story of the recall. The first was effective product traceability which enabled the company to identify the suspect shavers by location and production period. This restricted the scale of the recall to specifically marked shavers. The second was a defence-in-depth provided by a roving quality assurance audit team which reported directly to the parent company's headquarters at Bridgeport, Connecticut.

Samples awaiting despatch to retail outlets were checked by a member of the audit team at a warehouse in Germany. One of the checks included the application of 5,000 volts to a shaver as a test of the electrical integrity of its assembly. One sample failed this test. Investigation traced the cause to the presence within the casing of a small quantity of metallic swarf in the form of very fine strands of wire, approximately one eighth of the thickness of a human hair. It was discovered that this swarf had come from the unauthorised use of a metallic buffer to remove blemishes from the plastic casing during manufacture. In transit, the swarf had been distributed in such a way that it made the sample that failed electrically unsafe by the time it reached the German warehouse. Yet the original 5,000 volt check at the factory had been perfectly satisfactory.

Only M3 shavers made at the French factory were affected and then only M3 shavers coded 5MF1D and 6MF1D on the base. Some 90,000 units were involved. The chance of a customer suffering harm because of the swarf was considered to be very remote. But Remington's engineers had to say that there was an outside chance that a customer could receive an electric shock if, during transit and use, the random distribution of the swarf affected the shaver's electrical integrity.

Charles Carter consulted the parent company's lawyer and together they visited the Director of the British Electrotechnical Approvals Board, for the M3 carried the Board's logo. This was on 28 September. The next day, a Friday, they met again, in company with a representative of the DPCP. Charles Carter decided to recall the affected M3s and fully realised that it was a considerable operation to mount from scratch. On the Monday he briefed the company's advertising agency and two days later saw the roughs of an advertisement. He also briefed a field selling company whose personnel would replace the M3 shavers in retail outlets up and down the country.

Charles Carter told the DPCP of his proposed actions and the two-part campaign that he was in the process of arranging. The field selling company would cover the shops, while press advertisements would reach the customers who already had an M3. The recall advertisements had been booked for 20 October and 22 October (the earliest dates available) in 16 English, Scottish and Irish newspapers, and were an integral part of the overall scheduling. In the period running up to the advertisements' appearance, Remington had to brief personnel, arrange for replacement shavers to be in the correct places and ensure that the logistics were right. Unknown to Charles Carter, the DPCP put out the press release on the day following his visit to explain his actions. The first newspaper reports appeared on a Friday. On the following Monday, 27 newspapers phoned Remington at New Malden. So began the siege by telephone. The advertisement said:

WARNING

A small number of Remington M3 Electric Shavers sold since April 1977 may have an electrical fault which, under certain circumstances, could cause the user to receive an electric shock.

The shavers involved are those MADE IN FRANCE and they may be recognised by the markings on the base.

[Line drawings showing position of the codes 5MF1D and 6MF1D]

Similar models made in the USA are NOT affected and these may be identified by the wording MADE IN USA. Anyone who owns one of these M3 Shavers marked MADE IN FRANCE should

STOP USING THE SHAVER IMMEDIATELY

The shaver should then be returned to Sperry Remington at 9–11 New Oxford Street London WC1A 1BR.

Pre-paid adhesive labels are available for use and either a letter or a telephone call will ensure immediate despatch of such a label (call the operator and ask for FREEPHONE 2324).

Alternatively, the shaver may be sent postage paid and the postage paid by you will be refunded.

The FREE replacement shaver, which will be sent by first class post, will either be new or will have been completely reconditioned at the Remington factory and this will include a new shaver head and cutter together with a full one year warranty on the complete replacement shaver.

Should you be in any doubt as to what you should do you can telephone. Call the operator and ask for FREEPHONE 2324.

The day after the siege began, Tuesday 10 October, Charles Carter approved the final versions of the advertisement and sent copies to the DPCP and the British Electrotechnical Approvals Board. He also visited the Electricity Council. The next day was spent in finalising arrangements for exchanging the shavers in the shops. The instructions to the field personnel ran to 17 pages.

The object was to use 52 of the field selling company's merchandisers during a two-week period to visit all nominated Remington stockists and check their stock of shavers. Up to six units each of the M3 Mains shaver and the M3 Mains de Luxe were to be exchanged if they were marked 5MF1D or 6MF1D and MADE IN FRANCE. Further stock would be exchanged in a separate operation. Each girl was to make 11 calls a day, but the quality of calls took precedence over the number.

The girls were told to introduce themselves to the manager or owner of each store using a letter of authority to help explain the purpose of the visit. Every girl was to carry a letter on Sperry Remington letter-heading certifying her assignment. Photographs of the models to be checked, and those that did not need checking, were provided to help identify the suspect stock.

Each girl was to be supplied with 240 shavers to enable her to carry out the exchanges. They were told to keep the stock in the boot of their car or, if it was on the back seat, cover it with a rug.

A blue canvas bag was supplied to transfer the shavers between car and shop to disguise the fact that the girls were handling valuable merchandise. Special insurance would cover the 12,500 shavers held by the girls.

Instructions were given for dealing with multiples like Boots, Currys, House of Fraser and Trident. Some, which were being handled directly through the Remington warehouse, were to be disregarded – like Comet, Argos and Rumbelows. Others, like Shoppers' World, had already exchanged their stock but a check was required to ensure that the operation had been completed. Currys' managers had already been instructed to separate suspect and clean stock, but again this had to be checked. At Boots all M3 shavers were to be replaced, regardless of the coding.

In every case suspect stock was to be marked with a round, red label and all clean stock with a round, yellow label. At the end of each call the girl was to explain the exact situation to the store manager, complete a goods exchange note and have it signed and stamped by the store. Girls were told that they could obtain further supplies of shavers from the ten Remington service centres around the country. Each day every girl had to report back with full details of the calls made and those that could not be made. A 'highlight' system, was to be used to prevent any major outlet being missed.

On 12 October, a whole series of letters had to be written to the trade and to large customers explaining the situation before the advertisements appeared. They were told that the task force would be exchanging their stock of M3 shavers. All service dealers had to be sent a full explanation of the position and how to deal with it. Customers who 'phoned following the DPCP press release were sent a letter and a prepaid gummed label to return their shaver. Customers who returned shavers at their own cost were sent a letter accompanied by a refund of the postage. Replacement shavers had to be accompanied by a letter saying that the forthcoming advertisements would not apply – to prevent exchanged shavers being replaced a second time. Large customers were sent a letter and a supply of the pre-paid gummed labels to give to individual customers who wanted to return their shavers. Some customers had queries and these had to be answered individually. Charles Carter had to sign the 52 letters of authority for the merchandisers.

On the day that a special Freephone line was installed, 13 October, BBC radio warned of the suspected fault in the M3 shavers. A few days later, LBC and Capital Radio broadcast similar warnings. It was two weeks after the DPCP release that the trade advertisement appeared; the next day the national papers carried them and a couple of days later the national Sunday papers.

Remington's switchboard, scarcely relieved by an extra line even before publication, was swamped. Soon the local exchange itself was swamped, which produced a knock-on effect further back in the telephone system. The normal work of Remington's head office, already greatly attenuated, stopped dead. One example will illustrate the sort of problem that arrived on Charles Carter's desk. A solicitor representing a local doctor instructed Charles Carter to stop the recall immediately. His client was unable to run his practice in the usual manner because of the overtaxed telephone system. The reason was the recall, and therefore Charles Carter had to be responsible.

Extra space was hired for the reception and despatch of the shavers to be exchanged. Extra personnel were hired to help process the 16,000 customer exchanges, which represented twice that number of shavers. The sheer volume eventually over-whelmed attempts at adequate recording and checking. The Post Office made special daily deliveries and collections. New arrangements had to be instituted to dispose of the packaging rubbish.

Some people returned shavers outside the suspected code. Others returned shavers 10 or 20 years old. Some shavers had not even been made by Remington in the first place. Despite the warning letter, some people returned shavers that had already been replaced. Because an electric shaver is such a personal thing, the returned units could not be reprocessed and sold. In fact they were crated up and sent to the United States for disposal.

Charles Carter reckoned the whole company learned a lot during the frenetic weeks of the recall. 'I must emphasise two things', he said. 'The most important thing is that we did not receive one single consumer complaint regarding a defective shaver. Not one, and neither did we discover any faults ourselves. The second thing to remember is that we discovered the possibility of a defect ourselves, because we had an effective product safety programme. This was the first time in over 40 years, but it does show the need to check and double-check. It's impossible to mount a national recall in a couple of days – why, even getting the advertising placed at short notice is a major problem in itself. Premature release of information by the DPCP exacerbated an already difficult situation – and as you have seen we moved pretty quickly. I guess it cost us around a million dollars but it brought us some very valuable experience.'

In the three years to 1979, Remington had lost £30 million. A year after the recall Sperry-Rand sold Remington Products to Victor K Kiam II in a leveraged buy-out with a debt/equity ratio of 50/1. He took the company from £43 million sales to £350 million and second place in the world shaver market with a 25 per cent share. Manufacturing was concentrated in Bridgeport, Connnecticut, quality circles were introduced and a 100 per cent product inspection, which was claimed to yield 'a near zero defect rate'.

The company now has 4,000 employees and an extended product range with The Remington Fuzz-away, The Remington Lektro Blade, The Right Angle Beard/Moustache Trimmer and the Hygenic Clipper for those over-endowed on the nose and ear hair department.

Abbott, H , 'The Story Behind a Product Recall', *Product Liability International*, April 1980.

Kodak Instant Cameras

The cameras were recalled because of a patent action brought by Polaroid against Kodak in the United States. Polaroid originally filed a suit in August 1976 seeking an injunction and in 1985 after a 75-day trial, a court ruled that Kodak had infringed Polaroid's instant photography patents, forcing Kodak out of instant photography. On 9 January 1986, when the United States Court of Appeal rejected Kodak's appeal, the injunction became effective. This barred Kodak from manufacturing, using or selling instant camera and film that infringed any of 14 claims of five current Polaroid patents.

The problem that action presented to Kodak in the UK was that all their products came from the United States, so that they could no longer supply their market. This forced them into a recall, which was followed by others in Canada, Japan and Australia.

In the UK, separate recall packs were despatched to consumers, dealers and distributors. The latter two had to be recompensed for their work but the message was that the recall was also a way of getting customers into their shops. Kodak talked to Trading Standards Officers and the Consumers' Association, sent mailshots to dealer chains and put out press releases.

The recall offered customers the choice of vouchers to be used in exchange for Kodak products or a cheque. The recall ran for two years and involved much administrative work and needed extra staff. The total cost could have approached £1 million.

On 12 October 1990 a US judge in Boston awarded Polaroid $909.4 million in compensation for the patent infringement.

Nova Fritex deep-fat fryer

This recall demonstrates the problems and conflicts that can arise in a large corporation, even though it had in place an organisation to manage product safety. Of great interest are the disagreements that arose in trying to determine whether there was a product risk serious enough to justify a recall.

At the time of the Nova recall ITT Europe Inc was a conglomerate with huge telecommunications subsidiaries in every European country, an Industrial Products Group, an

Automobile Products Business with a $600 million turnover and, among others, a Consumer Products Division with a $200 million turnover. Nova was part of the Consumer Products Group, was based in Belgium and manufactured domestic electrical appliances.

The management system adopted by ITT included a local president for a company like Nova, who presented his plan to the European headquarters in Brussels once a year. One of the group staff would be a product manager responsible for the profit of the companies under his wing. There was a marketing department in Brussels and an ITT Product Safety Council, which had members from quality, legal, technical, marketing, safety and insurance departments; there was a similar Council in New York at the ITT Inc headquarters.

A product safety programme had been established as part of ITT's Policies and Standard Practices under the ITT Policy Guide, which had the intent of assuring that the products were safe and in compliance with all applicable laws, regulations and standards established for the protection of users. There were a number of very professional initiatives to carry the message home to all managers; and one Product Safety Reference Book weighed in at over 2kg.

Included in Nova's product range was the Fritex, a deep-fat fryer for cooking such things as potato chips. In construction the Fritex consisted of an aluminium casting, in the form of an open pot, to hold vegetable oil which was the typical cooking medium. In operation the casting was electrically heated by a separately manufactured heating element: a resistance wire heater contained within a metal tube and insulated from it. In the original Fritex design the heating element, in the shape of a toroid, was fused into the base of the main body unit as part of the casting (see Figure 7.1, p.192). The rest of the Fritex included the outer cover, an adjustable thermostat, the electrical flex, the connectors for the heating element and the thermostat. Units of this type worked well and without problem.

However, the manufacture of the casting, with the inclusion of the heating element, was difficult and costly; an independent consultant employed by Nova suggested that a channel should be cast into the base of the aluminium pan. The heating element would then be clamped into the channel as a separate operation, rather than be cast in. Production of the Fritex 3 to this design started in August 1975.

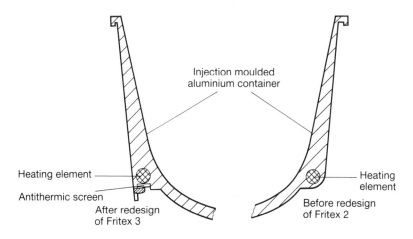

Figure 7.1 *Nova Fritex heating element before and after cost reduction*

On 6 January 1976 Nova after-sales service received a defective Fritex 3 from a customer. Analysis showed that the heating element had moved in the groove so much that one of the ends made contact with the aluminium casting. A test on 10 Fritexes heat-cycled without oil confirmed that this was a potentially repeatable failure mechanism. On 10 January a second customer complained by telephone that he received electric shocks from his Fritex. Nova management stopped production of the Fritex 3 on 14 January and, after review of the problem with the Appliance Division Director of ITT Consumer Products Group based in Brussels, a letter was sent on 30 January to all Nova's dealers. It informed them of a possibly serious defect in the Fritex 3 and asked them to return all their stocks to Nova, and where possible to get them back from final customers.

At this stage the recall level extended only as far as the dealer network and no attempt would be made directly to approach end-users with a Fritex 3 in their kitchen. This decision had been taken at a meeting in Brussels between the product manager and members of the Product Safety Council. The quality and marketing representatives pressed for further action but were told that the facts needed further examination.

The arguments against a full recall at this point deserve to be given prominence, as they have a familiar ring to them for anyone who has been in a similar situation.

- A recall damages the reputation of a brand with the final customers, both existing customers and potential new customers.
- The more effective the announcement about a defective product the more damage is done to the reputation of the product.
- Belgium ownership of the Nova Fritex was very high. In one sample of 25 housewives with telephones and friteuses 23 had the Nova Fritex. Clearly such a dominant supplier had a great deal to lose from bad publicity.
- A press product recall cost a substantial amount of money, which came straight out of profits.
- The carefully built-up image, based on years of good product quality and reliability, could be destroyed, and there would be no way of restoring the damage except over a very long period.

The Product Safety Council set up a working party to determine just how serious the risk was, because the only information at this point was the two reports of electric shock at the beginning of January.

Nova's technical department conducted an urgent investigation of the problem and made a comparison between the original design and the new design. They showed that in two respects the new design was worse than the old. Firstly, the thermal contact between the heating element and the aluminium casting was much less effective. In operation, the power input was the same, as was the final temperature reached by the casting which was controlled by a thermostat, but extra thermal resistance had to be overcome and this caused the heating element to reach a higher temperature, about 180°C higher in the new design. Secondly, the expansion and contraction stresses caused by this excessive temperature, together with the less firm anchoring of the element given by the clamp system, allowed the heating element slowly to creep around the channel as the Fritex was switched on and off. Life tests on 10 Fritexes indicated that a high proportion might fail in this way.

This failure mechanism markedly reduced the useful life of the Fritex so the design was clearly unsatisfactory. However, the Fritex 3 was always sold in Belgium with a three-lead flex terminating in a standard European plug with an earthed connection, and the instruction sheet enclosed expressly stated the need for the product to be properly earthed. In the UK the Fritex was supplied without a plug, as is customary, but the instructions required the use of an earthed plug on the three-lead flex; if used correctly in this way the failure would not be dangerous. Unfortunately, the standard European plug could readily be forced into a two-pin socket and it was believed that many kitchens in Belgium did not have properly earthed outlets. It was this deficiency that made the failure dangerous.

The marketing department were given the task of producing a forecast of the casualties that could occur from the defect. The questions that needed to be answered were capable of being set out in a classical probability tree form; probabilities could be assigned to each fork to the ultimate scenario of over 25,000 people in their kitchens. There were six questions that had to be answered:

1 How many had been sold which had the defect?
2 How many of these would now be in the homes of buyers in use?
3 How many hours of use were required before the product became electrically unsafe?
4 What was the forecast of the total number becoming unsafe over the total life of the product?

5   What were the chances of a user of an electrically unsafe Fritex suffering a severe shock, leading to hospitalisation?

6   What was the forecast of the total of such shocks that would be received as a result of the defective product remaining in the kitchens of users?

There were no official data on earth connections in domestic kitchens. However, the electricity and gas distribution company's own estimate was that only 25 per cent had an earth meeting legal standards, 25 per cent had a non-legal make-shift earth, and 50 per cent had no earth at all.

The market research departments in each of the major companies in ITT provided additional information. The German company came up with a crucial figure for mortalities for all those admitted to hospital suffering from electric shock: over 5 per cent of those admitted died within two weeks.

The risk analysis of the Nova Fritex 3 is given in Table 7.2.

Table 7.2   *Risk analysis of Nova Fritex 3*

	Min %	Max %
Proportion of Fritexes expected to short-circuit	25	50
Proportion of Belgian kitchens with no earth	50	75
Proportion of short circuits giving electric shock	100	100
Proportion of shocked users requiring medical attention	2	2
Overall product of proportions	0.25	0.25

The proportion of Fritexes expected to short-circuit was derived from the life-test experiments. Later results indicated that this initial assumption was somewhat pessimistic. Tests at 1000 cycles up to operating temperature and then cooling gave no more than 25 per cent of short-circuit failures. For larger numbers of cycles the predominant failure mechanism was wear-out of the heating element resulting in a safe open circuit.

Finally, it was assumed that a Fritex in the short-circuit condition, working on a non-earthed outlet, would sooner or later give someone an electric shock. Overall, the risk analysis showed that electric shocks from about 1 per cent of the Fritexes left in the field might cause a customer to seek medical attention; it indicated that a full recall was required.

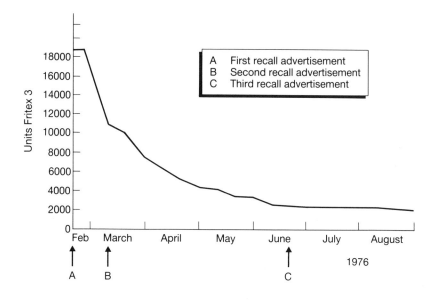

Figure 7.2 *Nova Fritex recall response rates*

The first step in the recall had been the letter to dealers on 30 January. Now three announcements were made in all the papers in Belgium (a country with a large number of local papers) in both French and Dutch on 17 February, 12 March, and 14 April 1976, see Figure 7.2). A similar announcement was made in the UK national papers on 3 March. In addition, a statement was made about the withdrawal on a television consumer programme in Belgium.

The first recall notification was unremarkable and had the heading 'Avis aux utilisateurs' in an attempt to be discreet. With the later notices a policy of making them as effective as possible, irrespective of the adverse effect on product image, was adopted. Market research was conducted to determine the effectiveness of the advertising. This showed that 10 from a sample of 15 understood the message of the second advertisement. The research also showed that fears about an adverse effect on market image were apparently groundless; on the contrary, Nova received credit for conducting the recall honestly, this being the first time any company had conducted a recall in Belgium.

However, the market research also showed that, despite the extensive advertising, most consumers remained unaware that there was a defective product. For example, from a sample of 25 friteuse-owning telephone subscribers in Flanders only nine had seen a further advertisement, especially directed at that group on 13 July, and only 10 saw yet another advertisement made on 15 August.

After a number of repeats of the press advertising and additional publicity on radio and television the recall was extremely effective. One of the initial actions during February 1976 was to establish exactly how many Fritex 3s were in the field and to get a precise record of the returns. It turned out that there were initially 18,703 in Belgium and 7,798 in the UK. The 47th report issued by Nova on 6 May, 1977, showed that all but 1,570 of the Fritexes had then been accounted for in Belgium and all but 719 in the UK. In both cases well over 90 per cent of the number sold had been recovered. The professional marketing view was that 'the remaining portion of the population of owners of defective friteuses are a residual fragment that it is impossible to reach.' Fortunately, as the population of Fritex aged, it became progressively more likely that failures would be by safe open circuit rather than unsafe short circuit.

In the UK customers were offered either a refund or a repair. The latter was to 'replace the fixing which attaches the element to the case, which after 18 months or so of continuous use might weaken and allow the element to touch the casing.'

The companies of ITT in Europe learned many lessons from the Nova Fritex recall. The first was the need to give added urgency to the existing programmes on product safety. Product safety seminars led by the ITT Director of Consumer Affairs were conducted throughout Europe; product safety was re-emphasised in design guidelines for engineers; individual companies conducted their own training; and many hundreds of existing products were re-examined for their safety.

The Fritex failure also represented a serious breakdown of the ITT Product Qualification system. Since 1972 ITT had had a policy requiring each new product to be subjected to defined qualification tests to give assurance that it conformed to all specified requirements, including safety requirements. Qualification testing was a formal quality assurance procedure additional to normal development testing. The important design change on the Fritex 3 was not subjected to this discipline and only a small amount of life testing was included during the development testing. The design change was proposed and tested by a consultant unfamiliar with the requirements for product qualification and this had also contributed to the problem. The fact that the Fritex 3 had been tested and approved by approval authorities in a number of countries only emphasises that there are no substitutes for rigorous internal qualification testing.

The Fritex case led to a major re-emphasis on product qualification, particularly for consumer products. At Nova a comprehensive safety checklist was established and all existing products were reviewed against this by a joint technical/quality team, assisted by the quality and technical directors of the Consumer Products Group. A complete schedule of qualification testing for all new products was established, including milestones for preparation of qualification test specifications, performance of tests, and issuing of qualification test reports. Safety and life characteristics were emphasised.

The conduct of the recall itself showed the great importance of co-ordinated actions from a whole series of general and functional managers acting within the operating unit and headquarters. In the end there were only two accidents with the Fritex, one involving personal injury and one damage to property, and the probability was that neither of them was in fact caused by a defective unit. The June 1977 issue of the Dutch consumer magazine *Consumentengids* gave an improved, safe Fritex the only 'good' rating among seven types of friteuse tested.

One senior manager involved in the Nova recall subsequently said, 'Product recalls involve arguments, and what is good for profits becomes entangled with what is right or wrong, and what is right or wrong gets confused with issues of the admission of culpability, and so on. The actual issue of how many people were likely to get hurt was crucial to the recall and will be a critical factor in all recalls. To calculate the probabilities of injuries is an essential activity in the period before a recall, and it should be done with dispassionate care.'

In 1990 five executives completed a management buy-out and formed Nova Electro International NV. In 1990 unit sales were £36 million with the deep-fat fryers accounting for 60 per cent. Nova remained the market leader in Belgium with a 50 per cent market share.

Groocock J M, Clifton P, Mueller A K, 'The Recall of the Nova Fritex', *Quality Assurance*, Vol 14 No 2 June 1978.

Extra-Strength Tylenol capsules[2]

This is by far the best known incident of malicious product tampering and is frequently mentioned in a variety of ways. It is of great interest for our purposes for two reasons. The first is that the regulatory body, the US Food and Drug Administration, strongly urged the company *not* to recall the product and yet, in the event, that is just what it did. The second is the way in which the manufacturer recovered its market share by a brilliant public relations campaign, and it is this aspect that the following account examines.

In many ways the Tylenol recall was unique. It is important to remember that it happened in the United States and that it

2   Source: Burson-Marsteller.

would be virtually impossible to repeat the exercise anywhere else. Furthermore, the manufacturer, Johnson & Johnson, did not want any adverse publicity to affect all its other products, so in a sense Tylenol was recalled to protect them. The story is the classic example of the concept of the demonstrable difference. When the new product reaches the market after any recall, the public will ask what is different about it. They need to be able to see a clear change from the previous product in order to reassure them that everything is now satisfactory. In the case of Tylenol, the demonstrable difference was the triple-sealed tamper-resistant packaging. After the second episode, four years later, J & J withdrew the capsules and replaced them with caplets, which presented the same drug but in a different form.

The background to the tragedy can be briefly told. In 1982 seven people died in Chicago after taking Extra-Strength Tylenol capsules used for the temporary relief of minor aches, pains, headaches and fever. The capsules had been filled with cyanide. No one was ever charged with the crime. In 1986 an eighth victim died from the same cause and the manufacturers withdrew all medication in capsule form. Three more people died that year through taking capsules laced with cyanide that were not Tylenol.

It started on Thusday 30 September 1982 with the TV news stories.

'Good evening! This is the CBS evening news. Dan Rather reporting. A bizarre and terrifying story today in the Chicago suburbs of Arlington Heights and Elk Grove Village. A twelve-year old girl and two men who were brothers are dead after taking poisoned capsules of Extra-Strength Tylenol.'

And later: 'In the Chicago area five people are now dead and another is in a critical condition after taking Extra-Strength Tylenol capsules laced with cyanide. A nationwide recall of the capsules marked lot number MC 2880 is underway. The numbers are on the upper left-hand corner of the bottles' label. Authorities are treating the cases as possible homicide and have warned people not to take the Extra-Strength Tylenol capsule.'

The first that James Burke, Chief Executive Officer, and Dave Clare, President, of Johnson & Johnson, knew of the tragedy was when their meeting was interrupted by Art Quilty, Executive Vice-President, who told them of the cyanide deaths in Chicago.

Tylenol had $400 million sales in 1981 and this represented 15 per cent of Johnson & Johnson's profit; it had a one-third share of the over-the-counter analgesic market, with the capsule version having sales of $175 million. About $40 million a year was spent on advertising.

On Friday 8 October 1982 the *New York Times* said, 'A drug's image has been devastated by tracing the deaths to cyanide-laced Extra-Strength Tylenol capsules.' Early on investigators absolved J & J of any blame but the marketing and advertising experts were very gloomy. Ben Lichstein, Marketing Professor at NYU Graduate School, said that if J & J could just hide under a rock for a while and pray the problem would go away, they should. Stephen Graser, Marketing Professor at Harvard, said that there were special problems which would impair the effort to resurrect Tylenol stock. The main one was that the consumer had a number of alternative brands to choose from. Jerry Della Femina, Chairman of his own agency, said, 'A flat prediction that I will make is that you will not see the name Tylenol in any form within a year. I don't think you can ever sell another product under that name. There may be an advertising person who thinks he can do it and if they find him I want to hire him, because I want him to turn our water cooler into a wine cooler.'

The competition rushed their own products onto the market as the story began to break and J & J received 'phone calls from pharmacies, doctors, hospitals, poison control centres and the media. Thousands of consumers asked for clarification, which at that time J & J could not give. Many other consumers called to make false reports of possible poisonings. 'It looked like the plague' recalled Dave Collins who had just become President of McNeil Laboratories, the J & J subsidiary which sold Tylenol. 'We had no idea where it could end and the only information we had was that we didn't know what was going on.' James

Burke took on the job of Brand Manager for Tylenol and delegated the running of the rest of the company to the members of the Executive Committee. This bruised the egos of some of his subordinates at first, but Burke took the central position.

He set up an incident room and what follows is a typical exchange between Burke and Collins when they were discussing when it would be appropriate to advertise again.

Collins: First, let me take you through the logical sequence. Number one shows us very clearly that the consumer was waiting to hear from us and when she heard from us she responded positively. No question about it.

Burke: Number two says that when we show the package she will do the same thing and until we have done that . . .

Collins: And in number three she says I know what went wrong, okay, but down here a substantial percentage of me can't buy their product. So until we bring the third lady in, which is commercial advertising, we're not using all the weapons available to us.

Burke: It's a non-sequitur. What she's saying is that she needs reassurance and we're giving it to her. But what she's also saying is that the most positive reassurance you can give me is a tamper-resistant package and we're going to give it to her. And what she's saying is that in spite of all that, deep down, I am still concerned and we have to track this as we go. Your conclusion is since she's concerned we ought to go out and sell to her. I don't agree with that.

Collins: No, hold it, what I am saying is that the conclusion is not that. The conclusion is that not going out and selling her doesn't mean we'll bring in 100 per cent of our resources to bear on that fear.

Burke: Quite the contrary. You may be bringing your resources to bear on exacerbating and freezing that fear.

Collins: The bad guy in this scenario is that fear. Okay?

Burke: Yes.

Collins: I don't see that for all of our testing that we are coming to grips with that bad guy.

Burke: That group of people who are scared are getting smaller and smaller. But let's not offend them. There is nothing more offensive to me, if I am frightened and somebody tells me I ought to buy their products, and I know I ought to buy it, and I feel I ought to buy it, but I can't. That's what I don't want to do.

On the fourth day of the crisis the FBI and FDA were arguing that J & J should *not* recall the Tylenol capsules. Their theory was that such an action would be giving in to the terrorist. 'Don't let them bring you to your knees' they said. Burke was advised by the company's public relations agency to seek an interview on the TV programme, Sixty Minutes, on the theory that it always took the contrary position to the established one. Since J & J were already taking heavy criticism in the daily press the odds were that the programme might give J & J a break. Burke went to each network in person to explain the situation and the true dimension of the problem. This was not an attack on J & J, he explained, but an act of terrorism against the entire national health care delivery system and by extension the food delivery system: everyone was being terrorised.

On Tuesday 5 October, the agency presented the results of some telephone research into what the public was really feeling about the problem. It showed that 94 per cent of the public knew about the Tylenol tragedy and had associated it with the murders in Chicago. Over 40 per cent of the people, up from 1 per cent a couple of days before, knew that Johnson & Johnson made Tylenol. This research was repeated every day to provide the best possible knowledge base.

Burke followed J & J's long-term credo which was displayed outside his office. It had been written by Robert Wood Johnson in the early 1940s and said, 'We believe our first responsibility is to the doctors, nurses and patients, to mothers and all others who use our products and services. In meeting their needs everything we do must be high quality.' This was reflected in a TV interview when Burke said, 'This whole corporation has built its reputation over 90 years on helping people. Helping people to heal, trust in all the things that are just the opposite to what happened here.'

A drop of nine points on the stock market cost J & J shareholders $2 billion in equities. The head of the FBI and the FDA continued to urge Burke not to surrender to the terrorists by recalling the capsules. However, J & J's public relations agency had come to the opposite conclusion and recommended that the company should recall, because until that was done nothing that J & J did would have credibility. Burke agreed and ordered the recall of $100 million worth of products for destruction, which eventually cost 50 cents a share.

In the incident room Burke announced the future aim of the company: 'Gentlemen, the idea here is not just to save the franchise or some part of the franchise but to restore the franchise to a full blooming health, the thirty-five share and build it.' In a TV interview Burke said, 'Have no doubt. None of us have any doubts, that we are going to have a business in Tylenol. The question is how big it is going to be and how long it will take to get back that 35 per cent share we enjoyed before this happened.'

As the medical profession had built Tylenol in the first place with their recommendations, J & J moved quickly to begin to communicate with them to rebuild the franchise. Over two million pieces of literature were sent to doctors and nurses, dentists and hospital managers. The key fact was that the problem had not originated at the factory. The advertising began, not to sell the brand, but to tell people who had thrown away their Tylenol capsules that they could get replacement *tablets* free, from their retailer or by writing directly to J & J. It was also a way of blocking the medicine chest from the competition and telling people that the tablets were safe.

Burke studied the statistical information from the daily research carried out by the agency but he also had direct communication with consumers all over America. He ordered McNeil Laboratories to shoot tens of thousands of feet of film of interviews with users and non-users. He wanted them to talk about Tylenol; talk about the tragedy; say what they felt about it; explain what they were going to do next; would they ever buy it again? So when he decided to recommence advertising, one month after the tragedy, he had a very good idea about what people wanted to hear. To say it he got the networks to allow J & J to use a doctor to talk about the situation: Dr Thomas Gates of McNeil Laboratories.

About this time it was estimated that $2 billion of free press had been given to the story linking Tylenol and death. Johnson & Johnson wanted to get the equivalent kind of media money behind the positive side of the story when it came out. The only way to do that was to turn editors and reporters into copywriters and use their interest by giving them the positive facts from Burke himself. It had to be a nationwide message all at once, because the competition was nationwide. To do this a unique press conference using satellite transmission was arranged. The tele-conference connected 30 cities at the same time and gave hundreds of reporters access to Burke and J & J – access that was not subject to the interruptions of the press or television networks and which turned the reporters into copywriters.

A typical question at this conference came from Peter Dometrao of PLAC radio. He asked, 'Is this the model for tamper-proof packaging as far as Johnson & Johnson is concerned? Is it going to apply to all pharmaceuticals that Johnson & Johnson and McNeil are going to be putting out in the future? What would be the projected cost of shifting over to that tamper-proof packaging for all pharmaceuticals over-the-counter that you will be selling?'

The publicity started again on 11 November 1982 with KPRE-TV Houston saying, 'From Houston this is Channel 2 news. Johnson & Johnson is ready to reintroduce Tylenol capsules nationwide. The capsules will be sold in triple-sealed tamper- resistant containers and should be on the store shelves in a few weeks.' The WDVM-TV Washington DC Eye Witness View said, 'Because it is good business the chairman of Johnson & Johnson says the company will not change the name Tylenol but will try to rebuild its business with a new type of resistant packaging.' WNBC-TV New York said, 'This is Live At Five with Jack Cafferty and Sue Simmons. At a nationwide news conference today the makers of Tylenol showed off their new tamper- resistant triple-sealed package for the remedy and promised to begin the task of getting it on the store shelves immediately.'

ABC started its World News Tonight with 'An unprecedented move by Johnson & Johnson today to bring its Extra-Strength Tylenol capsules back on the market. The company revealed the new tamper-resistant package and offered to provide one free to everyone in the country. Johnson & Johnson held a news conference today in New York to reintroduce Tylenol. Transmitted by satellite to reporters in 29 other cities, J & J chairman James Burke displayed a new Tylenol package with sealed flaps and two seals on the bottle top. Burke then announced newspaper coupons and a toll-free number that would be available for anyone wanting to try the new Tylenol free of charge.'

The 60-second commercials on TV said, 'Tylenol has had the trust of the medical profession and a hundred million Americans for over 20 years. We value that trust too much to let any individual tamper with it. We want you to continue to trust Tylenol.'

On the Sixty-Minute TV programme, anchor man Phil Donahue opened the new packaging before his audience, during an interview with James Burke. The following dialogue then took place:

Donahue: Okay, now here is the 64,000 dollar question. We can only speculate on the number of conversations that have taken place within the advertising community on what to do now. Let me just ask you what you think about this for a moment (pause). Would you change the name?

Audience: No. (Burke applauds)

Donahue: An awfully fast response class.

Burke: Well, that's a very interesting question because most of our experts had said the reverse. Most said change the name, change the colour or do both. We really never gave that much consideration at all. First of all it seems to me that you would not be playing it straight with the consumer if you did that. If you are going to sell Tylenol again and sell it under another name it is kind of asking you to change your name after you have had a serious disease or something.

On 12 December 1982 a commentator summed up the situation, 'Only a few weeks ago many business experts were asserting that Tylenol was dead. Today they are beginning to hedge their bets. Change their minds. For they have seen the men who run Johnson & Johnson use the facts, the media and huge amounts of money, as in the recall, in a way that confounded the crepe hangers. Instead of stonewalling, Johnson & Johnson has been forthcoming and apparently they have managed to avert disaster. Wall Street expects Tylenol to survive and flourish for Johnson & Johnson stock is back where it was before the episode. With the capsules temporarily off the market Tylenol tablets are now selling better than they ever did. And the capsules outfitted with new tamper-resistant packaging are slowly making their way into the stores. National advertising for them is scheduled to resume come January 2nd.'

In February 1986 a woman in Westchester, New York, died after taking cyanide-laced Tylenol capsules. Right away J & J reacted by recalling all the product and announcing that they would cease using the capsule form for the medication. In addition between $100 million and $150 million was spent in the advertising and promotion of the replacement form called caplets. Full-page advertisements were placed in 400 news-papers offering a free exchange of customers' capsules for caplets. Mailgrams were sent to 100,000 doctors, hospitals and pharmacies promoting and explaining the new caplet form, and a major information sampling programme was undertaken by the company's sales force. Consumer research conducted shortly afterwards showed the public felt that J & J had made an adequate response to the crisis.

Formula Shell petrol

Strictly speaking this was not a product recall as stocks of Formula Shell were allowed to work their way through the system and be replaced by petrol that did not contain the troublesome additive.

Launched worldwide in May 1986 Formula Shell petrol had been developed at a cost of $75 million and was part of a marketing strategy to re-establish brand loyalty with the motoring public. The launch cost in the UK was £6 million. The new petrol was claimed to offer a 'smoother and more responsive drive' and 600 cars had been tested over two million miles before it was introduced.

Shell scientists at Thornton, Cheshire, found a higher risk of inlet valve problems with Formula Shell. Importers and service agents in New Zealand said almost-new models of the Critroen BX, Fiat Uno and Volvo 360 and 760 had suffered burnt inlet valves. In Norway and Denmark the petrol was reported to have damaged valves in about 3,000 Volvos, Volkswagens and General Motors cars before the product was withdrawn.

In the UK the first reports of damage came from Scotland when Vauxhall cars run by Fife police began to get sticking engine valves. Vauxhall alerted its dealers and fleet owners and found that about 400 Cavaliers and Astras had been affected. In May 1987 Shell changed the carrier fluid but the problems in other countries emerged publicly in August. A further modification to the formula was made in October.

In January 1988 Shell announced the withdrawal of Formula Shell because it was concerned that some of its customers were worried by media reports of inlet valve problems: 'It had got to the point where the confidence of the public in Shell petrol could be affected', said a spokesman. The *Daily Telegraph* of 4 March reported that Bill Bentley, Group Marketing Co-ordinator, estimated that 10,000 cars out of a worldwide total of 20 million in 33 countries using the petrol had been affected. Claims would only be considered if motorists first checked with the car manufacturer, as 'spurious' claims had been received, such as the petrol being blamed for flat batteries. It was thought that it would cost £200 for each affected car. Insurance cover was available by a Sedgwick product liability policy.

Wall's canned stewed steak, steak & kidney pudding and steak & kidney pie

This recall was due to incorrect information and not because the product was dangerous in any way.

At the beginning of 1981 Wall's (part of the Unilever Group) recalled some of its canned products because there was a possibility that they could have been the victims of malpractice, when buying meat supplies for their canned meat factories.

An advertisement in a national daily on 20 January 1981 said:

Wall's CANNED Stewed Steak
CANNED Steak & Kidney Pudding
CANNED Steak & Kidney Pie

You may have read in the press that an unscrupulous element in the meat trade is alleged to have added horse meat to boxes of frozen beef. We regret that there may have been an occasion when we were victims of this malpractice when buying meat supplies for the **canned meat factory** only. If so, it would have happened at the time when the codes given below were applied.

There is a chance that the meat in some of these cans was not all beef. This does not involve any risk to health. However, if you have any doubts about cans carrying these particular codes, please return them to the shop where you bought them. Retailers are being asked to provide a replacement or refund.

The code consists of five digits. Ignore the first two and look for numbers ending in 323, 324, 325, 326, 327, 328, 329, 330, 331, 332, 333. The codes are stamped on the top of bottom of the cans.

The following month it was reported that there was a growing illegal traffic in horsemeat, with Wimpy the hamburger chain admitting that in 1980 it had twice come close to marketing horsemeat hamburgers. One of the country's biggest meat wholesalers, part of the Vestey empire, was said to be the latest victim of the illegal traffic. The firm was Weddel in Croydon, which had 40 depots throughout Britain.

In August 1982 some of the Wall's canned meat pies, taken off the British market 18 months previously, were being shipped to the Lebanon to feed refugees, with the Department of Health closely monitoring the progress of the shipment. It had given certificates for 288,000 cans, stating that the contents could be for human consumption as long as it was outside the United Kingdom and Western Europe.

Walton v. British Leyland

This case examines the standard of the duty of care owed by a manufacturer to users of his product, in circumstances where a defect was known to the manufacturer but was not a matter of public knowledge. In practical terms, it provides an illustration of the dilemma facing manufacturers when a fault is identified affecting a number of products: whether or not to institute a recall campaign. The failure of the manufacturer to undertake a recall was held to be a breach of the duty of care, and the company was consequently liable for damages for the accident that occurred as a direct result of a known product defect.

The accident occurred on the M1 motorway during the evening of 22 April 1976. Mr and Mrs Victor Walton, on holiday from Australia, were passengers in an Austin Allegro owned and driven by the first plaintiff's brother, Mr Albert Walton. Near Newport Pagnell, when the car was travelling at 50 to 60 mph, the rear nearside wheel came off, the driver lost control and the car collided with the central crash barrier. Mr Victor Walton, who was handicapped, escaped with minor injuries; Mrs Walton was thrown from the car and was left a quadriplegic.

It was accepted that the driver had not been negligent in any way. The case therefore turned on the apportionment of blame between the manufacturer, the selling dealer who had carried out certain servicing work, and a third dealer who had worked on the car on other occasions.

From the evidence, it seems that the manufacturer had been aware of a problem affecting the rear hub assembly of cars of this particular model for at least two-and-a-half years before this accident occurred. One hundred cases of 'wheel adrift' had been reported to the company, 50 of them in a seven-week period.

It had been recognised that incorrect adjustment could lead to overtightening with consequent overheating and bearing failure, which in turn could lead to the loss of a wheel. Advice had been circulated to the authorised dealer network, drawing attention to the way in which the new type of rear hub bearings should be adjusted and the importance of 'end float'. Despite this, numerous cases of bearing failure including instances of 'wheel adrift' had been reported. In September 1974 a decision was taken to fit a modified washer on the rear wheels to stop the wheels coming off, in the event that the bearings failed.

The court dismissed the arguments put forward on behalf of the manufacturer that it had in effect discharged its duty of care adequately when, having concluded that there was no defect in assembly, it introduced the modified washer and alerted its own dealer to the problem. To do so, and accept the manufacturer's argument that the problem leading to the accident was caused by mechanics carelessly or ignorantly overtightening the bearings, and not allowing sufficient 'end float' to avoid the seizing up, would have passed the burden of negligence to one or both of the two dealers who had carried out servicing work on the car in question.

In the case of the authorised dealer, who had also been the original selling dealer, there was evidence that he had indeed taken notice of the bulletins from the manufacturer, and when attending to the plaintiff's complaint about noisy wheel bearings had fitted the larger recommended washer to the other rear wheel.

The judge rejected arguments that the dealer should at that time have fitted the larger washer to both wheels, as he took the view that the service bulletin did not give clear advice on this point. The other defendant garage was not an authorised dealer and therefore was unaware of the bulletins issued by the manufacturer. As to whether staff should have noticed when working on the car, subsequent to its visit to the authorised dealer, that a larger washer had been fitted on one side than on the other, and thereby elected to make further checks and enquiries, the judge took the view that the company's own duty of care did not extend this far.

In dismissing all the other factors which may have contributed to the accident, and finding the manufacturer alone liable, Mr Justice Willis summarised the extent of their duty as follows:

> In my view, the duty of care owed by Leyland to the public was to make a clean breast of the problem and recall all cars which they could, in order that the safety washers could be fitted. I accept, of course, that manufacturers have to steer a course between alarming the public unnecessarily and so damaging the reputation of their products, and observing their duty of care towards those whom they are in a position to protect from dangers of which they – and they alone – are aware. The duty seems to me to be the higher when they can palliate the worst effects of a failure which, if Leyland's view is right, they could never decisively guard against.
>
> They knew the full facts; they saw to it that no one else did. They seriously considered recall and made an estimate of the cost at a figure [£300,000] which seems to me to have been in no way out of proportion to the risks involved. It was decided not to follow this course for commercial reasons. I think this involved a failure to observe their duty to care for the safety of the many who were bound to remain at risk, irrespective of the recommendations made to Leyland dealers and to them alone. It was, in my view, their duty to ensure that all cars still in stock and unsold by the time the washer palliative was proven were fitted with this safety feature device before sale.

This case not only illustrates the extent of the duty of care required of a manufacturer, but also indicates ways in which that duty may be fulfilled – to discharge or at least reduce the liability arising from that duty.

The manufacturer could have taken steps to warn all dealers, not just franchised ones, in unequivocal terms of the danger and the action to be taken.

The manufacturer could have instituted a recall campaign to ensure that all vehicles in service were modified without delay.

Ashworth J S (ed), *Product Liability Casebook*, Lloyd's of London Press, Colchester, 1984.

Product extortion and malicious product tamper

These two actions are crimes which are an attack on a company through the medium of its products. They involve the deliberate contamination (or the threat of contamination) of a product, the corruption of which would cause illness or even death. Product extortion is akin to blackmail and the demand is usually for money. Malicious product tamper (MPT) is akin to sabotage and seeks to harm the company's reputation; it can be used to settle a grudge or to obtain publicity for a radical group. The products attacked include food, drink, confectionery, pet foods, drugs, hair preparations, cosmetics, toiletries, tobacco, household products and the like. The companies attacked include many famous names such as Mars, Cadbury, Boots, Heinz, Cow & Gate, Bernard Matthews, Smith Foods, HP Foods, Heineken, and L'Oreal. The crime of product contamination or the threat thereof was included in the Public Order Act 1986.

Those companies aware of a potential threat establish crisis management plans to help them manage an attack – if it should ever happen. It is important to distinguish between a crisis management plan and a product recall plan (PRP). It is possible to have a product crisis without a product recall and to have a product recall without a product crisis. The two are separate but complementary. About half the deliberate incidents lead to a recall or the withdrawal of the product from sale. The crisis management team must have the ready-prepared option to recall, if it believes that it would be in the interests of the company to do so. Often a crisis management plan will refer to the recall option without there being a plan to substantiate it.

The two plans must be linked, and indeed some of the key players will feature in both; but the fundamental difference is that a crisis management plan deals with criminals, whereas a product recall plan is a civil affair.

A product recall initiated in response to an extortion or MPT is different from one initiated in response to an accidental contamination. In the latter case a company should be able to identify the source of the defect, locate the affected products and prevent a repetition. In the former case none of these will apply: the source will be unknown, with no indication of who is responsible and consequently the location of contaminated products is problematical; whether the criminal will attack again has to be a matter for conjecture.

Product recalls that stem from a criminal attack can be forced on a company to help protect its brand, more than to recover defective products. With MPT the aim of the criminal may be to force a company into a recall and so make it suffer damage in this way.

But if a recall is the only option should it be public or silent? It could be argued that a silent recall may deter the criminal because it would appear that he had failed, or it could goad him into further attack. For a nationally distributed product attacked in one area, the question could arise of whether to restrict a recall to that area or to initiate a national recall. These are particularly difficult decisions which must be judged on the merits of each case.

The number of worldwide incidents of product extortion and all forms of contamination, whether accidental or deliberate, peaked in 1989 at just over 250 compared to 125 the previous year[3].

---

3 Control Risks Group, London.

In the UK the figure was 89 compared to 28 for 1988. The highly publicised incidents concerning Heinz and Cow & Gate baby foods in April 1989 led to a great increase in reported cases which peaked in July, August and September, with 46 of the 89 occurring during these three months. The Heinz extortion of April 1989 resulted in an outbreak of copy-cat incidents. The food industry is most often affected by extortion and MPT, with 83 per cent of the incidents being in this sector in the period November 1989 to April 1990.

Fifty-two per cent of all contamination incidents recorded during the period under review led to a recall or withdrawal. This was a slightly higher percentage than in the previous six months when 46 per cent led to recall or withdrawal.

Substantial publicity was given to the recall in January 1990 of three hundred thousand packs of Mr Kipling Apple Pies after customers had found glass in the product. The findings of the investigation set up to discover the origin of the contamination are not publicly known. In the majority of tampering incidents, the motive and identity of the culprit are rarely discovered.

Companies can be vulnerable to tampering on the part of their employees following closure announcements, redundancy or disappointing pay rises, etc. In January 1990, Henry Telfer Ltd claimed that a disgruntled employee was responsible for placing a mouse in one of their pies. They were, however, fined £500 for the contamination. This is a very small sum compared with the losses sustained by other companies when faced with malicious tampering by their employees. For example, in July 1989, Smith's Crisps were forced to withdraw packs of Smith's Square Crisps and Crispy Tubes after objects, including broken glass, were found in sealed bags. The tampering was almost certainly the work of employees at their factory, although the precise motive is not publicly known. The incident was believed to have cost the company around £1 million.

Employees seeking revenge against their companies may not restrict themselves to malicious tampering but may also make extortion demands. This occurred in France in April 1990 when the pharmaceutical company, Smith Kline Beecham, received an extortion demand for six million francs. The extortionist claimed he had placed a contaminated sample in a storage bay and that other samples had also been distributed. The company had announced in March that the factory was to close and they were, therefore, fairly certain that the extortion was the work of one or more of their employees. The company had no alternative but to halt production and withdraw all products manufactured since the date of the closure announcement.[4]

The most notorious MPT was the Tylenol case in 1982 when seven people in Chicago died after taking headache capsules contaminated with potassium cyanide. At the time of the incident, the US Food and Drug Administration urged Johnson & Johnson (which owned McNeil Laboratories who manufactured and sold Tylenol) *not* to recall as it could be seen as capitulating to an attack on the country's health care system. In the event Johnson & Johnson did not accept the advice and recalled the product in a brilliant public relations campaign. The cost of the recall was put at $100 million and the loss of sales in the following year at $400 million (See the separate case history, p.199).

An example of how the perceived risk of a MPT can lead to an expensive recall occured in 1984. The Animal Liberation Front telephoned the *Sunday Mirror* and claimed that contaminated Mars bars had been placed on the shelves of retailers, including Boots. The reason for the attack was that Mars had given grants to Guy's Hospital for research into tooth decay using monkeys. A Mars bar injected with rat poison was delivered to the *Sunday Mirror* and the BBC. These were the only bars to be poisoned; however, 20 bars reached the public in eight cities containing leaflets claiming that they had been poisoned. Mars recalled 3,000 tons of bars and the reported loss of sales was £15 million and a profit of £2.8 million.

The tobacco company, Gallaghers, received an extortion demand for £500,000 in 1986 from a man saying that he had terminal cancer from smoking the company's cigarettes. He

4 Control Risks Group, London.

threatened to contaminate products with cyanide unless the money was paid over, which had to be carried out in an unusual way. The money was to be thrown from an 8.40pm Inter-City 125 train travelling from St Pancras to Leeds on receipt of orders given by CB radio. After three test runs, the order was received one night in May as the train pulled out of Nottingham. Police arrested two men who were later jailed for four years each. No recall took place, although Gallaghers worked intensively in planning for one while negotiations with the cri minals were going on.

In March 1989 the first report of glass in baby food appeared; Sainsbury, Gateway, Tesco, Safeway, the Co-op and Asda all had examples. On 25 April John Patten, Minister of State at the Home Office, told the House that there had been 17 reported incidents of baby food contamination since 7 April and 11 more on the day he was speaking. A reward of £100,000 was offered by Heinz and Cow & Gate for information leading to the arrest of the person responsible, after it was revealed that a black-mailer was demanding £1 million. The newspaper headlines about the affair dominated the front pages. Although the police at one point advised Heinz not to take the product off the shelves, Heinz and Cow & Gate recalled 100 million jars worth £32 million and were to repackage a further 60 million jars; Heinz decided to introduce tamper-evident packaging. There were 700 copy-cat threats and 24 people were subsequently charged with wilfully misusing police time. A former detective, Rodney Whitchelo, was convicted of a £3.75 million blackmail plot against Heinz and Pedigree Petfoods and sentenced at the Central Criminal Court on 17 December 1990 to 17 years' imprisonment, reported *The Times*.

Vehicles

United Kingdom

Recalls of motor vehicles are a fact of life, which the motoring public accepts as one of the ways in which they are protected from possible harm. Behind vehicle recalls is a complex network of which the motorist is unaware, and an unknown cost which runs into many millions. Most of the time the recall campaigns – as they are called – run smoothly without publicity, apart from the occasional paragraph in the press.

Table 7.3 *Number of vehicles subject to recall under the vehicle and motorcycle codes of practice*

Year	Number of campaigns	Number of vehicles
1979	43	314,544
6 months only		
1980	60	383,478
1981	63	501,687
1982	55	275,030
1983	68	252,056
1984	72	219,528
1985	90	877,041
1986	96	1,112,426
1987	67	945,592
1988	87	1,333,673
1989	78	624,944
1990	89	736,224

(Department of Transport Vehicle Inspectorate Executive Agency)

Up to a million vehicles a year are recalled, which represents 4 per cent of those on the roads (see Table 7.3, p.218). It can involve two government agencies, the society of Motor Manufacturers and Traders and the vehicle manufacturers themselves. All the famous names appear at one time or another, for none can be immune from the possibility of some rogue vehicles slipping onto the market sooner or later. Perhaps the surprising thing is that they succeed in getting back such a large proportion for rectification.

The Secretary of State for Transport has a statutory responsibility for ensuring the road-worthiness of the 24 million vehicles in use in the UK. The Vehicle Inspectorate of the Department of Transport (DTP) is the national testing authority which meets this responsibility mainly through the annual testing of vehicles, vehicle spot checks and the inspection of operators' premises. The Inspectorate is based in Bristol, with 54 district offices employing 1,600 people, more than half of whom are qualified engineers and vehicle examiners.

The Inspectorate plays an important role in vehicle recalls. The Code of Practice on Action Concerning Safety Defects – the Recall Code – was drawn up by the DTP and the Society of Motor Manufacturers and Traders (SMMT) (see Appendix 3 p.256). The Code defines a safety defect as '... a feature of design or construction liable to cause significant risk of injury to the driver or occupants of the vehicles or to other road users.' Safety defects include those relating to components bought by the vehicle manufacturers from other manufacturers and suppliers, and sold with the vehicle as original equipment.

It is the responsibility of the vehicle manufacturer to decide when evidence of a safety defect amounts to a case notifiable under the terms of the Code. The Inspectorate will require details of the size of the vehicle park, build years, chassis numbers, type of vehicle, description of the defects, the proposed remedy, the name of the recall co-ordinator and the launch date of the recall. The Inspectorate allocates a reference number to each recall.

Strictly speaking there is no legal requirement for a manufacturer to inform the Inspectorate about a proposed recall. But in practice this is invariably the case because the Inspectorate could make life so difficult for a recalcitrant manufacturer that it would be forced into a 'voluntary' recall; for example by taking advertising space to publicise what it considered to be a safety-related defect brought about by design or manufacture. This has never happened but the fact that the possibility is there may well influence manufacturers to co-operate.

About 90 per cent of vehicle recalls are initiated by manufacturers. The Inspectorate receives information about defects from the district offices and the heavy goods vehicle testing station network, which is staffed by qualified engineers and vehicle examiners. In addition the Inspectorate is responsible for the MoT testing stations of which there are about 18,000, which carry out 15 million tests annually on cars, light goods vehicles and motorcycles. It investigates over 2,000 serious accidents a year. When the Inspectorate becomes aware of a possible safety defect either from one of its own sources, or from other external sources such as the police, Trading Standards Departments or members of the public, it contacts the manufacturer to seek action.

The Inspectorate monitors the progress of a recall and will receive a status report from the manufacturer every three months for 18 months, when the situation is reviewed. If the response rate is below expectations, discussions will consider ways of improving the situation by, for instance, sending a second mailshot by recorded delivery using a fresh tape of names and addresses from the Driver and Vehicle Licensing Agency (DVLA) (see p.222).

The Inspectorate expects the following response rates: 6 months after launch 50 per cent; 12 months after launch 70 per cent; 18 months after launch 90 per cent.

A recall is terminated by agreement between the Inspectorate and the manufacturer when 100 per cent of the vehicles have been corrected or the response rate has remained static for a considerable time.

The Inspectorate maintains contact with similar organisations in other countries. On occasion a recall in a foreign country has resulted in the launch of a recall in the UK, although the Inspectorate is always careful to make sure that a foreign recall is not indigenous to one particular country before initiating one in the UK.

The Society of Motor Manufacturers and Traders' voluntary Codes of Practice were formulated following discussions between the Department of Transport and representative bodies of the motor industry. The Codes set out the guidelines on procedures for the recall of vehicles and components. The first Code was introduced in 1979 and applies to all motor vehicles. In 1982, a further five Codes were introduced: for trailers under 3,500kg GVW; commercial trailers of 3,500kg GVW and over; tyres, wheels and valves; motorcycles; parts and accessories.

The vehicle manufacturer needs to know who has the vehicles he wishes to recall. There are two sources: the DVLA at Swansea and the company's own records.

Local county and borough councils were made responsible for driver and vehicle licensing in 1903, seven years after the man with the red flag was no longer required. Driving tests were made compulsory in 1935 and the vehicle tax, called the Road Fund, began to be collected in 1910. The vehicle registration system, also administered by the local boroughs, gradually evolved as more and more identifying letters and numbers were needed. The current system of using a letter to identify the year of registration was introduced in 1963. In 1965 the government decided that a central national system was needed to cope with the increasing number of documents passing backwards and forwards each year. The Swansea Centre began operating in 1973 and in the 1980s a major computer replacement exercise took place. In April 1990 the Swansea operation became an Executive Agency of the DTP.

A record is maintained of the 30 million people who are licensed to drive, together with associated information. The Agency has a central record of over 24 million vehicles and keeps a history of each one, including changes of ownership. The density of car ownership is 2.7 persons per car, well below the US figure of 1.7, West Germany at 2.1, Italy at 2.4 and France at 2.5. Cars registered in company names account for 13 per cent, while over half registered cars are imported. There are 10 million transactions a year for drivers and 60 million for vehicles. All original documents are microfilmed for retrieval.

When a car first goes on the road all the information about it, registration number, chassis number, colour and details of the first keeper, are keyed into the computer. The vehicle excise duty reminders, that are returned when the tax is paid, are fed through optical character readers. These store the information on forms for matching up with the correct computer record, print a number on the form itself and finally microfilm it. The microfilm department stores 750 million documents in over 200,000 cassettes.

If a vehicle manufacturer wishes to initiate a recall, it asks the DVLA for a list of the registered keepers who have to be contacted. The company provides the relevant Vehicle Identification Numbers (VINs), which is a comprehensive code of seventeen digits, the first three are the World Market Indicator which gives the manufacturer and the location of the plant concerned, the next six are the Vehicle Description Section with details of the individual vehicle such as model, style, engine and so on, and the last eight digits are the chassis number. In return they receive a tape with the names and addresses of the registered keepers from the Agency's records. The company have to pay for this information at £1,500 plus 10p per vehicle up to a maximum of £6,500 for large recalls, provide a disclaimer that the information will only be used for the recall and eventually return the tape to Swansea.

The regular analysis of recalls published by the DTp shows that the average response rate for the industry is about 83 per cent, with occasionally 100 per cent being achieved for small numbers of specialised vehicles. Objective response rates for other industries are unknown and published figures are sometimes best seen as part of a public relations exercise. However, it is unlikely that any other industry could achieve such a high response rate as vehicle manufacturers, given the scale and complexity of the campaigns.

Canada

The law that makes the recall of a defective vehicle necessary is the Motor Vehicle Safety Act, which is part of the Criminal Code of Canada. Although there is no actual power to order recall the notice of a defect has the same effect. The Act requires manufacturers and importers to notify the owners of the cars, trucks, buses, trailers, motorcycles and snowmobiles of any safety problem relating to these vehicles.

Section 8(1) says, 'Every person is guilty of an offence who, being a manufacturer, distributor or importer of a motor vehicle of a class to which safety standards have been described fails to give notice of any defect in the construction, design or functioning of that motor vehicle or its components that affects or is likely to affect the safe operation of that vehicle of which he is aware to, among others, the current owner of the vehicle.'

The notice has to be given by prepaid registered mail and must contain a description of the defect, an evaluation of the safety risk and a statement of the means to correct it. If owners cannot be located the Minister of Transport can order that the notice is published for five consecutive days in two major daily newspapers in each of the six regions of Canada, or by an alternative approved medium. Every manufacturer, distributor or importer recalling a vehicle has to submit a quarterly report to the Minister for a period of two years.

An inspector, authorised by the Minister, can at any reasonable time enter the premises of a manufacturer, distributor, importer or consignee of vehicles or vehicle components and examine the products and records. An inspector can seize any vehicle or component that contravenes the provisions of the Act for 90 days.

A person who is found guilty of an offence under Section 8(1) is liable on conviction on indictment to a fine of up to $5,000 or two years in prison or both. A corporation can be fined up to $100,000.

On average 800,000 vehicles a year are recalled, with the numbers varying from 200,000 to 1,000,000, in about 150 campaigns. Response rates average 60 per cent, with new vehicles reaching 80 per cent to 90 per cent and older vehicles only 20 per cent or 30 per cent. There is no central data bank of owners. The VIN number of cars and trucks is fixed to the left side of the dashboard near the windscreen.

Japan

The Type Designation Regulations for Motor Vehicles provides that, if a manufacturer finds that certain vehicles are not in compliance with the requirements of the Safety Regulations for Road Vehicles, and that the cause is design or manufacturing, it must report the following to the Minister of Transport:

- the position of the defect and its cause;
- the measures for correction; and
- the method of informing the owners and garages.

A public notice must be published and the repair carried out free of charge. This recall system was established in 1969.

Table 7.4 *Cars recalled in Japan*

Fiscal year	Domestic made cars		Imported cars		Total	
	Notific- ations	Related cars	Notific- ations	Related cars	Notific- ations	Related cars
1969–81	228	9,560,773	205	80,775	443	9,641,548
1982	15	467,577	6	5,277	21	472,854
1983	20	470,907	8	1,877	28	472,784
1984	11	585,767	8	28,481	19	614,248
1985	6	138,397	21	26,377	27	164,774
Total	280	11,223,421	248	142,787	528	11,366,208

Table 7.4, p.224, gives the number of cars recalled in Japan. Between 1969 and 1985 there were 528 recall campaigns involving more than 11 million cars.

United States

Traffic accidents are the cause of 50,000 deaths annually, the primary cause of paraplegia, the major cause of epilepsy and the major cause of death of Americans under 44 years of age. It is estimated that the annual economic loss to society is more than $50 billion.

The National Traffic and Motor Vehicle Safety Act, originally enacted in 1966, gives the Department of Transportation's National Highway Traffic Safety Administration (NHTSA) the authority to issue vehicle safety standards and require manufacturers to recall vehicles with safety defects. Since that date more than 141 million cars, trucks, buses, recreational vehicles, motorcycles and mopeds, as well as 25.6 million tyres, have been recalled. Half of these recalls were initiated voluntarily by the manufacturers, while the others were influenced or ordered via the courts by NHTSA. If a safety defect is discovered the manufacturer must notify the NHTSA, as well as vehicle or equipment owners, dealers and distributors. The manufacturer is then required to remedy the problem at no charge to the vehicle owner. The agency is responsible for monitoring the manufacturer's corrective action for adequacy and for compliance with statutory requirements.

A recall is necessary when a vehicle or item of equipment does not comply with a Petrol Motor Vehicle Safety Standard or when there is a safety-related defect. The Federal Motor Vehicles Safety Standards set minimum performance levels for those parts of the vehicle which most affect its safe operation or which protect drivers and passengers from death or serious injury in the event of a crash. They are applicable to all vehicles and equipment manufactured for sale in the United States. A safety-related defect is one that exists in a vehicle or an item of vehicle equipment which poses an unreasonable risk to safety, and is common to a group of vehicles of the same design and manufacture, or to items of equipment of the same type and manufacture.

The NHTSA operates a free Auto Safety Hotline telephone service which collects information on vehicle safety problems. In response to a call, the vehicle owner will be sent a pre-addressed, postage paid questionnaire which will help the agency's technical staff evaluate the problem. Information provided on the questionnaire is entered into a computer databank and catalogued according to vehicle make, model, year, manufacturer and type of problem. A monthly trend analysis determines whether an unusual number of complaints has been received on a specific line of vehicles, tyres or equipment. The seriousness and number of complaints are then measured against the number of cars manufactured.

In addition to receiving safety complaints, the Auto Safety Hotline provides callers with vehicle defect recall information. On-the-spot information on safety recalls and agency investigations will be provided to drivers regarding their particular vehicle. This is especially useful to used-car buyers who want to be sure that any recall corrections have been made before they purchase a vehicle.

The NHTSA engineers have three stages of investigation. The preliminary analysis screens problems that are alleged to be associated with safety-related defects. This is intended to discriminate quickly between problems that are isolated in nature, do not represent a safety-related defect, or do not indicate an emerging defect trend, versus problems that could be safety-related. If no recall ensues and questions remain as to whether a safety defect exists then the investigation proceeds to the next stage. The engineering analysis determines the character and scope of the problem and collects sufficient evidence to influence the manufacturer to conduct a voluntary recall where appropriate. After the engineering analysis phase there is the formal investigation stage. At this point the manufacturer will be requested in writing to conduct a voluntary safety recall. If no recall occurs, and the evidence continues to justify one, the matter is presented to a Defect Review Panel with a recommendation that a case be opened.

If the evidence developed at the formal investigation stage demonstrating a defect poses an unreasonable risk to safety, an initial determination of a safety defect is made and publicly announced. A public meeting is then scheduled to allow the manufacturer and other interested parties the opportunity to present additional data, views and arguments.

Once the NHTSA has made a final determination of a safety-related defect and ordered a manufacturer to recall, the order may be challenged by the manufacturer in a Federal District Court. The Agency can go to court to compel a manufacturer to comply with this order where the burden of proof lies with the Agency. While the case is in the court, the manufacturer may be required to notify consumers by letter that the Agency had made a final determination of a safety defect, but that the decision is being contested by the manufacturer.

Most decisions to recall and remedy defects are made voluntarily by manufacturers, prior to a decision by the NHTSA that a safety defect exists and a recall must be initiated.

Within a reasonable time, after the determination of a safety defect, manufacturers must notify all registered owners and purchasers of the affected vehicle, by first-class mail, of the existence of the defect and give an evaluation of its risk to motor vehicle safety. In other words, the manufacturer must explain to consumers the potential hazards a defect may pose to the safety of the public. Names of vehicle owners are obtained from State Motor Vehicle offices that register vehicles. The letter must instruct consumers on how to get the defect corrected, remind them that corrections are to be made at no charge and inform them when the remedy will be available.

Once a defect determination has been made, the law gives the manufacturer three options for correcting the defect: repair, replace or refund. The manufacturer may choose to repair the vehicle; replace the vehicle with an identical or similar vehicle; or refund the purchase price in full, minus a reasonable allowance for depreciation.

In order to be eligible for corrective action at no cost the vehicle cannot be more than eight years old. The law requires tyre manufacturers to repair or replace at no cost to the consumer only those purchased within three years of the defect determination. In order to obtain free replacement or repair of a defective tyre, customers must bring the tyres to the dealer within 60 days of receiving the notification letter from the manufacturer.

Under the law if a vehicle recall has been initiated, consumers are entitled to the remedy without charge within a reasonable time.

In the US there is no national vehicle licensing authority, as there is in the UK; the activity is handled at state level. Manufacturers are responsible for identifying owners of recalled vehicles and in addition to their own information, they use commercial sources for vehicle registration information where necessary.

Table 7.5, p.229, gives recall completion rates over a 20-year period. Little more than half the vehicles on recall are corrected and the average number recalled in a year is about 1.5 million.

Other Countries

In Sweden cars are required to be tested at the National Car Testing Agency's stations, which report 600 to 800 unusual defects a year. If these point to a model defect the Agency contacts the manufacturer which may lead to a recall, although there is no mandatory recall.

In the Netherlands the inspection of cars is the responsibility of the Rijksdienst voor het Wegverkeer (RDW) which works with the Organisation of Motor Car Producers (RAI) to provide details of owners of cars being recalled. Response rates are said to vary between 50 per cent and 90 per cent. In one recent month there were 30 recall campaigns, with the number of cars varying from 5 to 5,000 for any one action. There is no mandatory recall.

In Germany the Federal Officer for Motor Traffic maintain a control vehicle register for vehicles and their owners. Response

Table 7.5 *United States National Highway Traffic Safety Administration Recall Completion Rates by year and vehicle age*

Year	Recall completion rates per cent			Number of vehicles by age of vehicle at time of recall		
	Domestic	Foreign	Total	0–4 yrs	5–8 yrs	8+ yrs
1966	84.5	76.2	83.4	743, 874	0	0
1967	67.1	90.0	68.1	1,611,094	0	0
1968	79.0	73.9	77.1	1,304,465	0	0
1969	70.5	57.8	69.9	945,242	0	0
1970	64.2	49.8	58.6	621,389	52	0
1971	43.5	40.3	43.3	1,116,679	1,742	0
1972	46.5	38.3	46.0	1,679,040	2,977	17
1973	64.4	43.5	63.4	2,382,200	0	0
1974	75.4	48.0	70.1	954,620	0	0
1975	55.1	47.3	54.2	1,241,941	165,119	0
1976	49.2	64.1	51.2	1,718,056	11	0
1977	44.6	22.7	40.1	968,905	585,429	13,793
1978	53.4	34.2	51.5	2,455,895	198,818	0
1979	59.2	40.5	55.3	3,473,464	1,448	33
1980	33.8	42.7	35.2	968,861	1,154,856	276,701
1981	73.9	43.9	67.7	645,849	2,808	0
1982	79.8	43.1	69.2	1,192,731	89	0
1983	61.7	40.4	51.5	1,248,356	328,228	0
1984	55.2	41.8	53.6	767,838	339,905	2,342
1985	55.2	45.7	54.1	679,734	4,662	282
Average	56.4	41.5	54.1	1,406,328	146,639	15,430

rates are claimed to be between 74 per cent and 94 per cent but one source has questioned these figures. In a recent three year period 2.3 million vehicles were recalled. The number of vehicles involved in 26 recall campaigns ranged from 200 to one million in any one action. There is no mandatory recall.

Medical products

The total National Health Service spending on prescription pharmaceuticals in manufacturers' prices in 1989 was £2.6 billion, which represented about 10 per cent of NHS costs. The sales of consumer medicines and allied goods (over-the-counter (OTC) products at manufacturers' prices) was estimated at £780 milion in 1989 giving a total close on £3.4 billion. The number of NHS prescriptions in 1989 was 436 million, which is an average of 7 to 8 for each person in the country.

The manufacturers of pharmaceutical products deliver to the 120 wholesale houses, which in turn deliver – often two or three times a day – to retail chemists and hospitals in the area which they serve. The proportion of direct business done between manufacturers and retail chemists is relatively small, except in the case of a few firms. Manufacturers deliver direct to hospital authorities, usually on special contract terms for bulk supplies. Otherwise hospitals are increasingly tending to utilise the service which the pharmaceutical wholesalers provide for their retail chemist customers. Less common distribution points, which hold supplies of pharmaceuticals, are country doctors who do their own dispensing, and local authority clinics covering specialised services, such as child welfare and family planning.

The products reach the patient through the hospital pharmacy department, the retail pharmacist or a dispensing doctor, usually against an NHS prescription.

In 1968 the wholesale distribution body, the National Association of Pharmaceutical Distributors (NAPD), started a scheme of co-operation between their members and the manufacturers in the event of a recall. The actions involved receiving products returned by retailers, completing a wholesale recall card, crediting the retailers, sending recall cards to the manufacturer together with the returned products and a separate card showing their stock level. Manufacturers use a batch issue system which enables a trace to be obtained from the manufacturer downstream to the customer.

In 1974 the Association of British Pharmaceutical Industry set up a working party to produce a recall guide (see Appendix 4, p.262). The first indication of a defect can come from a doctor, a pharmacist, the manufacturer or the Medicines Inspectorate, which can lead to the manufacturer putting an embargo on further distribution of the product concerned while an evaluation takes place. According to the individual case the decision may be taken to restrict the recall to trade channels only and inform the Medicines Inspectorate, or it may be for the urgent recall of a particular batch. The responsibility for action lies with the manufacturer in close liaison with the Medicines Inspectorate.

The Medicines Inspectorate was set-up under the Medicines Act 1968 (see Chapter 2, p.46). The Inspectorate advises the Medicines Control Agency (MCA) on a manufacturer's suitability to hold a Manufacturer's Licence; it can check that a product is being manufactured in accordance with the Product Licence and advise the MCA accordingly. When the Act finally came into force in 1969, there were 39,065 products already on the market which were automatically granted licences as of right. All manufacturers are inspected at least every two years and it is during this process that the recall procedures are examined.

The Inspectorate, which is part of the Department of Health, maintains a 24-hour emergency telephone service manned by pharmacists for problems relating to possible product defects concerned with prescription drugs and over-the-counter preparations. It is usually pharmacists, and in particular hospital pharmacists, who inform the Inspectorate of possible problems with a product.

When a notification is received, a case file is opened and all available information obtained. The Inspectorate takes a medical doctor's view and a pharmacist's view in reaching a decision on whether to recommend a recall or a withdrawal. A recall relates to a particular batch while a withdrawal would be a product safety matter and apply to a product as a whole.

If the hazard risks are serious enough the manufacturer would be asked to initiate a recall or a withdrawal. This would be backed up by a letter from the Inspectorate to the Regional Health Authorities and the Family Practitioner Committees, supported by a telephone cascade system when appropriate. Publicity would be provided in the weekly *Pharmaceutical Journal*. The Inspectorate use the media only on very rare occasions.

The Medicines Inspectorate receives about 200 notifications a year of product defects, with approximately half being substantiated. They do not maintain a record of response rates for recalls and withdrawals.

The restrictions imposed on the supply of drugs, and the tight control of the distribution channels, means that recall information can be rapidly passed down the chain.

Although there is tight control of the distribution chain, traceability can break down when dispensing from bulk by pharmacists or doctors, for instance. Original pack dispensing would enable a trace to be maintained further down the chain, but the UK and Ireland are virtually the last European countries not to adopt this modern method.

Medical devices, such as pacemakers, are the responsibility of the Medical Devices Directorate of the Department of Health which runs the National Reporting and Investigation Centre. All health authorities are required to report incidents or potential problems to the Centre, which categorises them into a three-tier system. The lowest level is low risk or one-off incidents which are investigated with the manufacturer. The medium and high risk reports are investigated by one of the Centre's specialist product groups; about half the 2,000 reports received each year are in this category.

Product recalls are made by the Directorate's hazard notification system, which alerts all National Health Service hospital managers, private hospital groups and some professional and purchasing organisations. Manufacturers and other organisations in the UK and abroad alert the Directorate to product problems. The manufacturer can institute a recall, with the approval of the Directorate, which will be followed with notification in the monthly Safety Action Bulletin and possibly a Hazard Notice if distribution is widespread.

The Directorate operates a Manufacturers' Registration Scheme, which is voluntary, and based on self-declaration of compliance with the Deparment of Health's published Guides to Good Manufacturing Practice, two of which specify recall procedures. The 400 registered companies are audited for compliance with good manufacturing practice.

The recall of medical products is dealt with in EC Directives (see p.42) and in the UK Medicines Act 1968 (see p.46).

Renault Owners' Handbook

It is not only design defects and manufacturing errors that lead to a recall: a failure of product information can be the catalyst as well. In this case the child was very lucky to escape with only cuts to her face and hands but the accident could easily have been considerably more serious.

Seven-year-old Karen Hirst of Woodthorpe, Nottingham, fell out of her father's Renault 20 when it was going round a bend in 1979. Fortunately she hit the side of the road, which was a mixture of earth and grit, and was not seriously hurt. The car's handbook said that the child-proof lock in the door operated when the lever was down, when in fact it should be kept up. The AA supported Rodney Hirst, the father, in his version of the accident.

Renault had to correct the 21,000 handbooks of British owners of the Renault 20 and Renault 30, of which 2,000 were in use.

Larousse cookery dictionary

This unusual recall was initiated because of the risk that defective information could result in injury or death, even though the product itself (a mushroom) was not involved. The directors of the French publishing company Larousse ordered the recall of 180,000 copies of the latest edition of its popular dictionary, Petit Larousse, at the beginning of August 1990. A company spokesman said, 'An error has occured on page 203 of the Petit Larousse in colour in the captions for the illustrated colour plate on mushrooms.' A deadly mushroom had been labelled as harmless. The recall would extend to France, Switzerland, Belgium and Canada.

Snecma aeroengines[5]

Snecma, the French state-owned aeroengine maker, is to recall almost 1,800 engines at an estimated cost of £18 million to £21 million in order to fit safer fan blades, following the British Midland Airways crash on the M1 in 1989 in which 47 people died.

The engines that power the popular Boeing 737, were developed jointly with General Electric of the United States. They will now be fitted with modified blades to eliminate high-altitude vibration, identified as the cause of engine failure in the British Midland crash.

The massive retrofit programme will cost between £10,000 and £12,000 per engine. The company will replace all 36 blades on

5 Dunn J, 'Snecma recalls aeroengines after enquiry into M1 crash', *The Engineer* 12 July 1989.

two versions of its CFM56–3 engines, which account for almost half the company's fleet of CFM56 engines in service. The new blades will allow Snecma to restore the climb thrust of the engines to their design maximum.

The fault, which escaped normal ground testing of the engine, was discovered after two similar aircraft developed almost identical faults six months after the M1 disaster.

Snecma has now received aviation authority approval to alter the angle of contact between the snubbers, or dampers, on the blades. These small fins, sticking out either side of the blade about two-thirds the way up, effectively lock the blades together in the fan ring.

Poor snubber contact angle in the M1 engine blades allowed the blades to vibrate, causing premature metal fatigue. This led to a broken blade tip which then caused the catastrophic failure of the engine.

Snecma will modify the blades by cutting off part of the snubber, welding on a new section and cutting the modified angle.

In 1989 Snecma made a profit of £8.5 million on its aeroengine business. It is expected to share the re-blading bill with its partner, General Electric.

Arsenic in beer

Recalls are not a modern affair; one that happened in 1900 was the result of over 70 deaths and 6,000 people becoming ill. The tragedy centred on Liverpool, Manchester and Salford but its source was far away in another country.

The first direct tax associated with beer was in 1614 when James I put a levy of four pence a quarter on malt. Thirty years later Parliament levied a duty on each barrel of beer to help pay for the Civil War and added a 5 per cent *ad valorem* tax on hops as well. By 1830 the only tax was the cumbersome and impractical malt tax. In 1849 an Act was passed allowing the use of sugars in brewing and in 1880 Gladstone repealed the malt duty. This enabled a brewer to use whatever he liked to produce fermentable matter, and as sugar was more economical than malt it soon accounted for a tenth of the beer produced.

This relaxation led to a chain of events that started in Spain and ended with a Royal Commission. Pyrites (iron sulphide) mined in Spain was imported into Leeds by a firm called Nicholson, where it was heated in kilns to extract the copper. A by-product of the process was sulphuric acid, which came in two qualities, depending on its arsenic content.

Just after Gladstone's repeal, Nicholson started supplying sulphuric acid to a sugar manufacturer at Garston, near Liverpool, called Bostock. The acid always carried a red label to distinguish the pure product – the one without arsenic. In April 1900 the lower quality acid containing arsenic was sent to Bostock who used it, as usual, to produce glucose from various starches. The sugar was sold to local brewers and by May the beer made with it had reached the public. A month later the first deaths occurred among beer drinkers; the cause was poisoning by arsenic, which had originated in the pyrites.

It was not until November that it was realised that the deaths were due to arsenic poisoning and not, as first thought, to alcoholism, peripheral neuritis or multiple neuritis. One of the six Manchester breweries affected was Groves & Whitnall, whose Chairman and Managing Director was James Groves. By the end of November, Groves was in a classic recall situation. He issued his first recall notice on 27 November, advising all his customers to stop selling or using any beer they had in stock until it had been further examined. On the same day 20 travellers and clerks from the brewery set out to visit each customer, carrying with them a list of brews that were certified to be pure. Those that were found to be safe had a certificate of purity attached to the casks. All the others, pending results from further analyses, had a red label affixed: 'Not to be used until further examined'. This severe action caused many of the public houses to be closed until stocks could be replaced with acceptable brews of beer.

A second notice was sent out to customers on 1 December which repeated the warning given in the previous notice and went on to say '. . . we shall regard it as a serious breach of duty on the part of anyone who permits any of that [uncertified] beer to be used or sold under any circumstances whatever, and further, that whoever does so will incur a grave personal risk.' Less than two weeks later a third notice was despatched asking the customers to make a stock return so that the brewery could monitor the success of their efforts.

Groves & Whitnall had difficulty in persuading many of their customers to return their beer stocks to the brewery for destruction. A publican would draw a sample of beer and say, 'Look at this – it is beautiful. Do you want to ruin us, and close the house?' The brewery traveller would reply, 'You will have to close the house if necessary but you must not sell a gill' (a half-pint). Many of the travellers reported having such difficulties, particularly in persuading people that it was not all a put-up job.

A full investigation was carried out by Lord Kelvin which set the limits on the amount of arsenic that should be present in food and drink. When the Food Standards Committee reviewed the limits in 1955 it found no reason to change them.

This recall was the result of a manufacturing error and had some of the actions described in this book. James Groves was the recall co-ordinator and the risk evaluation team consisted of Dr Tattersall, the Medical Officer of Health for Salford, Dr Cran, one of the district medical officers for Salford, and the head brewer. The independent laboratory was that of Gordon Salmon in London. The trade body, the Manchester Central Brewers' Association, was involved. The initial recall notification was a personal visit by brewery employees and this was followed by further notifications.

Perhaps the public relations aspect was not as good as it could have been. The only beer at Groves & Whitnall to be contaminated with arsenic was the 'fourpenny', but their name became associated with the 'arsenic scare' at a very early stage, in spite of the fact that a large number of breweries was involved. Groves said, 'It takes a long time to eradicate a misconception of that kind. It is in that way that I think we suffered considerably more than we have deserved.'

Glossary

A list of some of the terms used in the book

Cut-off
The period after which proceedings against the producer of a defective product may not be instituted.

Development risks
The residual chance that unforeseen failure modes will be revealed in a new product once it has been put on the market.

Duty of care
The legal duty to take responsible care to avoid acts or omissions which are likely to injure those to whom the duty is owned. Breach of this duty gives rise to liability for negligence.

Effectiveness check
Verification that relevant customers at the recall depth specified have received notification of the recall and have taken appropriate action.

Merchantable quality
Goods of any kind are of merchantable quality if they are as fit for the purpose or purposes for which goods of that kind are commonly bought as it is reasonable to expect, having regard to any description applied to them, the price (if

	relevant) and all other relevant circumstances.
Negligence	In legal usage it signifies the failure to exercise the standard of care which the doer, as a reasonable man should, by law, have exercised in the circumstances. The name negligence is given to a specific kind of tort, the tort of failing in particular circumstances to exercise the care which should have been shown in those circumstances, the care of the reasonable man, and of thereby causing harm to another in person or property.
Negligence, contributory	A partial or complete defence to liability in negligence when it could be shown that the plaintiff was partly or wholly responsible for his injuries.
Recall classification	A means of indicating the risk of the hazard presented by a product being recalled.
Recall depth	The level in the distribution chain to which a recall can extend, e.g. consumer, retail, wholesale.
Recall, mandatory	Occurs when a public authority or regulatory body uses its legal powers to order a manufacturer or supplier to recall.
Recall, product	Generally, the action taken to remove, repair, replace, retrofit or correct a defective product. Putting the distribution chain into reverse. For pharmaceutical products it is limited to the batch of a product only.

Recall, public   One in which the media are used to warn the public of the potential danger associated with a particular product. It has the advantage of immediacy and can reach many people, but it carries with it the possibility of public odium.

Recall, silent   One in which the public are unaware of the action being taken. It is most usual when a company, such as a supermarket chain, controls major parts of a distribution system.

Retrofit   Replacement *in situ* of a defective or worn-out part.

Withdrawal   Often the removal of a product for a minor problem with little publicity: except for pharmaceutical products when it is a full-scale operation akin to a major recall.

Appendices

Appendix 1

Some consumer products recalled in the United Kingdom

Apple drink
Aquarium pump
Baby dummy
Baby feeding bottle
Baby food
Baby frame carrier
Baby monitor
Baby sleep-suit
Bubble-blowing kit
CB radio
Cable reel
Camera
Car ramp
Cassette radio
Central heating boiler
Cheese
Child-resistant cap
Child's swing
Chocolate
Cider
Coffee
Coffee pot

Computer
Cooker hood
Cookpot
Cordless telephone
Cot bumper
Cycle light
Deep-fat fryer
Dishwasher
Doll
Electric blanket
Electric cooker
Electric shaver
Extension lead
Fan heater
Film
Fireworks
Fluorescent light
Food processor
Footbath
Game
Garden tool
Gas barbecue

Gas cartridge
Gas oven
Hair dryer
Ham
Heated duvet
Hot-air brush
Illuminated globe
Jug kettle
Lasagne
Lawn mower
Light bulb
Light fitting
Marine radar
Measles vaccine
Medicine container
Microwave oven
Motorcycle helmet
Mouth organ
Paint
Paté
Pencil set
Pen light

Petrol
Petrol can
Plug 13 amp
Powder drink
Push chair
Rum
Salami snack
Spa water
Spin dryer
Spotlight
Storage heater
Suncare gel
Sun lamp
Swimming arm bands
Table lamp
Toaster
Toy
Tyre
Vacuum cleaner
Washing machine
Washer/dryer
Weed-killer

Appendix 2

A survey of some consumer recalls

Australia

Recalls between 1 July 1986[1] and 30 June 1990

Total number of recalls

Year	Total		Product	Total
1986 half year	69		Vehicles	181
1987	182		Therapeutic goods	456
1988	224		Food	32
1989	191		Other	162
1990 half year	165			
	831			831

There were 369 public recalls, which were those advertised or otherwise brought to the attention of the public. Non-public recalls are those conducted without the need to inform the public, such as for a specialist therapeutic device only supplied to hospitals or a motor vehicle with a limited number of customers.

1 The date that the Trade Practices Act was amended to incorporate new provisions relating to product recalls (see Chapter 2, p.15). Federal Bureau of Consumer Affairs Australia.

Recalls between November 1989 and April 1990[2]

Canada

Incident cause	Accidental
Company/target	Nabob Foods
Product affected	Traditional caffeinated coffee
Location	Nationwide
Date	6 January 1990
Incident	The company recalled the product because of numerous complaints from consumers that it had a sour taste. It was found to have been made from inferior coffee beans.

Incident cause	Not known
Company/target	Martin Feeds Mills Ltd
Product affected	Technical Growth Puppy Food
Location	Toronto, Ontario
Date	16 March 1990
Incident	The product was recalled by the company after 15 puppies had died after eating the food. It was found to be contaminated with poultry vaccine. The possibility of sabotage was not ruled out.

Eire

Incident cause	Accidental
Company/target	CPC Foods
Product affected	Hellman's Mayonnaise
Location	Nationwide
Date	27 November 1989

2 Control Risks Group, London.

Incident	The company recalled 615gr jars of Hellman's mayonnaise because of a possible flaw in the glass which could cause it to break.

France

Incident cause	Accidental
Company/target	Société Général des Eaux Minerales de Vittel
Product affected	Hepar Mineral Water
Location	Nationwide
Date	10 January 1990
Incident	The company announced a recall of 1–2 million bottles of domestically consumed Hepar mineral water. It was contaminated when water in an above-ground tank came into contact with a filter clogged with alkane. At first there was a quiet withdrawal, then, because of the publicity surrounding the Perrier recall (see case history p.165), a full recall was initiated to avoid confusion.

Incident cause	Accidental
Company/target	Source Perrier
Product affected	Perrier mineral water
Location	Worldwide
Date	10 February 1990
Incident	Sales of Perrier were suspended in the USA because traces of benzene were found in tests. A worldwide withdrawal followed because of the contamination. It was believed that one of the filters at the plant, whose function was to remove the benzene, had not been well maintained. The cost of the recall and withdrawal has been estimated at around US$60 million (see case history p.165).

United Kingdom

Incident cause	Accidental
Company/target	Asda
Product affected	Own-brand Gold Coffee
Location	Nationwide
Date	15 November 1989
Incident	Asda recalled their own label Gold decaffeinated coffee when 12 jars were found to contain metal particles.

Incident cause	Intentional
Company/target	Gateway
Product affected	Nappies
Location	Poynton, Cheshire
Date	16 November 1989
Incident	Gateway removed disposable nappies made by Blueridge Care from their stores when a mother found a razor in one of the packs.

Incident cause	Accidental
Company/target	National Trust Shops
Product affected	Christmas puddings
Location	Nationwide
Date	24 November 1989
Incident	The National Trust withdrew 35,000 Christmas puddings from their 200 retail outlets and from mail order services because they were suspected of being contaminated with mould. The loss was expected to be £50,000.

Incident cause	Accidental
Company/target	Nestlé
Product affected	Build-up and Slender powder drinks
Location	Nationwide
Date	25 November 1989

Incident	Nestlé recalled batches of Build-up and Slender powder drinks because a factory production fault might have affected them. One positive salmonella find was made.

Incident cause	Accidental
Company/target	Plumrose
Product affected	Canned Hotdog Sausages
Location	Hull, Humberside
Date	25 November 1989
Incident	Plumrose Limited recalled tins of hotdog sausages after defects were found which caused leakages of the brine.

Incident cause	Accidental
Company/target	Gubeen Cheese
Product affected	Cheese
Location	Nationwide
Date	13 December 1989
Incident	An Irish cheese, Gubeen, was withdrawn in the UK after being linked to salmonella. The Department of Health warned the public not to eat the cheese.

Incident cause	Not known
Company/target	Manor Bakeries
Product affected	Mr Kipling Apple Pies
Location	Eastleigh, Hampshire
Date	22 January 1990
Incident	A customer found a piece of glass in a Mr Kipling apple pie. Several batches were recalled.

Incident cause	Accidental
Company/target	Plumrose
Product affected	Packed meats
Location	King's Lynn, Norfolk
Date	26 January 1990

Incident	Public health authorities found traces of listeria in packs of chilled meat made by Plumrose. Production was halted and 50,000 packs worth around £80,000 were withdrawn. Production was not restarted until the beginning of March 1990.

Incident cause	Not known
Company/target	Heinz
Product affected	Baby food
Location	Monmouth, Gwent
Date	29 March 1990
Incident	Jars of Heinz baby food were removed from shelves at a Gateway store following the discovery of an inch-long metal spike in a kidney dinner.

Incident cause	Intentional
Company/target	Chilean Wines
Product affected	Chilean Wines
Location	Various
Date	1 April 1990
Incident	Sainsbury's removed a number of Chilean wines from their stores, including one of their own-label products, following the discovery that some producers had been using sorbitol. The discovery of the illegal but harmless additive was made in the course of routine tests.

Incident cause	Intentional
Company/target	L'Oreal
Product affected	Beauty products
Location	Northern Ireland
Date	13 April 1990
Incident	A range of L'Oreal beauty products were removed from supermarket shelves

throughout Northern Ireland after animal rights extremists claimed to have spiked them with paint stripper. The contaminated items had all been clearly marked with labels or messages on the cap or front of the bottle.

United States

Incident cause	Intentional
Company/target	Boyers
Product affected	Boyers Peanut Butter Cup Candy
Location	Paterson, NJ
Date	1 November 1989
Incident	A four-year-old boy suffered a seizure after eating a Peanut Butter Cup made by the Boyers Candy Company. It was found he had ingested a drug used for diabetes. The rest of the product was removed from the shelves and investigations were carried out.

Incident cause	Intentional
Company/target	Gerber
Product affected	Baby food
Location	Bakersfield, CA
Date	12 November 1989
Incident	A woman found a needle in a jar of Gerber baby food. The store checked its supply. The jar appeared to have been tampered with. The incident followed the recall by Gerber of dry rice cereal packages after aluminium chips were found in some packages.

Incident cause	Intentional
Company/target	Apple
Product affected	Red Delicious apple
Location	Bronxville, NY
Date	15 November 1989

Incident	A woman found a needle in a Red Delicious apple. It was believed to be a case of malicious tampering. All similar apples were removed from shelves for checking. No other contamination was found.

Incident cause	Not applicable
Company/target	Veryfine
Product affected	Veryfine Orange Juice
Location	Glassboro, PA
Date	30 November 1989
Incident	A girl became ill after drinking Veryfine orange juice which was found to contain small quantities of antifreeze. The product was removed from the stores in the area. After investigations, it was found that the girl had drunk the antifreeze and then orange juice and made it look like tampering.

Incident cause	Accidental
Company/target	Continental Baking Company
Product affected	Bread/snacks
Location	Memphis, TN
Date	5 December 1989
Incident	The company recalled its bread and snacks when they found a broken light bulb in a flour bin. It was not certain that any products were contaminated but the recall was precautionary.

Incident cause	Not known
Company/target	Bubblicious Bubble Gum
Product affected	Bubble gum
Location	Westford, MA
Date	27 December 1989
Incident	A girl bit on what appeared to be glass in the bubble gum, although it was thought that it

was possibly gum resin which had crystallised. The bubble gum was removed from the shelves of the store where it was bought while investigations were carried out.

Incident cause	Accidental
Company/target	Pocono Pure Mountain Spring Water
Product affected	Mineral water
Location	Six states
Date	2 January 1990
Incident	A woman became ill after drinking the water. It was recalled from stores in six states. It was thought that the problem was with the bottles rather than the water.

Incident cause	Intentional
Company/target	Plum tomatoes
Product affected	Plum tomatoes
Location	Ardsley, NY
Date	22 January 1990
Incident	A man became ill after eating from a tin of plum tomatoes. It was found to be contaminated with mercury. The rest of that batch was removed from the shelves for testing. No other signs of contamination were found.

Incident cause	Intentional
Company/target	Aldi
Product affected	Astromike Creme Pies
Location	Gary, IN
Date	29 January 1990
Incident	A woman found sewing needles in the Astromike Creme Pies she had bought from an Aldi store. Aldi withdrew the product from all stores in NW Indiana and the Chicago area.

Incident cause	Not known
Company/target	Thornapple Valley
Product affected	Sausages
Location	Oakland, MI
Date	7 March 1990
Incident	A man found several pieces of glass in two packets of sausages. Both packets had been purchased from A & P supermarkets in Independence Township. The manufacturers withdrew the sausages.

Incident cause	Intentional
Company/target	Frito-Lay
Product affected	Frito-Lay's Chee-tos snacks
Location	Indianapolis, IN
Date	30 March 1990
Incident	Sewing needles were found in two packets of cheese snacks, one consumer was injured by one of the needles. The stores that sold the snacks removed all other packets of the product and notified other stores to do the same.

Appendix 3

Code of Practice on action concerning vehicle safety defects (Society of Motor Manufacturers and Traders)

1 Introduction

This 'Code of Practice on action concerning vehicle safety defects' (hereinafter referred to as 'the Code'), which has been drawn up by the Department of Transport and the Society of Motor Manufacturers and Traders Limited (SMMT), concerns cases where vehicle manufacturers and concessionaries become aware of the existence of safety defects (as defined in paragraph 3 of this Introduction) in vehicles that have been sold in Great Britain.

The Code deals with information to be given to the Department and to the owner/registered keeper in respect of passenger cars, commercial vehicles, passenger service vehicles and components fitted as original equipment. This document does not cover motorcycles, trailers, motor caravans or components supplied to the automotive aftermarket.

A 'safety defect' is a feature of design or construction liable to cause significant risk of injury to the driver or occupants of the vehicle or to other road users.

The following are outside the scope of this document:

(a) any defects which are not attributable to the original design or manufacture of the vehicle;

(b) passenger cars more than five years old;

(c) defects caused by non-compliance with any reasonable instructions or warnings that accompany the vehicle at the point of sale, or due to abnormal use.

2 Cases covered by the Code

The cases covered by the Code are those where:

(a) the evidence indicates the existence of a safety defect in the vehicles;

(b) the defect appears to be common to a significant number of vehicles; and

(c) some of the vehicles involved have already been sold for use in Great Britain.

In some cases, it will be a matter of judgement to decide whether the number of vehicles affected by a defect is sufficient to justify invoking the Code. No fixed numerical limit can be specified because the decision must also take account of the degree of seriousness of any possible road hazard involved.

3 Arrangements with individual manufacturers

Due to different operational structures within member companies of the SMMT, the Department may require a vehicle manufacturer to supply it with the names of a co-ordinator and his deputy responsible for dealing with vehicle safety recall campaigns.

4 Cases affecting components

Safety defects covered by the Code include those relating to components bought by vehicle manufacturers from other manufacturers and suppliers and sold with the vehicle as original equipment.

5 Notification of the Department of Transport

The primary responsibility is with the vehicle manufacturer to decide when evidence of a safety defect amounts to a case notifiable under the terms of the Code. The Department will be notified as soon as the vehicle manufacturer has concluded that there is substantial evidence of a safety defect which requires remedial action. The vehicle manufacturer shall at that stage indicate:

(a) the nature of the defect and estimated number of vehicles involved;

(b) the nature of the safety hazard involved;

(c) the action planned at the time to remedy the defect.

In cases where the defect appears to stem from a fault in a component produced by another manufacturer, that other manufacturer will also be notified and the Department advised accordingly.

The vehicle manufacturer will also inform the Department of all subsequent decisions on remedial action. This includes cases in which component manufacturers are involved, unless in the circumstances of the case it is agreed between the vehicle manufacturer and the appropriate component manufacturer for all remedial action to become the responsibility of the component manufacturer, in which case the latter shall keep the Department informed.

6 Initiatives by the Department in particular cases

The Department may wish to seek information from a vehicle or component manufacturer on safety defects which have been brought to the Department's notice. In these cases, the manufacturer will supply all the relevant information known to him.

The primary responsibility for deciding on remedial action also lies with the vehicle manufacturer, but the Department may, at its discretion, put its own views on this.

7 Notification of vehicle owners

As soon as a decision has been made by the vehicle manufacturer on the action to be taken to deal with the identified defects, that manufacturer will take all reasonable steps to notify all owners/registered keepers of the vehicles affected. The vehicle manufacturer may use any method at his disposal to notify the owner/registered keeper to call in his vehicle from in-service for the purpose of examining and, if necessary, rectifying components or assemblies which the vehicle manufacturer believes are safety defective. The vehicle manufacturer will arrange the despatch of a letter to the owner/registered keeper of the affected vehicles, either directly or through the franchised dealer network. If the vehicle manufacturer or franchised dealer receives no response from the owner/registered keeper then a further letter will be sent by recorded delivery.

If requested by the manufacturer, the Driver and Vehicle Licensing Centre will, on repayment terms, and in accordance with existing procedures, either supply the vehicle manufacturer with the name and address of the owner/registered keeper shown on the Centre's records, or address and despatch a letter from the manufacturer to the owner/registered keeper. Vehicle manufacturers will notify the Department at three-monthly intervals over a period of 18 months of the response rate of all recall campaigns.

8 Publication by the Department of Information on vehicle defects

The Department reserves the right, under ministerial authority, to publish at any time any information of which it is notified, where this seems necessary in the public interest. Before doing this, the Department will consult the vehicle manufacturer, and where appropriate, the component manufacturer concerned, and will not disclose publicly information on matters of commercial confidence unless there appear to be overriding safety considerations. Subject to this proviso, the Department will also make public at regular intervals summary information on action taken on cases notified under this Code. It will normally divert to a manufacturer more specific requests on particular cases.

9 Imported vehicles

The above provisions of the Code are also to apply to imported vehicles, other than those imported by a private owner, with the qualification that the appropriate UK concessionaire will assume on behalf of his vehicle manufacture the obligation of the latter under the Code.

10 Exported vehicles

The Code does not cover exported vehicles. Measures to be taken in relation to these will depend upon the legal and administrative arrangements prevailing in the country of import. However, the Department and the SMMT are prepared to participate in any international discussions designed to harmonise arrangements governing notification of defects and related remedial action.

Appendix 4

Code of Practice on recall procedures for pharmaceutical products (Association of British Pharmaceutical Industry)

Company responsibility

Responsibility for the decision to recall must remain with the company; this decision to include the level of recall, i.e. should the recall extend to patient level? Company medical advisers will play an important part in any decision to recall by determining the degree of possible hazard to patients.

Liaison with Department of Health

The need for liaison with the Department of Health should be adjudged by individual companies according to the circumstances which give rise to the recall. In cases of patient risk immediate notification to the Department is essential.

Written procedures

Each company should ensure that their recall systems and procedures are set out in written form and made known to all who may be concerned in their operation. Such written procedures should nominate a responsible individual, or group of individuals, (whose name(s) should also be known to the

Medicines Inspectorate) to deal with all incoming reports which call for consideration of a need for recall.

The document should be revised at regular intervals to take account of changes in procedure and the responsible individual(s) listed therein.

Immediate action upon receipt of a report suggesting a need for recall

Reports should be referred immediately on receipt to the responsible individual(s). Incoming reports may be expected to emanate from one or more of the following sources:

    (i)   Users or distributors, probably received through the company's professional service or sales staff.

   (ii)   The company's own quality control organisation.

  (iii)   The Medicines Inspectorate.

According to circumstances, an immediate embargo may be placed on the distribution of any remaining stocks of the batch, or batches, which are the subject of the report until the report has been evaluated.

Recall categories

If it is decided that a recall must be undertaken, a further decision must be made as to the extent of recall. For example, a *restricted* recall involving trade channels only (including hospitals, pharmacists, and dispensing doctors).

Prior notification to the Department of Health will not be required, but the Medicines Inspectorate should be informed at the same time and by the same means adopted for notification of trade channels.

An *urgent* situation, involving potential risk to patients, which would require immediate notification to, and discussion of recall plans with, the Department of Health.

In a *restricted* recall situation the notification may be limited to organisations or persons supplied direct by the company, e.g. wholesalers, direct account pharmacists, hospitals, dispensing doctors. The return of the goods may be facilitated by members of the sales force calling on those supplied (both direct and indirect) or by using the NAPD Recall Scheme, [see Medical Products case history, Chapter 7, p.230]. A wider notification (for example by mailing or trade journal announcement) may also be deemed necessary, according to circumstances.

An *urgent* recall situation will involve all the measures above. In addition, immediate consultation with the Department of Health is essential. Agreement will then be reached on further measures to be taken, e.g. the dissemination of recall information to 'patient' level by means of other media such as local or national press, television and radio. Midwives, district nurses, etc. may need special consideration since it may not be possible for them to be contacted through 'trade' channels.

Recall communications – identification, content, etc.

Recall notifications sent by post should be despatched by first-class mail in a readily identifiable envelope as already recommended by the Association.

In every recall, it is essential that adequate information be provided to purchasers or users, including:

Name of product.

Presentation(s) involved.

Strength(s) of presentation(s).

Pack size(s).

Batch/lot number(s).

Mention of the need for an immediate embargo on issues of remaining stocks of the relevant batches.

Reasons for the recall with indication of the health risk and urgency involved, where relevant.

Methods of recovery and compensation by the manufacturer.

Where circumstances make it appropriate, the notification should remind distributors of the need to take into account goods in transit to them when the recall is initiated.

Monitoring systems

A system for monitoring of the recall should be instituted to ensure that the original batch quantity is reconciled with the amount which is either embargoed or returned from distributors as a result of recall action.

Note. Where there is patient risk such arrangements are particularly essential to provide information, both for the manufacturer and for the Department of Health, on the extent of the risks for patients which may remain. An initial statement should be prepared giving the amount packaged, the amount distributed, and the quantity remaining in stock. A reply-paid 'Inventory of return' card may be distributed as part of the system for monitoring the recall.

Use of batch numbers

Adequate batch documentation is essential to the efficient operation of the measures outlined above; specific recommendations on this aspect of manufacturing procedures are outside the scope of this report. Ready identification of the batch number by the user or stockist is essential. It is recommended therefore that, subject to any legal requirements, batch identification figures or letters on labels must be preceded by either of the words 'batch' or 'lot' to distinguish them clearly from other numbers which may be included. This identification should appear on all manufacturers' packagings with the possible exception of unit dose packs, e.g. ampoules.

Recall envelope design as approved by the Commercial Affairs Committee

The block should be printed in COATES SIGNAL RED, positioned 10mm from the left hand edge of the envelope. The space between the top edge of the envelope and the top of the word 'URGENT' should be 10mm wide, i.e. the colour should bleed off the top and bottom of the envelope.

Appendix 5

Code of Practice for pedal cycle recalls (The Bicycle Association of Great Britain Limited)

1 Introduction

The 'Code of Practice on action concerning pedal cycle safety defects' (hereinafter referred to as 'the Code'), which has been drawn up by the Department of Transport, The Bicycle Association of Great Britain (BAGB) and the Association of Cycle Traders (ACT), in conjunction with the Royal Society for the Prevention of Accidents and the British Standards Institution, concerns cases where pedal cycle and component manufacturers, suppliers, or retailers become aware of the existence of safety defects (as defined in paragraph 3 of this introduction) in products which have been sold in the United Kingdom.

2 The Code deals with information to be given to the Department and to owners in respect of cycles used for social, domestic, leisure, sporting or commercial purposes and for components fitted to the aforesaid as original equipment or sold for use in the aftermarket.

3 A safety defect is a feature of design or manufacture liable to cause significant risk of injury to the rider of the cycle or to other road users.

4   The following are outside the scope of this Code:

(a) Any defects which are not attributable to the original design or manufacture of the product.
(b) Defects caused by non-compliance with any reasonable instructions or warnings which accompany the cycle at the point of sale, or are subsequently issued.
(c) Defects caused by abnormal use of the cycle.
(d) Exported cycles. Measures to be taken in relation to these cycles will depend upon legal and administrative arrangements in the country of import.

5   Cases covered by the Code

The cases covered by the Code are those where:
(a) The evidence indicates the existence of a safety defect in the cycle or component.
(b) The safety defect constitutes a significant risk of injury to the rider/other road users.
(c) Some or all of the cycles involved have already been sold for use in UK.

6   Notification to the Department of Transport

The primary responsibility to decide when evidence of a safety-related defect amounts to a case notifiable under the terms of the Code lies with the manufacturer, supplier or retailer. No fixed numerical limit can be specified as the decision must also take account of the safety significance of the defect. The Department will be notified as soon as the manufacturer, supplier, or retailer has concluded that there is evidence of a safety defect which requires remedial action. The manufacturer, supplier, or retailer shall at that stage indicate:
(a) the nature of the defect and the estimated number of cycles involved;
(b) the safety significance of the defect;
(c) the action planned to remedy the defect.

In cases of doubt the manufacturer, supplier, or retailer should consult the Department of Transport.

7 The Department may require a manufacturer, supplier or retailer to provide the name of a recall co-ordinator responsible for dealing with campaigns to recall cycles.

8 In cases where the defect appears to originate from a fault in a component produced by another manufacturer, that other manufacturer shall also be notified and the Department advised accordingly.

9 The manufacturer, supplier or retailer will also inform the Department of all subsequent decisions on remedial action. This includes cases in which component manufacturers are involved, unless in the circumstances of the case it is agreed between the cycle and component manufacturer that all remedial action will become the responsibility of the latter who should keep the Department informed.

10 Manufacturers, suppliers or retailers will notify the Department at three-monthly intervals for a period of at least 18 months of the response rates of all Code of Practice recall campaigns.

11 Initiatives by the Department in particular cases

The Department may wish to seek information from a cycle or component manufacturer on safety defects which have been brought to the Department's notice. In these cases the manufacturer, supplier, or retailer will supply all known relevant information.

12 The primary responsibility for deciding on remedial action lies with the manufacturer, supplier or retailer but the Department may, at its discretion, put its own views on this.

13 Notification of cycle owners

As soon as a decision has been made by the manufacturer, supplier or retailer on the action to be taken to deal with the safety defect, the manufacturer, supplier or retailer will take all reasonable steps to notify owners of the cycles affected. The manufacturer, supplier or retailer should use the most appropriate means to advise owners to take cycles to a dealer for the purpose of examining and, if necessary, rectifying, without charge any components or assemblies which are part of the remedial action of the recall.

14 A press release may improve the users response to, or awareness of, campaigns; and therefore the manufacturer supplier or retailer will be expected to consider use of the media to improve the responses to campaigns.

15 Publication by the Department of information on cycle defects

The Department reserves the right, under ministerial authority, to publish at any time any information of which it is notified, where this seems necessary in the public interest. Before doing this, the Department will consult the manufacturer, supplier, or retailer concerned and will not disclose publicly information on matters of commercial confidentiality, unless there appear to be overriding safety considerations. The Department will also prepare and issue at regular intervals, summary information agreed with manufacturers, suppliers, or retailers on action taken on cases notified under this Code. The Department will normally refer more specific requests on particular cases to a manufacturer.

Index

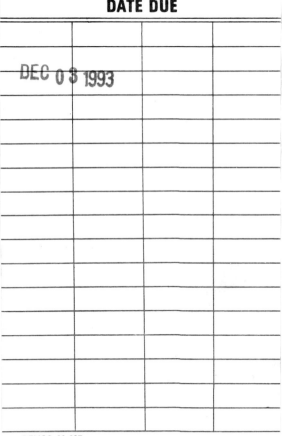

DATE DUE

DEC 0 3 1993			